THE
BUSINESS
DEVOTIONAL

LILLIAN HAYES MARTIN

STERLING INNOVATION
An imprint of Sterling Publishing Co., Inc.

New York / London
www.sterlingpublishing.com

STERLING, the distinctive Sterling logo, STERLING INNOVATION,
and the Sterling Innovation logo are registered trademarks of
Sterling Publishing Co., Inc.

2 4 6 8 10 9 7 5 3

Published by Sterling Publishing Co., Inc.
387 Park Avenue South
New York, NY 10016
© 2009 by Sterling Publishing Co., Inc.

Distributed in Canada by Sterling Publishing
c/o Canadian Manda Group,
165 Dufferin Street
Toronto, Ontario, Canada M6K 3H6
Distributed in the United Kingdom by
GMC Distribution Services
Castle Place, 166 High Street, Lewes,
East Sussex, England BN7 1XU
Distributed in Australia by
Capricorn Link (Australia) Pty. Ltd.
P.O. Box 704, Windsor, NSW 2756, Australia

Design by Barbara Balch

Sterling ISBN 978-1-4027-5642-9

For information about custom editions, special sales, premium and
corporate purchases. Please contact Sterling Special Sales Department
at 800-805-5489 or specialsales@sterlingpublishing.com

ACKNOWLEDGEMENTS

THIS BOOK WOULD NOT HAVE BEEN POSSIBLE without the help of many people. I'd like to thank Erin Clermont, Cheryl Kimball, and Pamela Liflander for their invaluable assistance. These women helped me make this book a reality. I would also like to thank Carlo DeVito at Sterling Publishing Company for fostering such a great project and for his infinite patience. Lastly, I would like to acknowledge my husband, Adam, for supporting me throughout the project, and beyond.

INTRODUCTION

T HE *BUSINESS DEVOTIONAL* OFFERS A UNIQUE VIEW OF the world within your office, whether you work for a large company or from a small room in your basement. In this volume I've collected 365 quotations that apply to the business world. Each entry is meant to be read either at the start of your day or as you unwind later, offering you simple advice or words of encouragement to help you improve your profits, manage your team, or motivate you to reach new heights of excellence.

You will meet some of the most outstanding business leaders from the past and present. You will learn from them, and you will laugh with them, too. You will understand what motivated them to excellence and see how their ideas connect directly to your work. Whether you are an entry-level employee or a seasoned business professional, reading this book will help you improve your skills and become more productive. If you are a team leader or a managing professional, you'll discover better techniques to deal with your peers and your employees. And for entrepreneurs, you'll learn a few tricks from some of the master inventors and marketers known throughout the world.

You'll receive advice from likely suspects, including Tom Peters, Peter Drucker, Harvey Mackay, Bill Gates, Warren Buffett, and Ken Blanchard, as well as nuggets of wisdom from sports heroes, literary figures, historical leaders, hysterical comedians, and some of today's most celebrated business gurus. There are also plenty of surprises that will make reading this daily devotional an enlightening practice instead of a deliberate chore.

Each day of the week highlights a unique aspect of business life:

MOTIVATION MONDAYS

TEAM-BUILDING TUESDAYS

CAREER WEDNESDAYS

SALES THURSDAYS

LEADERSHIP FRIDAYS

ENTREPRENEUR SATURDAYS

MANAGING PEOPLE SUNDAYS

Enjoy. Now get back to work!

MOTIVATION | MONDAY

Your attitude, not your aptitude, will determine your altitude. —*Zig Ziglar*

IN ELEMENTARY SCHOOL, REPORT CARDS SHOWED A LIST of virtues that were important for succeeding in school. Chief among them was attitude. Even if you were getting decent grades, if the teacher felt you were not working up to your potential, your attitude could pull down your report card. And when your parents read, "If Johnny would only apply himself, he could be doing so much better in science," they'd get on your case to study harder.

So, it's not surprising that even though our school days are long gone, we're still getting graded on attitude. If someone thinks you're not delivering as well as you should, or the customer isn't buying what you're selling, you've got an attitude problem. It doesn't matter if you've got the aptitude and you know you can do the job; if the attitude isn't right, your boss isn't happy.

Zig Ziglar points out that attitude in business is all about enthusiasm. Getting excited about your work and maintaining that excitement shows others that you believe in whatever it is you do. If you don't believe in yourself or your company, or you show even the slightest discouragement or disinterest, it's going to creep into your attitude. Nothing great is ever achieved with a bad attitude. Your level of enthusiasm will determine how high you're going to fly.

TEAM-BUILDING | TUESDAY

Never commit your team unless you are confident your team will support your decision. —*Christopher Avery, Ph.D.*

TEAMWORK GURU CHRISTOPHER AVERY KNOWS THAT people don't like a decision being made for them, especially when they don't agree with the consensus.

Avoid this situation whenever you can. Always involve the team from the beginning. You'll improve team morale when you work on commitments that they support. More important, your team leadership status will increase if your staff knows you won't put them in an awkward position. Then, on the rare occasion when you have no choice in the decision making, your team will still support you, even if they do not agree with the decision made for them.

When you inform your team that they are going to work on a project that they don't believe in and/or have no control over, it is your job to help the team take ownership of the decision. You can start by acknowledging that this particular case is not the best scenario for the team. Let them air their grievances. Keep the conversation from getting nasty, but don't make excuses for every complaint. Sometimes being allowed to vent is enough. Then, turn the tables to see if the team can come up with any positive aspects to the project. Maybe they can test a new idea, or perhaps the department can get some new software they've wanted to complete the task. If you show them how to identify the upside, it will help them come to your side.

CAREER | WEDNESDAY

Men are anxious to improve their circumstances, but are unwilling to improve themselves. —*James Allen*

MANY PEOPLE DESIRE TO MAKE MORE OF THEIR BUSINESS life, whether it's getting a promotion, finding a better job, or simply having the opportunity to take time off for a once-in-a-lifetime extended vacation. But we often miss these chances because we unintentionally hold ourselves back from success. For example, if you are stuck in a dead-end job, you've got to find a way to get out of it. If you stay in that position, you will never move up to the next level professionally, and you'll miss out on longer vacation time, more money, and even more job flexibility.

Over one hundred years ago, British writer James Allen aptly remarked in his essay, *From Poverty to Power,* "To know that justice, harmony, and love are supreme in the universe is likewise to know that all adverse and painful conditions are the result of our own disobedience." Positive, lasting change starts by knowing who we are and taking ownership for the dissatisfying aspects of our lives. We can't rely on others, to improve our station. We must learn to act now.

Change in your career can require looking deep within yourself to find out how you can best succeed. Spend some time each day reflecting on where you want your career or your business to head. You will find that your dreams and goals will begin to take shape. It's not going to happen overnight, and it's not going to be easy, but it will work.

SALES | THURSDAY

> Only knowledge put to use can create
> capital. —*Mikel Harry and Richard Schroeder*

S IX SIGMA WAS DEVELOPED BY MIKEL HARRY AND
Richard Schroeder when they were working at the
Motorola Company in 1986. It is a dynamic management
process designed to streamline operations and maximize
profits. Its fame derives from an innovation in quality control. The Six Sigma system teaches managers how to quan-
titatively hone in on specific information to find out what's
working and what's not. These measurements and analyses
of the business processes provide statistics, which give you
the knowledge you need to make your business more profitable. Knowing this information enables a business to re-
create its operation and eliminate defects entirely.

Without data, you're at best guessing why you're either
winning or losing, or what the cost of defects means to your
operation—from creating product to keeping files of purchase orders and billing. With the right data you can make
sense of your past sales problems, show what needs to be
improved or fixed, and then implement the changes to
increase your profits. It applies to the manufacturing process
as well as the sales process.

Knowledge put to work this way, focusing on improving virtually undetectable defects, creates capital. See if your
company can benefit from a Six Sigma orientation, and then
put the results to work for you.

LEADERSHIP | FRIDAY

The man who never makes a mistake
always takes orders from one who does.

—Anonymous

SOMETIMES BEING PERFECT CAN BE HARMFUL WHEN attempting to move up the ladder. If you are a consistent top performer in your current job, but have been passed over for promotions, it's time to rethink what your diligence is doing to your career. After all, if you successfully fulfilled your duties and responsibilities in a timely and efficient manner, your boss would surely see that you were ready for a promotion. Unfortunately, perfect performance is not always what gets you ahead—sometimes the imperfect performance demonstrates your potential.

Risk taking shows initiative—a trait valued by superiors. Whether your job requires complex processes or more mundane tasks, you probably see countless areas for improvement within the company. In terms of leadership, this spells opportunity. Let's say your department ships one thousand boxes of inventory each day. Over time you've noticed several processes that hinder the operation. You have some ideas for improvement, but are hesitant to present them to the higher-ups. If they work, and you double the amount of inventory moved, you will make the company a great deal of money. If they fail, all is not lost—you will have shown initiative, a trait of true leadership. The lesson here is obvious: don't be too eager to be perfect. Taking risks shows a certain aptitude bosses look for when looking to promote.

ENTREPRENEUR | SATURDAY

> Nothing is more difficult
> than the art of maneuvering for
> advantageous position.
>
> —*Sun Tzu*

HOW CAN AN ANCIENT CHINESE GENERAL BE CONSIDered a business guru twenty-five hundred years later? By having written a book on military strategy called *The Art of War*. Business people from all industries have considered this little book a classic for their own skill development. The book covers the intellectual side of war and lays out a strategy for "psyching out" the enemy. Many a business mogul believes that Sun Tzu's teachings are an indispensable guide to everyday life. Countless quotations are pulled from *The Art of War* and used not only by business people, but by sports coaches and military personnel.

"Maneuvering for advantageous position" refers to the strategy that before you march toward your business goals, you need to have a firm plan as well as the flexibility to change those plans as your needs arise. You won't just land in the right place to take advantage of a good business opportunity by accident. But with a good plan, you can create your own opportunities. And if things change in your favor, you can modify your plans for an easier journey.

With that in mind, consider this famous Sun Tzu quote that many entrepreneurs hang on the wall: "According as circumstances are favorable, one should modify one's plans."

MANAGING PEOPLE | SUNDAY

> A company is only as good as
> the people it keeps. —*Mary Kay Ash*

T HE FOUNDER OF THE MARY KAY COSMETICS EMPIRE
proved early in her sales career, long before she became
a household name, that she could break sales records by herself. But once she started the cosmetics line, she realized
that she needed lots of people to support her success. Mary
Kay Cosmetics Inc. is one of America's largest privately held
companies not because of one person, but because of its hundreds of thousands of sales reps. They are the ambassadors
who turn women onto the company's products and recruit
new reps by living the company's values: recognition, motivation, support, and financial success.

Ultimately, Mary Kay Cosmetics is nothing without its
employees. Sadly, many companies (and managers) don't see
this big picture. They get more jazzed about technological
advances, manufacturing efficiencies, or stock options. They
don't recognize employees for jobs well done. They don't
motivate employees to stretch their skills. Too often they see
employees as little more than "cost centers" because compensation is often their biggest expense. But there's a good
reason employees cost so much: they hold tremendous
knowledge and possess unlimited potential. Sometimes you
might hire a bad egg, but that's a correctable mistake. But
when you hire the right people, you and the entire company
look like a million bucks.

MOTIVATION | MONDAY

When walking through the valley
of shadows, remember, a shadow
is cast by a light. —*Aeschylus*

S HADOWS REPRESENT THE DARK SIDE, LIKE GLOOM AND
depression. Shadows are metaphors for negatives. Yet on
the other side of a shadow is light. Shadows could not exist
without light.

Aeschylus, a revered Greek playwright, often referred to
as the founder of tragedy, wrote about the Persian invasion
of Greece. He wrote about the dark days of war and turbu-
lence and the shadows of pain and suffering that accompa-
nied these wars. Aeschylus knew pain and suffering was not
what life was all about. He knew to juxtapose them with the
life-affirming light behind these shadows. He offered a brilliant lesson to those who came to see his plays: life was not
always exactly what you saw.

When you find yourself enmeshed in a modern-day
Greek tragedy—conflict provided by the cast of characters
that is your office team or someone in middle management
who just won't listen to either the bad or good news that
you must pass along—go past the shadows, weed out the
conflict, and find where the light beams through.

TEAM-BUILDING | TUESDAY

We never get to the bottom of ourselves on our own. We discover who we are face to face and side by side with others in work, love and learning. —*Robert Bellah*

Y OU CAN'T SEE YOUR OWN REFLECTION WITHOUT A mirror. At work, your team members function as that mirror, allowing you to see how others perceive your true character. Not only do coworkers provide you with the ability to learn about yourself, but surrounding yourself with different kinds of people can bring out aspects of your personality that even those closest to you haven't seen. This is when working on a team can be revealing, rewarding, and also frustrating.

Famed sociologist Robert Bellah comments that being a member of a community, or a team, offers the opportunity to learn things about yourself you didn't realize. You may find that you have the ability to relate to someone twenty years younger than you are; that you are compassionate; or that you can inspire confidence in someone who is feeling insecure. It can also be frustrating—maybe patience isn't your virtue, yet you need to muster every bit of it in order to get along productively with another team member.

When you discover traits you don't appreciate in yourself, working with a team can be a beneficial way to work through them that improves both your work and home life.

CAREER | WEDNESDAY

Charm is the quality in others that makes us more satisfied with ourselves.
—*Henri-Frederic Amiel*

W E ALL KNOW SOMEONE WHO WALKS INTO A ROOM and radiates charm. This person always seems confident, happy, and quick with a joke or story to tell. We can't help but gravitate toward her. We look forward to seeing her again and again. We find charming people to be captivating, yet not overbearing. Most important, charming people are often successful in business.

Poet and philosopher Henri-Frederic Amiel lived in Switzerland during the eighteen hundreds, a time for which charm could procure almost anything, except for social status. Even though he was denied access to the aristocracy, he knew that being around someone with a great personality makes others feel good. But how can someone always be upbeat, especially when charm seems unreal or exhausting for the rest of us to master? Even though they may seem disingenuous, charming people are very real. Unfortunately, many of us underestimate the power of charm.

On a scale of one to ten, how charming are you? Most people are probably a five. To raise your score, start by being friendlier towards your coworkers. Dole out compliments as long as they are sincere. Charm pays off by making people feel better about themselves. Try making your workplace a more pleasant environment. This will pay off in the long run and even the office grump might come around.

SALES | THURSDAY

One learns to itch
where one can scratch.
—*Sir Francis Bacon*

YOU'D THINK THE PHILOSOPHER, WRITER, AND SCIENTIST Sir Frances Bacon, who was said to have been the last man on earth to have all knowledge as his province, and who some have even theorized was the author of works attributed to Shakespeare, would be above concerning himself with itching and scratching. But he makes his point quite succinctly—you learn how to itch in places that you're able to reach to scratch.

The subject is adaptability, and Bacon spent a lot of time writing about it in his scientific studies. This led to the "Baconian method," or, as we call it four hundred years later, the scientific method. Yes, Bacon invented the scientific method, a practical approach to science that involves adapting next steps according to observational or experimental findings. Inflexibility does not have a place in scientific study.

This advice applies to sales: being rigid in sales will never work. To succeed, you must learn to adapt to changes in the market, in technology, and in your own attitude. Those who adapt often break new ground. Adapting to a situation or being able to reorient yourself in new directions—finding a place where you can scratch—is a win-win situation for you and your company.

LEADERSHIP | FRIDAY

> From the earliest days at eBay, I posted
> five core values on the site—not because
> they came from some business plan, but
> because they were values I've lived my life
> by—values I hoped would help govern
> the community. —*Pierre Omidyar*

PIERRE OMIDYAR STARTED EBAY AS A HOBBY. HE SAW A need for a marketplace that would empower people to sell things on the Internet. Since day one, Omidyar's social leanings have been "utopian," posting on the Web site a set of core values that his company espouses. These core values are so important that Omidyar added a feedback forum where users rate each other's honesty and reliability.

The five core values are the following:

- People are basically good.
- Everyone has something to contribute.
- An honest, open environment can bring out the best in people.
- Recognize and respect that everyone is an individual.
- Treat others the way you want to be treated.

Applying and adhering to a set of core values demonstrates true leadership. In turn, these values will help you define your business and life goals. With their coffers from eBay continuing to grow, Omidyar and his wife now finance an international microfinance fund for entrepreneurial efforts. The Omidyars exemplify how leaders who are true to their core values excel in any field.

ENTREPRENEUR | SATURDAY

> Birth and fortune are evidently the
> two circumstances which principally
> set one man above another.
>
> —*Adam Smith*

MANY PEOPLE WHO HAVE ACCUMULATED WEALTH— either through inheritance or their own hard work— have shown that it pays to be generous to those who aren't as fortunate. Bill and Melinda Gates started their foundation focusing on global health and learning. Warren Buffett set up his children with sufficient inheritance then pledged the rest of his great fortune to the Gates' foundation. Tiger Woods and other highly compensated sports athletes have created foundations to help less fortunate children realize their dreams. Most of these people have more money than they can ever spend in their lifetime, and perhaps their children's lifetimes, but even those of us with more modest fortunes can help raise the fortunes of others.

Think of ways that your company can contribute to the betterment of society. Let your employees know that this is an essential part of your business plan. Include them in the conversation about which organizations your company will support, or set up a matching fund so that your company will contribute to charities that match their personal interests.

Adam Smith, the founding father of modern economics, knew the value of social status. The same rules apply today, more than two hundred years later. Because of this, remember to use your good fortune to help others who are less fortunate.

MANAGING PEOPLE | SUNDAY

Don't shoot the messenger.
—*Anonymous*

HOW MANY TIMES HAVE YOU HEARD THAT PHRASE? Probably too many to count. The principle is simple: When you hear something that you don't particularly want to know or think about, don't automatically blame the person who brings the bad news to your attention.

Let's say you're a brand manager for a toothbrush company, and you learn from a subordinate at a morning meeting that the competition is developing a radically new product that brushes and flosses at the same time. The idea seems ridiculously far-fetched in your mind, as you believe that focusing on what works today is more important than worrying about half-cocked ideas that won't work tomorrow. Dressing down the subordinate for wasting precious time isn't going to help. And more important, it's not going to stop the competition.

Don't bother throwing around your authority by shooting the messenger. It's a natural reaction, but it's also a sign of emotional weakness. It's defensive and it makes you look foolish instead of powerful. Now think about the wondrously valuable alternative: there's usually an important message to be absorbed when you hear something you don't like. So be receptive to what other people have to tell you, especially when it's bad news.

MOTIVATION | MONDAY

> Only a man who knows what it is
> like to be defeated can reach down to
> the bottom of his soul and come up
> with the extra ounce of power it takes
> to win when the match is even.
>
> —*Muhammad Ali*

D EFEAT IS A MAJOR THEME IN BOXING. MANY GREAT writers have waxed poetic on the subject. Metaphors and analogies for everyday life abound. And within boxing, no star rises higher than that of Muhammad Ali. But his career was no straight and steady course toward victory. He was handed defeats on the world stage many times.

Ali's career could have ended when he was stripped of his heavyweight title by the World Boxing Association for his refusal to serve in the army during the Vietnam War, stating he was a conscientious objector. Ultimately, he was exonerated in the courts, but he didn't fight for three more years. In the meantime, he stayed in shape, always thinking of the day he would return to the ring to regain his title. This vision became a reality when Ali triumphed over George Foreman in the "Rumble in the Jungle." Against Foreman, Ali came up with that "extra ounce of power" to win.

Ali learned from his defeats. He never gave up, and when the time came, he brought forth all the inner strength he gained through years of defeat and used it to win against Foreman.

Be like Ali, and use defeat to find your inner strengths.

TEAM-BUILDING | TUESDAY

Purpose inspires performance and commitment. —*Ken Blanchard*

MANAGEMENT GURU KEN BLANCHARD TEACHES supervisors that if you assign a task that may appear pointless, spend the time to explain what the purpose of the task is. Explain why the results of their statistical analysis will allow the marketing department to better understand the buying habits of teens, which will in the long run save them from spending time and money developing a marketing plan that simply won't work.

Horseback riders see this in their horses. Riding in circles in a ring holds no excitement to a horse. Even though there is a purpose—getting ready for a dressage test or a show with the local club—the horse has no idea about this future purpose. Yet most horses will go through the motions without argument, getting a glazed-over look in their eyes. But, if you give the horse an immediate purpose—herding cows, trimming overhead branches on a trail, or just riding to the end of a long driveway to get the mail—you'll get a more lively, committed partner.

So, too, with your team members. Giving purpose to the tasks you give your team will energize their intensity. Then they will be able to perform the tasks they are given with commitment and a desire to excel.

CAREER | WEDNESDAY

*You never get a second chance to
make a first impression.* —*Anonymous*

WE ARE TAUGHT FROM A YOUNG AGE TO DRAW conclusions and make choices quickly. That's why it's crucial that we take full advantage of making a good first impression. People lead excruciatingly busy lives—juggling a career, family, and friends—so grabbing someone's attention is difficult. And, if you succeed in getting their attention, you will only have seconds before they move on to the next new thing. Automatically, someone will make a judgment about you in the first moments of seeing you.

It's easy to put your best foot forward when you meet new people in both your business as well as your personal life. Make sure to always be clean and well-groomed. After an initial introductory handshake, look your team members or business associates in the eye, smile, and stand up straight. Repeat their name, and then follow with your full name. Don't mumble. If your name has a strange pronunciation, briefly explain it. For example, "I'm Chuck Digh, spelled like High." People will not only appreciate the information, it will create a reason for them to remember you.

During an initial business encounter, don't interrupt others while they are talking. Don't take a cell phone call, fidget, or look at your watch. If the situation warrants, hold the door or offer a hand to help. And lastly, express gratitude for the opportunity to meet them. If you follow these common courtesies, you'll always make a great first impression.

SALES | THURSDAY

A brand for a company is like a reputation for a person. You earn reputation by trying to do hard things well. —Jeff Bezos

H IS COLLEAGUES WERE SKEPTICAL WHEN JEFF BEZOS left a promising corporate career to sell books on this new thing called the Internet. Amazon.com launched in 1994, and the rest is history. Today Bezos is ranked thirty-third on the *Forbes* list of America's wealthiest people.

As a computer scientist, Bezos was already familiar with online communications, and as soon as the World Wide Web debuted to the consumer market, he saw a great potential for a vast new sales vehicle. At the same time, he realized he had a difficult challenge ahead of him. He wouldn't be meeting his customers face-to-face, so he had to find a way to build a reputation for his start-up another way. He made people respect the reputation of his brand.

Amazon treated customers like friends. The praise about Amazon spread by word-of-mouth. This positive spin was followed up with outstanding customer service. If you needed to return something or make an exchange, Amazon handled these transactions immediately and efficiently.

As Bezos and his team improved the technology, Amazon became an even better friend. Its state-of-the-art artificial intelligence knows you—making clever suggestions for new books, CDs, and DVD. See how you can learn from his lead in your business, whether or not you ever meet face-to-face with your customers.

LEADERSHIP | FRIDAY

It is the mark of an educated mind to be able to entertain a thought without accepting it. —*Aristotle*

I F YOU'VE EVER QUESTIONED THE WAY A BUSINESS DOES something, only to be told, "It's always been done this way," you're in good company. It's the premise behind Aristotle's book, *Ethics,* which espouses "theoretical wisdom to be a more valuable state of mind than practical wisdom." To live your life following practical wisdom is to follow predetermined rules and work within set boundaries. This status quo provides a comfortable structure for most individuals.

Doing without thinking or accepting without questioning, however, is limiting. Aristotle understood that in order to be a leader, you need to think beyond what is already acceptable convention. Instead, you must entertain radical thinking or what he called, "a pursuit of theoretical wisdom."

It's the same in the business world. Most technical, social, and modern advances have come from inquisitive leaders, asking the simple question, "What if…?" Without questioning the existing rules that governed the human world, there is no hope for innovation. Instead of relying on conventional methodology, a true leader thinks of new ways to view everything.

Pursuing theoretical wisdom requires you to acquire a working knowledge of the boundaries that exist and to develop your mental ability to analyze and pursue a new way of looking at the subject matter.

ENTREPRENEUR | SATURDAY

For every failure, there's an alternative course of action. You just have to find it. When you come to a roadblock, take a detour. —*Mary Kay Ash*

ANY ENTREPRENEUR WILL TELL YOU THAT THE ENTRE-preneurial road is like Dorothy's yellow brick road in *The Wizard of Oz*: sometimes it's a beautiful thing, and other times there is danger lurking behind every talking tree. Talk about roadblocks! Take cosmetics giant Mary Kay Ash: during her sales career she was repeatedly passed up for promotions despite her sales success. Each time, the better jobs went to men, which was not an unusual experience for women in the mid-twentieth century. But these roadblocks led her on a path that would change her life. She started Mary Kay Cosmetics Inc. in 1963. Branding her company with trademark pink packaging as well as the legendary pink Cadillacs which were given to top performers, Mary Kay soon became phenomenally successful. When she died in 2001, Mary Kay Cosmetics had more than $2 billion in sales. Her many books have provided inspiration to millions of readers, including students at Harvard Business School.

It's hard not to get discouraged when your road to success is bumpy. So inspire yourself with a book or two that highlights other entrepreneurial success stories. Read how other entrepreneurs shook off failure and soldiered on to fulfill their dreams and accomplish amazing things. Follow their examples, and soon you will experience similar success.

MANAGING PEOPLE | SUNDAY

*You take people as far as they will go, not
as far as you would like them to go.*
—Jeanette Rankin

J EANETTE RANKIN WAS A DREAMER WHO DREAMED BIG.
A small-town girl from Minnesota, she was elected as the
first congresswoman to the United States House of Repre-
sentatives in 1916—a full four years before women officially
got the right to vote in a federal election. Talk about leading the pack.

Early on, Rankin knew that she wanted to be a voice for
women in America. She lived her life setting the example
that she wanted others to follow. As the lone woman on
Capitol Hill, Rankin was no stranger to controversy. A lifelong pacifist, she voted against the United States entering
World War I, World War II, and the Vietnam War. Trying
to persuade other members of Congress that going to war
was the wrong choice was considered political suicide. Nevertheless, Rankin stuck to her guns and continued to be
reelected.

The wisdom of Rankin's actions applies to any manager
in business. As a supervisor, you can only lead people so far.
Whether it's motivating a lazy employee to reach his or her
potential or persuading an eager newbie to slow down, you
can't be responsible for what others end up doing. All you
can do is try your best to show them the way.

MOTIVATION | MONDAY

The achievement of one goal should
be the starting point of another.
—*Alexander Graham Bell*

ACCOMPLISHMENT IS A GRATIFYING EXPERIENCE: IT offers the rare opportunity to sit back, relax, and revel in how great you are. And there's nothing wrong with enjoying the glow of your achievement. Take advantage and treat yourself to a fine dinner or a day at the spa. But after that, don't linger. There's a lot more to do. One achievement should lead to another. So start thinking about a new goal.

Alexander Graham Bell needs no introduction as the inventor of the telephone. He began inventing sound devices because his mother and his wife were both deaf. There were a lot of other sound-related experiments before that famous day in Boston in 1876 when he phoned his assistant down the hall, and said, "Mr. Watson, come here. I want to see you."

Bell didn't stop with the telephone, which even he realized would completely change the world. He went on to invent the phonograph, the metal detector, the hydrofoil, and a host of other things. Each achievement was the starting point and motivation for another.

Goal setting never stops if you build on your achievements. Once you accomplish one goal, set another for yourself. When you sit back on your laurels, remember that it will soon be time to start thinking of where you can go and what you can do next.

TEAM-BUILDING | TUESDAY

It's not the will to win, but the will to prepare to win that makes the difference.

—Bear Bryant

SUCCESS ON OR OFF THE FOOTBALL FIELD DOESN'T COME simply from the desire to be successful. Instead, you need to do the groundwork in order to "win." You may have a great business idea, but you just can't open shop and assume all you need is that one good idea. You need to create a business plan, investigate where your market is and how to reach it, figure out what you are going to need for sales materials, and research the best way to maximize sales. These steps are crucial if you want your business to last for any length of time. And in order to be fully vested in the project or the business venture, you need to believe that preparation is both rewarding and meaningful.

If you are a leader charged with overseeing your team doing the prep work of a new project, let them know how important their work is to the bigger picture. Legendary University of Alabama football coach Bear Bryant knew that no football team could win a game without many practices and workouts—pro baseball teams spend two months in spring training preparing for the season!

All the preparation in the world can't guarantee your success, but lack of preparation will almost certainly ensure failure.

CAREER | WEDNESDAY

What the world needs from you is not
to add to their number, but to figure
out, and then contribute to the world,
what you came into this world to do.
—*Richard Nelson Bolles*

FINDING A CAREER THAT IS BOTH CHALLENGING AND rewarding can be difficult, but it is worth the effort. Begin by determining if your current job fits into your life's purpose. If you are relatively happy at work, you may just need to make small adjustments like finding a new job in the same industry or switching departments within the same corporation.

If you are ready for a more radical change, you can employ Richard Nelson Bolles's methodology. His classic book, *What Color is Your Parachute?*, teaches that you can find the career you were meant for by prioritizing your values. The first step is to rank them in order of importance. Do you value stability, mental challenges, or a three-day weekend? If you like to work outdoors, then accounting obviously won't be a rewarding career choice.

Once you evaluate your priorities, new career options will begin to crystallize. Some of your current lifestyle choices, like having a new luxury car every few years, may not match your new earning potential. But, according to Bolles, identifying your unique business skills will ultimately lead to financial and personal success. And by doing so, you'll find yourself in a career, instead of just a job.

SALES | THURSDAY

> We're adding a little something to this
> month's sales contest. As you all know, first
> prize is a Cadillac Eldorado. Anybody want
> to see second prize? Second prize is a set of
> steak knives. Third prize is you're fired.
>
> —*Blake,* Glengarry Glen Ross *(1992)*

B LAKE, A CHARACTER PLAYED BY ALEC BALDWIN IN THE
film version of David Mamet's brilliant play, is the guy
from the central office who reads this blistering riot act to
the four salesmen in a losing real estate branch. He wants to
see "closers" on deals and taunts them with "leads" on the
hot new properties, Glengarry and Glen Ross. The month's
bottom seller will not only lose out on getting any of these
leads, he will also be fired.

The machinations that follow are not only career-ending
but criminal for some of the characters. Mamet makes the
point that, given a cut-throat competitive environment, the
pressure to be the best will make some people go to any
lengths to win. Sales careers are stereotyped by this type of
attitude, but you certainly don't have to behave this way in
order to succeed.

It's tough not to bow to pressure when your job—and
commissions—depend on it. Keeping your values in perspective and not compromising your integrity means a lot
more than keeping a job. And if your boss asks you to do
something unethical, find a new job. Life is too short to work
in a hostile environment.

LEADERSHIP | FRIDAY

> Politics is not a necessary evil in the leadership game—it is necessary. No leader achieves goals without playing politics. Politics is the air leaders breathe and an important source of an organization's energy and dynamism.
>
> —*Anthony F. Smith*

THERE IS A FINE LINE BETWEEN WORKING THE ROOM AND working someone over. While some people eagerly join in the carousel of cronyism, others cringe at the thought. However, being political can actually be a useful tool for someone working his or her way through the company's ranks. Anthony F. Smith writes in his book, *The Taboos of Leadership,* that politics serve a company by outlining who the players are and who really yields the power.

Politics get a bad rap, however, when management promotes blatantly obvious kiss-ups while ignoring the hard work of others. Although you might need to play politics to get to the top, a true leader shouldn't play politics overtly—it undermines her authority. Instead, as a leader, you must master the illusion that you are not playing politics. This will satisfy the underlings while you wheel-and-deal with the power players who also have their own agenda. Smith writes, "The political leader knows how to stack the deck, play the right cards, build solid alliances, triangulate issues, and isolate those with conflicting points of view."

Knowing how to play politics will only help you win.

ENTREPRENEUR | SATURDAY

Growth without prior planning can be
as fun as a hard kick in the stomach.
—*Tim Berry*

B USINESS GROWTH IS NOT ALWAYS A POSITIVE THING. Small businesses frequently fail as a result of growing too fast—overstretching their resources, taking on too much debt to finance growth, or losing their attention to detail and keeping track of additional costs. Growth, however, is usually a business goal and can turn out to be lucrative when it is carefully planned.

Planning for growth goes beyond just projecting increased sales and higher revenues. Be sure to factor in how you are going to get there. How do you pay for supplies until sales catch up? Do you have the human resources in place to accommodate the increased business? If not, where do you get them? What upfront expenses need to be covered before you can see the resulting revenue? Where will that money come from?

One of the first places you can turn to for consultation about growth is your accountant or a financial representative at your local bank. These people should be able to advise you and help you plan for expansion.

Entrepreneurs must guard against being swept up in the rush of the moment where expansion gets out of hand. As business planning expert Tim Berry knows, you must expect growth by planning for it.

MANAGING PEOPLE | SUNDAY

Effective leaders adjust their style to provide what the group can't provide for itself. —Ken Blanchard

A WINNING BASEBALL MANAGER KNOWS WHAT HIS TEAM needs inside the clubhouse and on the field. When his team plays its best, he can stay out of the way. In a pressure-packed playoff game, he might call for a clever pitching change, or during a losing streak, he can take the pressure off slumping batters with a day off or a lineup shift.

Whether it's baseball or business, the ability to adapt successfully to the circumstances often defines the best managers. After all, employees and players alike want to prove their worth to the team. Legendary consultant Ken Blanchard teaches that the most effective managers regularly adapt to the needs of the groups they lead. At various points, these leaders provide direction, support, encouragement—or nothing at all.

When a new project is in the pipeline, the need for direction from the start is paramount. Group members may be committed but unsure of what to do next. Later, they may start doubting other team members' commitment or wondering if their own ideas matter. At this point, rather than telling people what to do, effective leaders should solicit the group's best ideas to show everyone that teamwork is crucial. In the end individual members of the group may never realize what it takes to win without agile leaders giving them what they need when they need it.

MOTIVATION | MONDAY

Our fear of weakness seems to overshadow
our confidence in our strengths.
—Marcus Buckingham and Donald Clifton

D EEPLY ROOTED IN OUR CULTURE IS THE IDEA THAT
mistakes and weaknesses need to be fixed. Starting in
childhood, your parents might have done everything they
could to help you overcome your weaknesses: if you had
trouble in math, they got you a tutor; if you couldn't play
baseball, they found you a pitching coach. But if the situation was looked at from another vantage point, you might
have fared differently: if the focus was put on how well you
did in all subjects other than math or on how fast you could
run even though you couldn't throw a ball, you might have
succeeded in other areas.

Rather than focusing on perceived weaknesses in your
management of personnel or in the delivery of the duties of
your job, switch gears and focus on your strengths. Develop
confidence in those strengths and develop strategies to work
around your weaknesses.

If public speaking is your strong point but writing long
annual reports is not, see if you can redesign your job so that
more speaking is involved. As the authors of the bestselling
business book, *Now, Discover Your Strengths*, teach, concentrate
on building upon your strengths rather than fixing your
weaknesses.

TEAM-BUILDING | TUESDAY

Regardless of what you are doing, if you pump long enough, hard enough, and enthusiastically enough, sooner or later the effort will bring forth the reward.

—*Zig Ziglar*

SOMETIMES IT SIMPLY TAKES HARD WORK TO REACH success. You may seem like you are getting nowhere, but as Zig Ziglar instructs, by pumping harder and longer your muscles will start getting stronger, so you won't have to pump as hard in the future to get to success.

Convey your enthusiasm to your team, and never stop believing in your success. This doesn't mean going out and panning for fool's gold. But if you have done your homework and know your idea is of sound value, keep motivating your team to plug away. No one else is going to believe in your ideas unless you show that you do.

There are famous examples of those who didn't give up. A dramatic case is the Wright brothers and their crazy idea of flying a plane. They kept trying, each time tweaking their invention and getting a few feet further off the ground on the next flight. And look where we are now with aviation—from legs dangling in the air in an open cockpit to luxury airliners crossing the globe.

The Wright brothers were so enthusiastic and committed to flying, that they changed the world. And even though they aren't around to see its peak, they surely knew aviation was headed somewhere they couldn't even imagine.

CAREER | WEDNESDAY

> Office politics is just like the lottery.
> Dreaming about winning doesn't get
> you anywhere—there's no pay off if
> you don't buy a ticket. You have to
> play if you want to win. *—Jamie Fabian*

JAMIE FABIAN BELIEVES THAT SHUNNING THE POLITICAL scene at the water cooler will get you nowhere fast. "You'll be most effective if you can deal with things the way they are, not the way you think they should be," says Fabian, a business writer and columnist for Jobcircle.com.

Even though you might think you are above office politics, plan on embracing them. Rethink your perspective and determine how office politics can help your career. First, the heavy hitters are usually involved. Chances are that one of them is someone important who needs to know about you and your accomplishments. Second, make sure you can run in different circles and don't cast your vote too early. It takes awhile to ferret out the posers from the real power players: you don't want to risk aligning yourself with a persona non grata. Third, before jumping into the gossip mill, take a step back and listen for a change in political climate. People who listen get more information and can pick and choose their course of action.

And remember—just because you heard it, doesn't mean it's true. Steer clear of rumor mongering. It's bad for your career and your reputation.

SALES | THURSDAY

> Price is what you pay.
> Value is what you get.
> —*Warren Buffett*

THIS LINE EPITOMIZES THE INVESTMENT PHILOSOPHY OF the "Oracle of Omaha." His astute value investment strategy made him the richest person in the world in 2008. Buffett doesn't invest according to price. Rather, he invests on the basis of value or what the market or the customer gets in return.

It works this way. A customer will pay for a product if she thinks it has an intrinsic use. What assigns its worth is quality—the value. A product isn't necessarily quality just because a long manufacturing process makes it and it costs a fortune at retail. If it doesn't work for the customer, it has no value. And if the product has no value, then customers won't buy it, no matter how impressive the sales pitch.

Take software, for instance. The software manufacturer believes that the years of development that went into designing the upgrade determine the product's value. But if the customer isn't going to get anything new from an upgrade, then why pay for it? The software maker is then proven wrong.

Know that you are selling value, and the price tag won't matter. The customers will want it, no matter what the cost.

LEADERSHIP | FRIDAY

Effective leaders provide for succession.
—*Alan Axelrod*

QUEEN ELIZABETH I WAS NO STRANGER TO THE POLITICS of succession. As the only surviving heir of her father, Henry VIII, and mother, Anne Boleyn, she was favored for the crown—that is, until her mother was beheaded. Imprisoned and exiled by her own sister (Mary, Queen of Scots) because she wasn't a Catholic, Elizabeth never spoke out against her sister, but kept her counsel to herself. During her long reign as queen, Elizabeth never forgot the power of keeping a secret. Knowing that picking the right successor would be the only chance to ensure a peaceful transfer of power, she kept her subordinates guessing about her successor as she went on with the business of governing.

Alan Axelrod writes in *Elizabeth I, CEO* that a leader must keep her choice of successor a secret at all costs. If you make the information known too early, you risk alienating and undermining your authority. For Elizabeth, this meant possibly being overthrown or killed.

Although extreme, this metaphor might feel applicable to many CEOs. While not openly rejecting candidates or showing favoritism, a leader must scrutinize all potential candidates. After you have made a choice, give your successor the means to make decisions implicitly while maintaining the illusion that you are still calling the shots. Using this method of indirectly relinquishing power, you'll be able to adequately mentor and prepare your successor.

ENTREPRENEUR | SATURDAY

Good design can't fix broken
business models. —*Jeffrey Veen*

T HE BEST PRODUCT IDEA IN THE WORLD WILL UNLIKELY
reach its target market without fundamental manufacturing, marketing, and sales models representing good business. That doesn't mean you can't be innovative and original
in how you do business. Many companies have tried creative
ideas to stand out, either publicly or within the organization's makeup. Employee ownership, flexible work schedules, and other employee-oriented ideas can attract a loyal
and creative workforce.

Ford Motor Company's Saturn brand went straight for
the jugular of automobile purchasing by eliminating the
negotiation dance that customers feel compelled to do—and
often dislike—when buying a new car. And the brand is still
around today. Overnight service? Free shipping on Internet
sales? These and other "crazy" ideas have helped make many
companies stand out and be successful.

The innovations may be in the details, but the foundation
for models of good business are still intact. You can build a
bicycle with new toe clip design, put the shift levers on the
tips of the handlebars, or use solid disc wheels instead of
wheels with spokes—but in order for it to be a bicycle, it still
needs a framework that allows for it to move on two wheels.
Famed Web designer Jeffery Veen knows that you can tweak
the details, but you should leave the fundamental framework
of good business intact.

MANAGING PEOPLE | SUNDAY

Search others for their virtues,
thyself for thy vices.
—*Benjamin Franklin*

As A MANAGER, IT'S EASY TO PIGEONHOLE YOUR employees. You've seen them all in action—the leaders, the workers, the slackers, the confused, the wannabes, and the nobodies. People will eventually play into the stereotypes that you've created. Constantly reminding people of their bad habits and crowing about how you might as well do it yourself isn't very effective either.

One of the main reasons people change jobs hasn't changed since the time of old Ben Franklin. People often leave good employment opportunities simply because they don't like their immediate supervisor. Since turnover is costly and unproductive, rethinking your expectations as well as how you interact with your employees might benefit everybody.

Start by considering each of your employees as a unique person with the potential to become great at his job. If you let him know that you are expecting greatness, it might actually happen. Another trick to getting the most out of people is to let them know that you're on their side. If you empathize with employees, you'll develop a relationship of trust and understanding with them. When weakness rears its ugly head, your employees will seek your counsel and try to work with you in order to get better, because they are seeking your approval. Who knows? They just might do it.

MOTIVATION | MONDAY

*It's not so important who starts the game
but who finishes it. —John Wooden*

JOHN WOODEN WAS THE GREATEST COLLEGE BASKETBALL
coach in history. The record winning streak of the UCLA
Bruins (eighty-eight games), including ten National College Athletic Assoiciation titles, gave the "Wizard of West-
wood" plenty of statistical and practical evidence that the
players who start the game are not a big factor in who's
going to win. What counts is staying in the game, playing
at full capacity, and doing your best.

And so it translates into the game of business. Let's say
you don't launch a new product or discover a new sales technique before the competition—it doesn't mean you're going
to lose. Don't let someone else's innovation inhibit you.
Remember that your ability has gotten you where you are
today. Concentrate on what you do, and don't slow down
because you didn't get to market first.

Take advantage of being second. Capitalize on the lessons learned from your competition and use that valuable
knowledge to make your product or your plan better. Think
of Apple's success. They never invented the MP3 player;
they just invented the one that the market fell in love with.
Focus on continuing to deliver excellence, and you will not
only gain from the experience, but it's entirely possible you
might still win the market.

TEAM-BUILDING | TUESDAY

*We rarely confide in those who are
better than we are.* —*Albert Camus*

I ONCE TOOK A JOB RUNNING A SMALL DEPARTMENT OF A larger company. When I arrived to meet my new team, I was told by the human resources manager that under their former department head the group had developed low morale.

As time went on, I began to unravel the story of why the department had been so unhappy. One little discovery was especially revealing. The first time an industry weekly trade magazine landed on my desk, I read it and then made up a circulation list with the names of everyone in the department on it, stapled it to the top of the magazine, and put it in the next person's mailbox.

I quickly learned that this was a practice that had not been implemented before. The former manager did not circulate the trade magazine to the group: he read it and tossed it in the trash. That tale led me to believe that he was overly concerned that those who worked for him not become more knowledgeable than he was.

You don't lose anything by increasing your team's business savvy and industry knowledge. Heed Albert Camus's advice and be eager for your team to become experts on whatever project you assign. There's nothing more motivating than a well-equipped team that wants to succeed and feels like they've learned something along the way.

CAREER | WEDNESDAY

It's not who you know, it's who knows you. —*Jeffrey Gitomer*

MOST PEOPLE ASSUME THE MOST EFFICIENT WAY TO network is by positioning yourself to meet the right people. But if you think meeting people is the only way to network, you're missing out on a huge, free networking resource—yourself. In *The Little Black Book of Connections,* Jeffrey Gitomer writes that making a name for yourself can happen two ways. The conventional way is to attend parties, pass out business cards, speak at conventions, and follow up with phone calls. The unconventional way is having your name speak for itself. When people discuss who they think someone should call if they need an expert, you want your name to be at the top of the list.

Imagine being able to generate plenty of positive publicity when you are not even around. Joining a trade organization in your field is a great place to start. Most people join a trade organization, send their dues in, never attend any events, and then wonder why they bothered. But, if you become active, volunteering for the head of an important event, suddenly your name will be at the top of the list of "who's in charge," generating a large number of contacts and instant credibility. Get your name out there and become someone people want to meet.

SALES | THURSDAY

> Success is the result of your single-minded focus on what you want. The energy to sustain your drive must, and can, only come from within your own head. —*Kevin Hogan and James Speakman*

I N THE SPY GAME IT'S CALLED "COVERT ACTION." IN SALES, it's a more subtle version, as in the title of Hogan and Speakman's compelling book, *Covert Persuasion.* Covert persuasion is your own secret operation. You observe customers and anticipate how they'll react to your pitch. You are super-aware of whom you're dealing with, know what drives them, then single-mindedly focus on persuading them to buy what you're selling and land the deal.

Covert persuasion in selling requires you to anticipate problems or resistance and be prepared to change the mind of your customer with just the right words. Your job is to help the customer think about another outcome. Use questions to redirect your customer's thinking: "Well, what do you think about changing the color of the widget to make it more harmonious with your product line? We can do that for you." And never phrase a question that gives the customer the option of responding with a definite "no."

All the energy you use in persuasion comes from you—from within your own head. Sharpen your powers of observation and your verbal skills so your customers will make the choice you want them to make.

LEADERSHIP | FRIDAY

> The faculty of creative imagination is one which the majority of people never use during an entire lifetime, and if used at all, it usually happens by accident. —*Napoleon Hill*

DREAMERS, VISIONARIES, AND IDEALISTS ALL HAVE ONE thing in common. They identify something in the world they want to change, and they listen to their inner voice to find a way to do it. Napoleon Hill, in his ground-breaking book *Think and Grow Rich,* analyzed the habits of five hundred successful businessmen and found a startling conclusion. Successful people are those individuals who are able to tap into their unconscious mind through an intense level of focus, allowing a free flow of thoughts. These people were able to look outside the box, discover and invent products that never existed, apply them to the real world, and happily profit from them.

Your unconscious mind is an untapped reservoir that is full of information. You get an inkling of how powerful it is when you experience hunches. Hunches are the answers to questions that we pose to our inner voice. Don't dismiss your hunches as crazy ideas. Instead, ponder them, look at them from all angles, and be open to new possibilities.

Your inner voice can be active day and night. You can't consciously control it, but you can nudge it in the right direction. By planting words, concepts, or feelings into your internal thoughts, you will be able to access your subconscious and reap the financial benefits.

ENTREPRENEUR | SATURDAY

> Your talents are those recurring patterns
> of thought, feeling, or behavior that you
> can productively apply.
> —*Marcus Buckingham and Donald Clifton*

MARCUS BUCKINGHAM AND DONALD CLIFTON BELIEVE that once you can figure out what your talents are, you'll be able to choose a new business venture that's right for you. And once it is up and running, apply what you are good at to your business. If you are a good "people person," be involved in hiring new employees. If you are good with numbers, become your finance officer's right-hand person.

More important—and usually more difficult for entrepreneurs—is to learn how to delegate those things you do not have talent for. If you hate number-crunching, hire someone to do your books for you. If you are a klutz with scissors, hire a more craft-oriented person to create your window displays. Taking on tasks that don't use your best talents not only means they will be done less satisfactorily— it also means you will probably become quickly dissatisfied with your work life and experience entrepreneurial burnout.

When you delegate a task to someone else, be very clear what you want done. If you can, let others do your thing, their way. You need to concern yourself with the outcome, not the process.

Use your skills to their max; recognize which skills you don't have that your company needs, and go find someone with those skills. And then let them help!

MANAGING PEOPLE | SUNDAY

It helps a ton when you learn people's names and don't butcher them when trying to pronounce them. —*Jerry Yang*

S OMETIMES KNOWN AS "CHIEF YAHOO," JERRY YANG, the company's former CEO, offered this advice about people's names in a 1997 interview. Asked if he had any business secrets that aided in him as he logged two to three trips across the globe every month, Yang didn't bother with wonky techno-talk or financial mumbo-jumbo. He immediately raised the people issue.

Yang may not be considered a brilliant manager, but his answer should be admired by all managers who aspire to be brilliant. Whether you are traveling and meeting new clients or just traveling the halls of your company, learning people's names and knowing how to pronounce them is simple currency that earns those people's respect. You need that, desperately, to manage effectively. This skill is a simple marker for the quality of a manager's compassion, regardless of whom you are managing. It's a sign that you talk to your people, early and often.

MOTIVATION | MONDAY

> If you can't take a nap at noon, you can
> at least try to lie down for an hour before
> the evening meal. It's cheaper than a
> cocktail and, over the long stretch, it is
> 5,467 times more effective. —*Dale Carnegie*

P EOPLE ON A FAST-PACED CAREER TRACK OFTEN TEND TO
burn the candle at both ends. They are programmed to
believe that if they work harder and longer, they can get
ahead, solve that problem, or win that customer. But face it:
none of these things is going to happen if you're exhausted.

Dale Carnegie's bestselling book, *How to Stop Worrying
and Start Living,* is about stress management—in fact, it was
the first book ever written on the subject. Carnegie wrote it
because he was sick of stressing out over his position in life
and he wanted to stop feeling that way. So he analyzed what
he was worrying about, what it did to him, and devised
techniques to stop it.

One of his first realizations was that stress and worry
cause fatigue. So Carnegie's strategies for combating fatigue
include this simple technique: lie down for an hour before
dinner. He translated those hours into the course of a lifetime to get the technique he called "5,467 times more effective" than a cocktail.

Today it's even harder to find a free hour. But you can
adapt. Find time to take a break—even twenty minutes will
suffice. It will do wonders for your stamina and your peace
of mind.

TEAM-BUILDING | TUESDAY

> To succeed as a team is to hold all of the members accountable for their expertise. —*Mitchell Caplan*

PEOPLE ARE PROUD OF WHAT THEY KNOW AND ARE good at, so let your team members shine. Mitchell Caplan, former CEO of eTrade Financial Corp., believes you need to be sure these people really have the expertise needed to succeed. Most times, the best way to do that is to hire people who already have the right experience for the job.

Sometimes, however, you are better served hiring people with the skills for the job but perhaps not the specific expertise. For example, if you hire someone who has worked in a marketing department and is good at juggling multiple tasks but has never put together an entire marketing program, she may be the right person you need for a very busy office.

Even when you hire someone with the fundamental skills, it is your responsibility to make sure she gets the specialized training she needs. In fact, encourage employees to constantly further their education—no matter what interests them. Learning to play music teaches people how to be detailed; and learning to dance gives them energy and enthusiasm! Encourage employees to take seminars, workshops, and courses in skills that are directly related to their jobs.

By making sure you've hired the best people and continuing to train and groom them, you can confidently hold each team member accountable for their expertise.

CAREER | WEDNESDAY

Dare to be mediocre.
—*Ben Casnocha*

H OW MANY TIMES HAVE YOU WANTED TO TRY SOME-thing new, but were afraid to fail? Most of us usually operate within a zero-risk philosophy. Not Ben Casnocha. In 2000, he was just another sixth grader trying to pass his technology class. Ben created a piece of Web software that was designed to track citizen complaints for government agencies. He realized that a current market for his product existed, and at age twelve founded Comcast Inc. Being twelve has its advantages—most twelve year olds know everything and can do anything. (Just ask one if you doubt it.) And they certainly aren't worried if their work is not perfect all the time.

Ben Casnocha didn't initially realize the importance of taking risks and working with what was finished instead of what should be perfect. He was too busy being successful. Over time, however, he realized what an advantage it was.

What if you took a chance and discovered that not being perfect was actually good enough to make your business goals work? It would free up all that time you spend dwelling in the world of self-doubt. Next time you find yourself wanting to pitch a new client or develop a new product, don't worry if it doesn't go exactly as expected. Lower the bar and just do your best. You may find that being mediocre just might be good enough.

SALES | THURSDAY

> The best and fastest way to learn a sport
> is to watch and imitate a champion.
> —*Jean-Claude Killy*

JEAN-CLAUDE KILLY WON THE TRIPLE CROWN OF ALPINE Skiing with a sweep of all three gold medals at the 1968 Winter Olympics in Grenoble, France. Charming and handsome, Killy was probably referring to himself as the "champion" in the quote above. But for the rest of us mere mortals, the take-home message is "Get a mentor."

Sales, like skiing, is much harder than it looks. You've probably met a million people who think they are great at it. But surely you can recognize a master salesperson when you see one. A true, professional salesperson makes you feel excited about the product—even if you think you don't need it—conveying her deep belief in it. What's more, her passion and integrity show through.

Have a mentor, but choose carefully. You want to learn from a professional, not a con artist. Once you find this kind of salesperson, ask her to take you on as an apprentice/ understudy. Make a lunch date, and ask what are the techniques that work best. Even if this super salesperson isn't in your particular field, her knowledge would surely transfer to your line of work.

LEADERSHIP | FRIDAY

> Very few companies have meaningful
> evaluation systems in place. That's not
> just bad—it's terrible! —*Jack Welch*

HONESTY DOESN'T SEEM TO BE THE BEST POLICY IN corporate America. When it comes to evaluating people fairly about their work, most companies fail miserably. Jack Welch, former CEO of General Electric Co. and author of *Winning,* says companies who don't give honest feedback to their people can't expect to be very effective at managing them. Instead, leaders need to make sure the steps are in place so that people get relevant feedback.

Feedback should be based on criteria that both management and employees agree upon. This type of evaluation can come in many forms. Most companies base raises on performance evaluations that happen once or twice a year. But more frequent and informal feedback can make all the difference. Welch writes, "I evaluated twenty or so direct reports with frequent handwritten notes that included two pieces of information: what I thought the person did well, and how I thought they could improve."

According to Welch, even companies with good evaluation systems are usually missing the most crucial element—integrity. Since most companies focus on the bottom line, managers often overlook personal conduct when the result is big profits. Finally, merit-based awards and recognition, Welch says, should be standard. After all, everyone likes to know their work is appreciated.

ENTREPRENEUR | SATURDAY

In the business world, the rearview mirror
is always clearer than the windshield.
—*Warren Buffett*

HINDSIGHT IS TWENTY-TWENTY. IT'S EASIER TO TELL WHAT happened than predict what's going to happen. It's also safe! But no one ever said "safety" and "entrepreneurship" are synonymous.

Real entrepreneurs don't worry about history. They use it to their advantage and learn from their mistakes, but they don't spend their time looking through the rearview mirror. If you do, you are going to run into something up ahead. Or worse yet, you're going to miss an opportunity because it flew by while you were looking behind you. Spend your time concentrating on today and your vision for the future.

And don't forget, you probably hired people who are looking in the rearview mirror for you—accountants, lawyers, even a human resources person. They keep tabs on what has happened and help you on the road ahead.

Entrepreneurs also don't fret if the view through the windshield isn't crystal clear. Like driving in the rain, the wise businessperson assesses the conditions and drives accordingly. You may use all the tools you have available—in the case of driving, your windshield wipers, tires with good tread, and the white lines on the sides of the road. In your business, use the market conditions, your financial status, and your pool of talent to help you get safely to your destination.

MANAGING PEOPLE | SUNDAY

I can live for two months on a good compliment. —*Mark Twain*

A CONSTANT REFRAIN IN CORPORATE AMERICA CONcerns feedback: nobody gets enough until it's too late to do anything about it. In some industries, it's virtually nonexistent, unless of course it's negative. Managers frequently find fault with employees and let them hear about it before they would ever praise a job well done.

Criticism is important, but unless it's countered by praise, employees quickly brand themselves damaged goods and lose motivation. Alternatively, a little praise boosts the energy of the workplace and bolsters productivity. Indeed, managers who praise success breed more success, because employees know exactly what kind of performance to repeat. Plus, they come to work happy and leave happier. Compliments can be large or small—usually it doesn't matter. They can also be public or private—either works well. In all cases, managers should constantly look for reasons to praise their people. Employees never tire of hearing how great they are.

Mark Twain's famous line holds true even today: compliments don't cost much, yet they are priceless.

MOTIVATION | MONDAY

*Make a decision to give wherever you go,
to whomever you see.* —*Deepak Chopra, M.D.*

I F ASKED TO GIVE A QUICK ANSWER TO THE QUESTION OF which attributes contribute to success in our modern business world, most people might say, hard work, ambition, and planning. But is that definition of success the final statement on the subject? There are other values you have to acknowledge in your definition of success. You may be leaving out a critical dimension of what makes us human: our spiritual side.

Attaining success can't be all about you. You can't succeed without other people, and being aware of others and how you interact with them is crucial to success and good fortune. This is why it is so important to understand what "giving" means. Giving to others—not in a monetary sense, but in the sense of giving of yourself, and even listening— will signal that you feel others are valuable and worth your time. And this means giving to everyone you come across in your daily life, not just in the marketplace. These people in turn will pay you back in kind.

Deepak Chopra, a pioneer in mind-body medicine who has written extensively about spirituality, says that you have to "make a decision to give." Make that decision and stick to it, and you'll get a huge return on it. Just give it a chance.

TEAM-BUILDING | TUESDAY

> A committee is a cul-de-sac down
> which ideas are lured and then quietly
> strangled. —*Sir Barnett Cocks*

AS THE CLERK OF THE ENGLISH HOUSE OF COMMONS in the 1960s, Sir Barnett Cocks knew a thing or two about committees, and hated every one he was ever a part of. Committees are commonly thought not to be particularly effective. They are often pulled together to appease a certain group or client. And committees often fail because they are set up to fail.

However, committee work can be both efficient and rewarding. It's all about forming the team. When pulling together a committee, don't just take any warm body who volunteers. Figure out which skills your task requires and how the committee can fulfill the assignment. Then, actively seek out members who bring those skills to the table.

Next, as the committee leader, you are going to have to manage the team. Don't just leave them on their own to return a verdict several months later. Check in with the committee regularly. Make sure they are getting the cooperation they need from other departments. And be sure they have the resources needed to fulfill their mission. Most important, be sure the committee has a very clear mission.

If you are clear in your intentions, careful in your selection of committee members, and oversee the committee as it progresses, you will not strangle an idea, but instead help move it forward.

CAREER | WEDNESDAY

Stop trying to impress other people.
Other people are probably so busy trying
to impress you that they will, at best, not
notice your efforts. At worst, they will
resent you for one-upping them.

—*Joe Dominguez*

WITH MARQUEE PLAYERS MARKETED ON EVERY PROfessional sports team and the rest of us blogging about what we had for breakfast, it's easy to get caught up in the "look at me" game. The celebrity "flavor of the month" hogs the spotlight; her ideas, opinions, and interviews are plastered on every talk show and magazine cover. It might seem logical to conclude that being egocentric will make you more successful. However, Joe Dominguez, author of *Your Money or Your Life,* thinks differently.

In fact, he believes the opposite is true. It's commonly known that the need to impress others is a by-product of low self-esteem. In business, even though exuding confidence is important, it's not in your best interest to brag, no matter how great your golf game, your company, or your individual accomplishments are. When you focus exclusively on yourself, you inadvertently create a competitive environment.

Instead, you'll get better results when you enter into a conversation with valuable information that has little or no relevance to your personal greatness. Avoid showing off—and you will come out ahead.

SALES | THURSDAY

> Iron rusts from disuse, stagnant water
> loses its purity, and in cold weather
> becomes frozen, even so does inaction
> sap the vigor of the mind.
>
> —*Leonardo Da Vinci*

D A VINCI WAS THE ARCHETYPE OF THE RENAISSANCE man—painter, sculptor, architect, engineer, inventor, mathematician, and anatomist. His life was dedicated to achievement, invention, and acquiring knowledge. Da Vinci possessed a ceaselessly active mind, an abundance of energy for hard work, and most important, enthusiasm for learning new things. His friend, the great sculptor Cellini, remarked at Da Vinci's death, "There had never been another man born in the world who knew as much as Leonardo."

Da Vinci knew that nothing saps the energy of body and spirit more than complacency. After years in sales, there are surely days when you come home exhausted, wondering what happened to the spark you used to have. The truth is that you've got to refresh your spark on a daily basis. Staying on top of your game requires an active mind that you keep feeding with new knowledge. New ideas inspire renewed energy and the will to take on new challenges.

As you see your sales job turning into a long-term career, make sure that you don't let yourself rust or your mind go stagnant. Stay active and open to everything new. It's contagious—your customers will feel your enthusiasm and respond positively.

LEADERSHIP | FRIDAY

> Leadership is the key to realizing the
> full potential of intellectual capital.
> —*Warren Bennis*

WARREN BENNIS, THE FOUNDING CHAIRMAN OF THE Leadership Institute at the University of Southern California's Marshall School of Business, believes that companies don't realize they possess a vast source of untapped knowledge, what he refers to as intellectual capital. If even a fraction of a company's workers contributed their knowledge to problem-solving or production capabilities, a company's productivity would skyrocket. Unfortunately, studies also show that employees also frequently gripe that nobody listens to them.

To increase productivity and worker satisfaction, take a hard, long look at the way management handles worker input. In today's highly technical world, "knowledge workers" need to be retained and challenged. When you routinely marginalize creative thinking within a company, morale suffers. Even highly motivated employees eventually stop sharing their ideas. This leads to turnover and a host of other easily avoidable problems.

A good leader should acknowledge the contributions of his workers on a routine basis. Small incentives, such as gift cards, show your employees you appreciate their hard work. Get creative with your incentives and it won't be long before you'll be swimming in intellectual capital.

ENTREPRENEUR | SATURDAY

Never tell anyone what you are going to do till you've done it.—*Cornelius Vanderbilt*

NOVELISTS OFTEN ABIDE BY THIS AMERICAN BUSINESS tycoon's statement—they won't discuss their work-in-progress for fear of losing their creative spark. Your reason for keeping an idea to yourself may be something else—the fear of an idea being "stolen," the fear of losing momentum, or wanting to use the element of surprise when your competitors learn of your new product or service.

But you probably can't keep the idea completely to yourself if you want to accomplish your goals. There is no way you can open a business without revealing your plans to someone along the way—if only to get the required permits or help stocking your shelves. And if you are going to build a solid working team, it will help to build it from the ground up. That includes telling your team your idea.

Be sure everyone who is working with you knows that the idea is to be kept under wraps until you are ready to announce it. If you are concerned about your idea being revealed before you are ready, release it to the team slowly, on a "need-to-know" basis. Then if something leaks out, it is just a piece, not the whole idea. Or, ask them to sign a confidentiality agreement so that they realize you are serious about keeping things hush-hush.

MANAGING PEOPLE | SUNDAY

> Whenever there is a hard job to be
> done I assign it to a lazy man; he is
> sure to find an easy way of doing it.
> —*Walter Chrysler*

A T FIRST GLANCE, LAZY EMPLOYEES SEEM TO BE THE opposite of an ideal hire. While constantly complaining about how much they have to do, they never seem to be doing anything. But, a lazy employee might not be all that he or she appears to be. Lazy people have an important strength: finding shortcuts. Since they want to do as little as possible, they always find easy ways of getting the job done.

Walter Chrysler needed this kind of lazy genius on his side each time he was called in to save dying car companies. Early in his career, Walter toiled for Buick Motors while the company made forty-five cars a day. In less than a decade, he helped increase production numbers to six hundred a day. Chrysler streamlined the manufacturing process, putting people and parts in the right places. It was hard work that required easy shortcuts.

Do you manage people who never seem busy enough but appear to keep your organization humming? Chances are that they do something so well that they might seem lazy. Take a lesson from their attraction to shortcuts. Organizations with efficient employees can regularly increase their productivity—the route to a fatter bottom line. If you've got "lazy" employees, find out what they do best and ask them to do more of it.

MOTIVATION | MONDAY

Enduring trust in a relationship cannot be faked, and it is rarely produced by a dramatic, one-time effort. —*Stephen R. Covey*

ALL RELATIONSHIPS ARE BUILT ON TRUST AND TIME. This formula applies in business as well. Granted, the time factor can be a hindrance. In business you may meet people daily whom you may never again see in person. But you want to keep doing business with them and achieve a lasting trust. Bestselling author Stephen R. Covey teaches that while first impressions are critical, what's more important is that you build on those moments, and use that effective first meeting to create truly strong bonds: an enduring trust.

Each action that you perform in a relationship will either build it up or break it down. Be mindful of everything you do. If you say you're going to deliver something on deadline, deliver it. If you can't make that deadline, keep your customer informed every step of the way. Follow through on every promise.

The more you show that you are willing to invest in a relationship, the more meaningful it will become. Trust is built over the long haul, and your actions over time speak volumes about your character and motivations. A one-time effort to get the sale or the client, even if it is dramatic and a big feather in your cap, is not enough. Keep that trust and nurture it.

TEAM-BUILDING | TUESDAY

> The only way to deliver to the people
> who are achieving is to not burden
> them with the people who are not
> achieving. —*Jim Collins*

P ROFESSIONAL SPORTS TEAMS ARE PARTICULARLY CUT-throat when it comes to culling bench warmers from their teams. They give every teammate a chance to shine and live up to his or her promise, but at the end of the season the ones who couldn't perform are cut from the roster.

Famed American business consultant Jim Collins believes that you should not feel compelled to keep people on your team who are not working out. Give them a chance to achieve, and be sure you have given them the guidance they need to be successful. But when it is clear that they are not up to the task, cut them loose. If they have skills that are useful, just not for this particular team, find another team or project for them to work on.

Some people are simply not cut out to be part of a team. These people are often tagged as "not a team player." But that may not be the case. They may just not be able to work within a team approach.

CAREER | WEDNESDAY

Never do an enemy a small injury.
—*Niccolo Machiavelli*

I F YOU'VE EVER GONE HUNTING, YOU KNOW THAT WHEN you shoot at something, you better make it count. You always have to go for the kill, because there is nothing more dangerous than being in the area of a wounded animal. When a wild animal is injured, it becomes unpredictable and you have no way of knowing what it will do next. It turns out that business situations are no different.

Business peers and adversaries can both be deceptive, and those you think are allies can quickly jump to the other side. Machiavelli's teachings of "never trust anyone" unfortunately apply to the business world, as he instructs every leader to be prepared for any situation. You need to be ready for when your business partner suddenly decides to open a competing company right next door, or when your best friend steals your best account.

And when it does happen, Machiavelli suggests that you take no prisoners. If you choose to take them on, you need to incapacitate your foes completely. So when your best client jumps ship to your worst enemy, work hard to make that client regret this decision by doing outstanding work for all your other existing clients. This will be your best revenge and not only sustain, but boost your reputation.

SALES | THURSDAY

Real integrity is doing the right thing, knowing that nobody's going to know whether you did it or not.

— *Oprah Winfrey*

SOMETIMES, THE "REAL ME" CAN GET BOGGED DOWN in the trappings of success. You might have broken your six-figure record in sales this year, and are having fun showing off your Lexus. But listen to Oprah: remember to take a reality check.

The making of a great salesperson is not just the brilliant negotiation that led to the brilliant close. It lies in exceeding your customers' expectations. When you travel that extra mile for them, say, going into the office on a weekend to personally make sure the plant gets out the order with the last-minute color change, you guarantee the order will be in the customer's hands on deadline. You don't boast about this later, you just do it. It's the right thing to do because it's part of the trust you've built in the relationship.

True success in sales is only achieved by character. Reputation has its place—your giant sales figures, dazzling showmanship—but character is the enduring trait essential to greatness. You want a quality relationship with your customer, and true quality—integrity—begins on the inside.

No one needs to know exactly what you do and don't get points for. But you will know, and your pride will grow, helping you achieve great success.

LEADERSHIP | FRIDAY

Casting a critical eye on our weaknesses and working hard to manage them, while sometimes necessary, will only help us prevent failure. —*Marcus Buckingham*

IT'S COMMON PRACTICE FOR PEOPLE TO TRY AND COVER up their weaknesses—especially when it might mean getting ahead or left behind in the business world. However, despite the effort to minimize them, weaknesses tend to reveal themselves when you are under pressure.

In his book, *Now, Discover Your Sales Strength,* Marcus Buckingham writes that spending all of your time managing your weaknesses is pointless. Instead, a better approach is to concentrate on your strengths.

Building on your strengths makes sense because, ultimately, it will pave the way for a less stressful way to the top. First, you'll have a proven track record that demonstrates the skills you already do well. Second, playing to your strengths allows you to experiment within your comfort zone. When trying to branch out and expand your business, it helps to know that you can build on what you have already done well. Third, by relying on your strengths, you'll find the inspiration to set attainable goals. By seeking more challenges, your leadership will inspire others to do the same.

ENTREPRENEUR | SATURDAY

We don't think of ourselves as do-gooders or altruists. It's just that somehow we're trying our best to be run with some sense of moral compass even in a business environment that is growing. —*Craig Newmark*

CRAIG NEWMARK IS THE FOUNDER OF THE "CRAIGS-list" Web site, that brings together people interested in the same thing—whether an employer looking for an employee or people looking for romantic involvement.

The modern-day Wild West known as the Internet is filled with entrepreneurs like Newmark struggling to keep their principles intact. They realize, as you probably do, that it is easy to lose your moral compass in the hubbub of intense business activity.

The Internet has the greatest potential to deceive media: graphics can be manipulated, and blogs are filled with exaggerations and blatant lies. So it's important that everyone involved watch out for each other and stay honest in an environment where business occurs without the traditional watchdogs.

Whether your business is Internet-based or not, if you promise top quality, give it. If you say an order will leave your warehouse within twenty-four hours, live up to it. Stand by your products, take returns, and give back money or issue credit. Do all the things you would do if you had a storefront and had to stand behind a cash register every day.

MANAGING PEOPLE | SUNDAY

If you want something, you can always ask.
—*James M. Citrin and Richard Smith*

S OME PEOPLE SEEM TO HAVE IT ALL. FROM THE GREAT house to the perfect wardrobe, it's mind-boggling how they could be so lucky. But maybe it's just a matter of being smart enough to ask for help. Consultants Citrin and Smith, authors of *The 5 Patterns of Extraordinary Careers,* argue that the first and simplest strategy when you're striving to achieve is to simply ask for things. By asking for something, you demonstrate confidence that you are willing to accept the risks and challenges that go with the rewards.

If you want the corner office and you're two offices down, your boss may not believe you're ready. But you won't know the possibilities or the obstacles in your way until you ask for what you want. While this approach may seem naïve or overly bold, the ensuing feedback is bound to prove invaluable. If the boss says you aren't ready, chances are he'll tell you why. Now you have a clear list of next steps. If the boss is receptive, you've made his job easier. Now he knows who's ambitious and wants more responsibility. This tactic of asking for what you want is all part of "managing up," an often overlooked part of managing people.

MOTIVATION | MONDAY

What you have to do and the way you have to do it is incredibly simple. Whether you are willing to do it is another matter. —*Peter Drucker*

I T IS SIMPLE TO BE PRESENTED WITH A TASK AND FIND A way to do it. But what if you're not willing to do it? Suppose you know that in order to meet this year's scaled-back budget, you're going to have to lay off two people on your team. That sounds simple enough. But doing it may not be so simple. Or, say you need to write a long report on sales for your division. Simple. But you know that it's not easy because you don't like writing, working with Excel charts, or sitting at a desk for too long; you want to be out in the field doing what you do best.

Peter Drucker was a great business thinker who wrote many bestselling books on the subject of management. A basic tenet of his philosophy was to make everything as simple as possible. He proposed that too many managers fail to see simple solutions to problems and that all problems could be analyzed and broken down. Using this analysis, you can discover why you're unwilling to do something. And when your unwillingness has a credibile basis, perhaps it can point you toward a better solution.

If you find doing a task difficult, it's usually not because there isn't a way to do it; it's because you're unwilling. Know why you're holding back and you'll find an even better way to do it.

TEAM-BUILDING | TUESDAY

> Interdependence is a choice only
> independent people can make.
> —*Stephen R. Covey*

INFUSE YOUR TEAM WITH LOTS OF INDEPENDENT TEAM members, or so Stephen Covey believes. One way to achieve this is by planning ahead for resolving mistakes and bad decisions. How you react to a mistake is key to helping others learn to work independently and, when necessary, interdependently.

First, remember that mistakes happen. However, you also want your people to feel comfortable telling you about their errors right away. Then you can help them fix the problem before it becomes a bigger dilemma. Let's say you asked your assistant to write a press release. He took the initiative and had it proofread by someone else, and then had several hundred copies printed. The press releases were stuffed into envelopes before he realized a crucial word had been left out. Luckily, the envelopes were still sitting in the mailroom when your assistant discovered this error.

Your assistant could just let it go and hope the error isn't noticed. Or he could come to you and tell you what happened. If he is comfortable with the way you have responded to errors in the past, he will inform you of his mistake.

By staying calm you show great leadership. These are qualities that help build a great team player—one who will not lay blame, who appreciates the value of teamwork, and who feels comfortable enough to ask for advice.

CAREER | WEDNESDAY

> You are unlikely to learn the art and
> science of persuasion from some
> connect-the-dots corporate lesson plan.
> —*John Evans*

AFTER YEARS OF BEING A TOP SALES PROFESSIONAL, John Evans discovered an intriguing concept that increased his success rate at landing new business. He already knew that most of his profits were generated by only a handful of his best clients. In the course of doing business, these clients inevitably sang his praises to their friends, who in turn became clients in their own right. Applying research by Roger Fisher and Charles Dwyer, two pioneers in the field of persuasion methodology, Evans coined the term "Focinar" (pronounced FOH-kin-are). The focinar is a combination of the words "focused seminar," and it became the basis of how Evans honed his ability to secure profitable clients.

First, create a list of your top existing clients—you already have a deep bond with them. Most likely, they will know like-minded individuals who will also be interested in your products or services. Then offer to take the existing client and her friends to dinner so that the client can brag about how you have helped her, and you can explain your business in detail.

You've narrowed the field of prospective clients to a few who might be very interested in working with you and you won't waste valuable time chasing customers who may not pan out.

SALES | THURSDAY

> When you have to shoot . . . shoot, don't talk.
> —*Tuco,* The Good, The Bad and The Ugly *(1967)*

SUREFIRE TECHNIQUES FOR CLOSING DEALS AREN'T exactly synonymous with the "shoot first, ask questions later," approach Tuco (played by Eli Wallach) bluntly advocates in one of the great westerns of all time. In Sergio Leone's *Man With No Name* trilogy, Clint Eastwood spoke about five lines (slight exaggeration) in all three movies.

Tuco is talking about how he does his job—he's a bandit. However, the concept applies to nearly any job. There are times when actions are stronger than words. In sales, that time is when you are closing the deal. The possibility of a close is not what you discuss during the negotiation phase of the sales process. If you overemphasize closing, or, in your eagerness, start to apply pressure, it might work against you. Purchasing agents, for example, are well aware of the tactics salespeople use and grow irritated when pressured while still learning about your product or service.

As Clint Eastwood's character must know, talking too much puts a strain on any relationship. Knowing how to interpret and balance the flow of information makes a smooth and effective sales process. If you adhere to these rules, you'll instinctively know the right moment to ask for a decision. So when you have to close, close . . . don't talk.

LEADERSHIP | FRIDAY

> When rapid or radical change is called
> for, executives must turn to the networks
> within their organization. Key positions in
> the network mobilize it to flexibly adapt
> to the exigencies of the moment.
>
> —*Karen Stephenson*

KAREN STEPHENSON, A HARVARD-TRAINED CORPORATE anthropologist, theorizes that real information flows not through the official corporate hierarchy, but flows parallel in an informal network that happens in unofficial channels. "A network is a physical representation of trust based on relationships between a cluster of people," explains Stephenson. Because of a unique combination of physical proximity and sociably acceptable personality traits, only one or two people in the office "know what's really going on." Stephenson coins them "gatekeepers and pulsetakers," and they hold vital information and can make or break an organization.

As a leader, the challenge in this situation becomes eliciting trust from your workforce. An effective leader should encourage management to discover who is the hub of the unofficial office network. These key players will help foster a better relationship between management and the staff—unofficially, of course.

ENTREPRENEUR | SATURDAY

Investing other peoples' money, any fool could see, was far safer than investing one's own. —*Bryan Burroughs and John Helyar*

E NTREPRENEURS OFTEN FIGHT THE ENDLESS BATTLE OF funding. Start-up money or expansion capital can be hard to come by. Banks are reluctant to finance start-up businesses. People are understandably reluctant to borrow from family and friends, who in turn may be unwilling to turn over their hard-earned cash. There is a basic expectation that entrepreneurs should risk some of their own money—as it should be. But sometimes keeping your own reserves and investing someone else's money is not only safer, but wiser. Authors Bryan Burroughs and John Helyar found this while researching their bestselling book, *Barbarians at the Gate.*

If you look hard enough, there is always someone out there who might be interested in investing in a business. Find those investors by networking. Talk with everyone you know and keep an ear open for hints as to whether the person you are speaking with or someone she knows may be ready for a business investment.

One way to make applying for a business loan easier is to create a formal business plan. Even the smallest business start-ups can benefit from one. It gives you a map to the start-up years of your business' life, when a hectic pace make it hard to keep track of what you had planned. It should also include financial projections that allow you the chance to compare your projected plans against a more realistic version.

MANAGING PEOPLE | SUNDAY

> Often, just around the corner is where
> the solution will happen. —*Sir James Dyson*

MANY INVENTORS' DREAMS GO UNREALIZED, FILLING up the graveyard where old experiments get tossed. Plain and simple, they just gave up. It's too bad they didn't share Sir James Dyson's attitude that failure can be illuminating. It took Dyson 5,127 prototypes before he finally came up with the one he wanted for his new vacuum cleaner, the Dyson Cyclone, which has broken sales records around the world.

When Dyson went to school in the 1960s, design and engineering were two separate fields. Dyson learned quickly that to be an inventor, he had to be good at both skills and grow accustomed to dealing with failure.

Good managers should encourage experimentation. The first step is to create an environment of trust. People must believe they can fail without compromising their job security. Second, start by constructively coaching employees how to turn failure into progress. Third, bring mistakes, problems, or failures to a round table discussion. Invite suggestions on how to deal with them. An office manager's idea might just be the final touch you need for a new product's packaging. As Dyson implies, by embracing failure, success is just around the corner.

MOTIVATION | MONDAY

*I've learned that you can't have everything
and do everything at the same time.*

—*Oprah Winfrey*

WE ALL FACE MOMENTS, RUNNING BETWEEN JOB AND home, wondering how we can ever live up to the high expectations we hold for ourselves.

You're torn—obsessing about the job while watching your kid's soccer game, and obsessing about missing the soccer game while you're in Cincinnati closing a deal. The computer hasn't made it any easier. Now, no matter where you are, you can be at work.

Bringing balance to the situation is clearly necessary; attaining it is another matter. Oprah seems to have worked it out. She has a huge work schedule, but she also knows how to indulge at the spa, be a world-class shopper, and go on exotic vacations. She is also a gracious philanthropist and is actively involved in her charities.

Oprah surely knows about self-discipline, which is what it takes to achieve a healthy work-life balance. Through trial and error, she set up boundaries for the business, personal, and philanthropic aspects of her life. She has fashioned an awesome schedule for herself, and self-discipline gets her to stick to it.

Without self-discipline, you're not going to have it all. Setting up a structure for your day will allow you to get your job done and also have an enriched life at home. It's hard, but you can do it.

TEAM-BUILDING | TUESDAY

> A meeting moves at the speed of the
> slowest mind in the room. In other words,
> all but one participant will be bored,
> all but one mind underused. —*Dale Dauten*

Meetings are the classic "necessary evil." Business book author Dale Dauten believes that a team cannot be very effective if they don't get together and work on the mutual goal. Team members can go off in the interim and work independently, but you don't really have a team unless the participants gather and interact.

The key to a productive meeting is to not waste time. Perhaps you have a team member who is slow to understand new projects or ideas, but you keep her on board because her outgoing personality is a hit with the clients. It is your responsibility to take the extra effort needed to get this person up to speed before the meeting—provide her with materials to read in advance, perhaps give her a brief rundown of the meeting's agenda before the meeting starts. You may want to give her a team partner; but change the partner regularly so no one feels overburdened.

Keep everyone else engaged and focused during the meeting. Cell phones, pagers, and Blackberries must be turned off. Make sure everyone has something to contribute. If the information you are giving is only useful to one or two people at a table of six or seven, it shouldn't require a meeting. Keep to the agenda and make sure the meeting or presentation is well-outlined in case people's attention drifts in-and-out.

CAREER | WEDNESDAY

When we are truly passionate
about something, it's contagious.
—*Keith Ferrazzi*

P ASSIONATE PEOPLE ARE EXCITING TO BE AROUND, ESPE-
cially in business. Displaying your true passion is a
lightning rod; others will seek to find out what you offer. By
displaying a high level of enthusiasm for subjects that you
love, you automatically make a better impression, one that
will garner you more attention.

Keith Ferrazzi writes in his book, *Never Eat Alone,* that
the benefits of being passionate aren't something to gloss
over. Ferrazzi notes that people incorrectly assume that acting "business like" means being unemotional. However, as
the lines drawn between business and social life are blurred,
people are seeking deeper connections with those they do
business with. And what better way to let business associates into your life than sharing what gets you excited.

Passion also enhances the most routine interactions. If
you have a passionate interest that connects appropriately
with a particular business conversation, mention it. Once
you are "on display," switch the conversation back to the
business topic and show your passion for work. This demonstrates that you are a person who can make things happen.
Don't be afraid to shout from the roof top, or maybe just
your desk. Passion is still unexpected enough to get you
noticed.

SALES | THURSDAY

> When dealing with people, let us remember
> we are not dealing with creatures of logic.
> We are dealing with creatures of emotion,
> creatures bustling with prejudices and
> motivated by pride and vanity. —*Dale Carnegie*

FOR SOME LUCKY SALESPEOPLE, READING PEOPLE COR-
rectly is a natural talent, a heaven-sent gift. For the rest
of us, it's something we have to strive to achieve.

In sales relationships, buyers need to feel they got the
best deal you have to offer. Just as important, you have to
feel that way, too. This balance is what makes long-term
sales relationships—negotiation is required for everyone to
be equally satisfied.

People are not creatures of logic, as Carnegie says in perhaps too kind an understatement. When you're making a
sale, there's always the wild-card factor. The customer may
not go for the date you offer to deliver a product, the price,
the warranty or the maintenance deal, and who-knows-
what-else. Even if you feel you've worked out every detail,
the "creature of emotion" you're negotiating with may still
not behave logically.

You have to be prepared with backup solutions for all
contingencies of the sale. Also be prepared to say "no" to
some things, in a way that won't hurt the customer's vanity.
Every sales negotiation will teach you more about people.
As a result, you will grow more comfortable anticipating
their demands and reading their behavior.

LEADERSHIP | FRIDAY

*I believe more in the scissors
than the pencil.* —*Truman Capote*

B AD WRITING IS LIKE A VIRUS: EVERYONE BECOMES A victim sooner or later. Verbose language, dangling modifiers, and passive voice clutter not only the pages of unfinished novels, but also year-end reports, business plans, and presentations. Effectively written communication gets the message across—essential for any leader to succeed. Whether you are pitching for new business or looking for venture capital, you need to get to the point. Good writing uses fewer words, not more.

In her business writing blog, Lynn Gaertner-Johnston (whose mission is "to quash bad writing habits that linger in the cubicles of 21st-century organizations") says the number one goal is to keep it simple. In today's hyperbolic world, you lose your audience's attention quickly. This is especially pertinent in markets where competition is fierce. Worse, you send a subconscious message of uncertainty in your verbose sentences. Don't use jargon or phrases your reader won't understand. That technique often looks like you are trying to hide something.

The next important stage is editing. Don't settle just for grammatical corrections and perfect punctuation. Take the time to add value by reworking you message. Don't be afraid to redraft any weak points. This will help others understand your vision and help you stand out against the competition.

ENTREPRENEUR | SATURDAY

> I owe my success to having listened
> respectfully to the very best advice,
> and then going away and doing the
> exact opposite. —*G.K. Chesterton*

THERE ARE MANY TIMES WHEN YOU WILL DO THE opposite of the advice you get. But if you are seeking "the very best advice," don't cavalierly run off and do the exact opposite. However, as influential English writer G.K. Chesterton knew, make sure you consider whether the advice you've received is actually the best.

One barometer to gauge others' judgment is to think carefully about whom the advice is from. Does that person have an ulterior motive? Does she have experience in your business—in other words, is she qualified to give you advice? Is she a good listener? Did she hear what you are asking and offer advice accordingly? Or did she hear what she wanted to hear and respond with the advice that she was dying to give you no matter what your question was?

This doesn't mean you should seek only advice you want to hear. You might do well to seek advice from people outside your industry, from someone who has some outstanding knowledge he wants to pass along, or from someone else you respect. But then you need to listen carefully, and separate the wheat from the chaff. Learn what to use and what to discard.

MANAGING PEOPLE | SUNDAY

When in doubt, don't hire—keep looking.
—*Jim Collins*

N O PRINCIPLE DESCRIBED IN JIM COLLINS'S 2001 MAS-
terpiece, *Good to Great,* could be more valuable than
this: Great companies get the right people "on the bus" and
the wrong people "off the bus." By way of example, Collins
cites the remarkable history of banking giant Wells Fargo &
Company. In the early 1970s, it's CEO knew big change was
coming to banking, but didn't know exactly what form it
would take. So before mapping out a strategy, he carefully
set about hiring outstanding people. The results were incredible: not only did Wells Fargo outperform the overall stock
market three times, but virtually every executive hired by
the CEO went on to become CEO of another company.

Now imagine what would have happened had the company quickly picked a different strategy and moved fast to
fill openings in hopes of executing it's strategy with more
speed than competitors. Chances are it would have made
hiring mistakes and failed to soar to the same heights.

Companies and hiring managers are often under pressure
to fill openings. The pain of a position unfilled is often seen
as too great. But the pressure itself is a trigger for choosing
a failure, which will eventually cause even more pain. Unless
your due diligence reveals that a job candidate is exception-
ally bright and qualified for the job, the search must go on.
Otherwise, a hiring manager isn't doing the right job.

MOTIVATION | MONDAY

We cannot become what we need to be
by remaining what we are. —*Max Depree*

W HAT EXACTLY WILL IT TAKE FOR YOU TO REALIZE
your business goals? If you are looking for changes
in the job you have now, are you talking to your friends
about it, perhaps complaining at home every night about
the boss and the dead end you've reached? But are you actually doing anything to change the situation?

People often lose sight of the fact that wanting change
requires change. And that means you have to change. You'll
be passed over again and again for promotions if you don't
develop the skills to qualify. Or, if your current job is hopeless, you're going to keep treading water, stuck in that position, unless you start looking for a new job.

That future is never going to happen unless some
changes are made, beginning with the ones you make for
yourself. Max Depree, former CEO of the Fortune 500 furniture company Herman Miller, Inc., wrote several bestsellers on business leadership, including *Leadership Is an Art*.
As Depree says, knowing who you are, what you want to be,
and what you need to change in order to reach your goals is
the core ingredient for success.

TEAM-BUILDING | TUESDAY

*Sometimes you have to go slow first
to go faster later. —Carly Fiorina*

A TWO-WEEK PROJECT COULD EASILY TAKE TEN DAYS OF research and four days to actually complete. Those ten days may seem like an eternity with the work still looming ahead, but if you don't have the best information at hand when you begin the project, you will have to stop working and go back to researching.

It doesn't matter if the project is putting together an architectural model or writing a company report. In order to create the best product, you need to do your research first. This first phase may go slowly for the person who is anxious to dig in and get going. But that person won't enjoy his work as much if he needs to spend time later dismantling his efforts because he didn't have all the information he needed.

A lot of managers walk away after throwing a task to a team, and then they complain when the task needs to be done again. Carly Fiorina, former head of Hewlett-Packard, believes that this type of management is not only demoralizing to the team, it makes the second go-round even slower. Doing the task again takes far longer than taking time up front to explain exactly what you want.

It's the same experience when you are training a new employee or team member. Take the time to work with the new person in order for her to get familiar with the project and with the team's way of operating. Then the newbie can go forward as a productive team member.

CAREER | WEDNESDAY

> An overburdened, overstretched
> executive is the best executive,
> because he or she doesn't have the
> time to meddle, to deal in trivia,
> to bother people. —*Jack Welch*

JACK WELCH HAD A STRATEGY AND A VISION TO TURN around General Electric Co., which had become a bloated corporate entity when he was named CEO. He wanted to create a leaner business structure that rewarded the employees who shared his company vision. To do this, he knew he had to make drastic changes that his management team would have to buy into.

Welch first laid off 150,000 workers at all levels and forced those who remained to work harder. He then proceeded to create a work environment where people were excited to be a part of the team. As a result, they devoted more of themselves to their jobs, which in turn became personally rewarding.

Jack Welch believed that you must build your company with managers who are excited to go to work and are full of energy and passion. Keeping everyone moving forward leaves little time for water cooler malaise to set in. His efforts turned around GE, and everyone—both inside and outside of the company—began to see the benefits.

In your business, make sure to open communications and keep the energy levels high. Get everyone involved with the vision of the company.

SALES | THURSDAY

*Conflicts between your inner values and
your goals block your achievement.*
—*Ron Willingham*

SETTING UNREALISTIC GOALS, OR GOALS YOU NEVER intend to meet, wastes everyone's time. If you're so out of touch with your inner self that you spend time daydreaming about wealth and riches with no plan for achieving them, it's time for an attitude overhaul.

Ron Willingham is best known for helping organizations succeed with ethical, values-driven strategies. He teaches that the right mental attitude can make the difference in what you are realistically going to achieve. Knowing who you are and where you are going helps you set positive goals. It's fine to fantasize about buying a Mercedes Benz (and even to purchase one if your budget allows), but do not allow yourself to be motivated or driven by status. Keeping up with the Joneses is a dangerous game to play. If you find yourself more concerned with status than personal values take stock of your life. Change your mindset: read some good books, listen to music, and go to lectures. Redirect your thinking to focus on practical goals based on the reality of what is feasible in your life.

You may be young in the business and in need of a positive support system to plan exactly how you are going to reach your goals. Seek out a mentor, a super salesperson, and discover some of his or her tricks. Experience in the field and the right mental attitude combine to enable you to achieve.

LEADERSHIP | FRIDAY

An individualist is a man who says: "I will not run anyone's life—nor let anyone run mine. I will not rule or be ruled. I will not be a master nor [sic] a slave. I will not sacrifice myself to anyone—nor sacrifice anyone to myself."—*Ayn Rand*

A RUSSIAN SURVIVOR OF WORLD WAR II, AYN RAND defected to the United States at age twenty-one and embraced the individualism of the American character. Her most famous novels, *The Fountainhead* and *Atlas Shrugged,* praise the philosophy of Objectionism, which holds that logical reasoning should set the standards for human action. In the appendix of *Atlas Shrugged*, she offers, "My philosophy, in essence, is the concept of man as a heroic being, with his own happiness as the moral purpose of his life, with productive achievement as his noblest activity, and reason as his only absolute."

Objectionism promotes lofty goals—holding individuals accountable for their actions, and believing humans possess unlimited potential to reach great heights within their existing circumstances. It may seem obvious that people should hold themselves to high standards. However, a leader's moral code is always tested. If you feel your values being tested, logic and rational thought should be your weapons of choice. Holding yourself accountable will help clarify the reasons why you got into business in the first place.

ENTREPRENEUR | SATURDAY

*Success is the ability to go from one failure
to another with no loss of enthusiasm.*
—*Winston Churchill*

DETERMINE HOW YOU DEFINE FAILURE. DID YOU LOSE money the first year? (Most businesses do.) Did you come to the market too late? Did you think you had a winning idea and it turned out to be less popular than a used Chia pet at a garage sale? Whatever failure means to you, it doesn't have to get you down more than temporarily.

If you enter into a venture as prepared as you can be, no outcome can really be considered a failure. Sir Winston Churchill led his country by this example, instilling the belief that even when faced with great adversity, one should always continue to do the best one can.

One way to get out of the "failure" mode is to surround yourself with positive thinkers. An atmosphere of failure can promote negative thinking. Be around people who have "failed" and tried again. Let their stories convince you that whatever you tried that didn't work out as you planned was only a practice run for the real thing. Some of the most successful entrepreneurs we know—Walt Disney, Harry Truman, and Bill Gates—all had businesses that "failed." Yet all went on to achieve phenomenal success.

Why lose enthusiasm when you are presented with a chance to try again to succeed? Most entrepreneurs are like crossword puzzle addicts—when they finish with one, there is always another to solve.

MANAGING PEOPLE | SUNDAY

Never break another man's rice bowl.
—*Akito Morita*

WHILE WESTERN MANAGERS ROUTINELY WORRY ONLY about their own division's performance, a Japanese manager's success comes from the collective effort, cooperation, and achievement of the entire company. The Japanese culture of honor also requires businesses to operate with integrity.

Akito Morita founded Sony Corporation with management practices that embody the best of Japanese culture. It firmly embraces Wa, meaning "harmony;" Kao, meaning "personal pride;" and Omoiyari, meaning a combination of empathy and trust. In addition, Japanese culture believes that any kind of work someone does is honorable, so Akito Morita set his corporate culture in such a way that managers would respect and honor the personal space and lives of their employees. Morita also believed that excessive executive bonuses, posh offices, and perks sent the wrong message to the employees.

Talk to many American employees and they would probably agree with these tenets. If you don't show your employees you care about them, but expect them to care about the company, you won't earn their respect. You must create a community of pride, which will in turn demonstrate that honor and respect are good for business in any culture.

MOTIVATION | MONDAY

Only those who will risk going too far can possibly find out how far one can go.

—*T. S. Eliot*

HOW FAR WILL YOU GO? HOW HIGH CAN YOU JUMP? What risks are you willing to take to find your destiny . . . to find what's right for you?

Taking risks isn't easy. You often have to conquer your fear or insecurities. You have to be ready and eager to jump from the familiar into the unknown. Getting there is often downright scary: What if it doesn't work out? What if I fail?

The only way you're going to find out is to risk it. If you're having trouble making the change, look within yourself to see what is causing your resistance. Overcome it. This is part of having the will to take risks—overcoming fear to make that jump into the unknown.

The Nobel Prize-winning writer T.S. Eliot was talking about symbolism in poetry when he wrote the above-mentioned line, but it applies to every aspect of life. Indeed, the quote has been adopted as the slogan for numerous societies and organizations. Before he achieved international fame as a poet, playwright, and essayist, Eliot worked in a bank. By choosing the path of writing—at best, a chancy economic future over a salaried position at an institution—he was clearly willing to risk going too far to see just how far he could go.

Ready, set, go . . . make that same leap into the unknown!

TEAM-BUILDING | TUESDAY

> Nothing else can quite substitute for a
> few well-chosen, well-timed, sincere
> words of praise. They're absolutely free
> and worth a fortune. —*Sam Walton*

I T SEEMS LIKE SIMPLE ADVICE BUT IT IS SO OFTEN OVER-
looked. Walmart founder Sam Walton strongly believes in
the value of always praising your team. There are myriad
opportunities to give credit where credit is due; you need to
always look for them. Let your team know when they are
doing a good job; shower them with praise when something
turned out better than you expected. If the financial numbers
aren't as stellar as you'd like to see, at least tell them how
impressive the spreadsheet or the PowerPoint presentation is.

Praise is often overlooked when working with outside
contractors. Write a letter that their team leader can read to
the rest of the team. Give them permission to use a quote
from your letter to add as a testimonial to their brochures or
to be able to send a copy of your letter along as a testimonial when they are bidding for other jobs.

Praise doesn't have to be a financial reward or special
prize. Employees value hearing their boss say the simple
words "good job" and "thanks." When they do a good job,
you look good, too. But don't fake it—insincere praise is not
worth anything and is readily detected.

CAREER | WEDNESDAY

It has been my observation that most people get ahead during the time that others waste time. *—Henry Ford*

HENRY FORD WAS NO STRANGER TO TIME MANAGEment. He introduced the assembly line to automobile production, reducing the time it took to assemble each vehicle down to mere ninety-eight seconds.

Today, time management is something that no serious professional can ignore. Most people underestimate the amount of time it's going to take to accomplish certain goals. If you are interested in getting ahead, take a look at how your time is spent. For several weeks, take notice of the most time-consuming activities during your work day. After you identify your major time-devouring activities, formalize a plan to streamline them.

Nothing sets business priorities as well as an old-fashioned to-do list. First, make sure that your list is appropriate. A task list is not an activity list. "Go to New York" is not a single task—it's an activity. It needs to be broken down into get plane tickets, make hotel reservation, etc. Second, avoid generalized verbs, such as "do" or "make." Be as specific as possible; for example, "purchase" or "write." Third, make sure the task can be completed within a specified amount of time. Nothing is more frustrating than looking at a list of incomplete task items at the end of the day. If you find you are continually having this problem, you are probably listing activities, and you need to go back to step one.

SALES | THURSDAY

You do not have to be superhuman to do what you believe in. —*Debbi Fields*

AND LOOK WHAT DEBBI FIELDS BELIEVED IN: CHOCOLATE chip cookies. Yes, this is *the* Mrs. Fields, the young bride who turned entrepreneur at age twenty. She found a banker to back her cookie shop in Palo Alto. When no one came in to the store to buy the first day, she went outside and began handing out samples. Soon the store was mobbed.

Since the beginning in 1977, customer satisfaction and a quality product were her top priorities—"Good enough never is" became her motto. Her cookies were going to be the best cookies in the retail market. As her stores spread, she introduced a computer system to streamline operations and in 1990 started franchising her business concept— which is now a case study at Harvard Business School.

During this time she gave birth to five daughters. It all sounds superhuman, but Debbi Fields became a success by believing in what she was selling. She didn't listen to the naysayers who kept telling her no one gets rich selling cookies. Instead, she persevered and turned her childhood hobby of baking cookies into a $500 million company. She loved what she was doing, and the proof was in her delicious product.

LEADERSHIP | FRIDAY

*Waiting and acting, the latter always
being a riposte and therefore a reaction,
are both essential parts of defense.*
—Carl Von Clausewitz

L IKE VULTURES, COMPANIES WILL ATTACK A WEAKENED
prey. Carl von Clausewitz's writings in his famous strategy book, *On War,* show how defense is the better offense. Having a plan to defend your market share is crucial, especially if you're in a business whose primary products and markets are subject to encroachment from other companies. Defense, according to Clausewitz, consists of waiting and then acting. Waiting isn't a passive state, however. It's a state of readiness that requires vigilance.

According to Clausewitz, a counter-strategy to repel the offensive—in this case, the competition—must be in place before the other side "attacks" or launches their product. Insightful leadership determines the state of readiness of the company. It requires the company to develop plans to remain on top and commit to continuously reevaluate their position.

Clausewitz also believed the willingness to hold one's own position, without giving away any territory, was paramount to winning. It also hastened the demise of the enemy. Business leaders must be deeply committed to retain their share of the marketplace. If you haven't done so lately, perform an analysis of your company's position and strategies. It's not fun to be on the defensive, but it's sometimes your best offense.

ENTREPRENEUR | SATURDAY

> Most people who build important
> businesses build them on a rift, usually
> one that they find by accident, and
> usually only once. —*Seth Godin*

ENTREPRENEURS THROUGHOUT THE WORLD ARE LOOK-ing for the missing link in an industry, a rift, as marketing guru Godin describes it, an opening waiting to be filled. Successful new businesses often fill a need that no one even realized existed.

Many times new rifts open as industries progress. Take the television, for example. The digital age means that analog televisions will soon need a converter in order to tune in to the digital television world. Hands-free headset manufacturers made a bundle when lawmakers made it illegal to drive and talk on the cell phone at the same time.

Where do you think the next rift will be? Today's marketers are looking for the rifts where businesses can address the aging baby boomer.

Seth Godin has filled a rift, partly as the author of several bestselling marketing books. He has fully embraced the computer age, writing a popular marketing blog and founding a "recommendation" Web site. Although someone else will come along and replace Godin's ideas as fast as you can hit control/alt/delete, his early entry into the Web community brought marketing into a contemporary world.

MANAGING PEOPLE | SUNDAY

It's not personal . . . It's strictly business.
—*Michael Corleone,* The Godfather *(1972)*

I MAGINE IT'S TIME FOR YOUR WORST EMPLOYEE'S PER-
formance review. You need to tell him that his shoddy
work is hurting the bottom line and that his arrogant attitude leaves everyone around him cold, but you're afraid of
confronting him. You don't want to hurt his feelings,
because you think he might explode. Yet in the past year,
the same pattern played out every week: he underperformed
and you constantly cut him slack fearing a blow-up. Along
the way, the company suffered.

Let's face it: You can learn something from Mario Puzo's
fictional Michael Corleone. The Godfather knew that
avenging a personal attack was a messy but necessary job.
But he always had a plan to rectify the problem—and executed it with utmost aplomb. Of course, I'm not advocating
committing a crime or using violence in seeking revenge.
Hard work and persistence will better serve you.

As a manager, it's your job to rectify problems. When an
employee continually underperforms, the right course for the
company is corrective action. Sometimes the employee will
take your criticism too personally, creating an emotional
firestorm. But it's your job to explain and fix any problem in
an objective way. Caring about employees' feelings is healthy,
but if you care too much, you're liable to make excuses for
them and lose sight of your company's goals. Doing what's
necessary isn't personal. It's just good business.

MOTIVATION | MONDAY

Many of life's failures are experienced by people who did not realize how close they were to success when they gave up. —Thomas A. Edison

G IVING UP ON A CHALLENGE CAN OPEN A PANDORA'S Box of trouble for you and your career. But the saddest part about giving up is that when you do, you might be very close to succeeding. Trying one more approach to solving the problem might bring you success.

Thomas Edison is certainly a poster boy for perserverance. When he was inventing a light source, he tested over 3,000 filaments in his light bulb until he got it right. Besides being a genius inventor with over a thousand patents, Edison was a consummate businessman. He capitalized on his inventions and made a fortune, first from the stock ticker, then the phonograph, and later he accomplished that little thing of bringing light to the masses through his own power companies. In fact, 424 of his patents were for electric light and power.

Edison had rock-solid confidence in his abilities and never doubted he would ultimately achieve success in everything he did. Believing he was always close to success gave him the confidence to stick with a project and never give up until it happened.

Next time you're ready to give up, tackle the project again. Remind yourself that you may be close to success but just haven't realized it yet.

TEAM-BUILDING | TUESDAY

Competitors will eventually copy an innovative idea for a product or service, but an organization of highly motivated people is very hard to duplicate. —*Bill George*

HIGHLY MOTIVATED PEOPLE ARE THE REASON THAT ANY company can develop a successful product or service. But what motivates them to begin? Is it their compensation, or do they simply have tons of pride in what they do? Harvard Business School professor Bill George believes that the pride felt by inventing something valuable cannot be matched. An environment of innovation is much more motivating than an environment of copycatting. Creating a better mousetrap is a big step down from designing the original invention.

Let your team feel pride in their work by allowing them to be unique. Don't always send them off to repeat someone else's success. They should be able to experiment, innovate, and create successes of their own.

Breeding this kind of atmosphere entices the best people to come to work. Most creative thinkers don't want to do the same-old, same-old their entire career. They didn't spend four years in college, accumulating tens of thousands of dollars in debt to be a mimic. Almost everyone dreams of putting his or her unique stamp on the world, and this alone creates the motivation needed for success. So give your highly motivated industrious team the time they need to come up with something great.

CAREER | WEDNESDAY

Do the big stuff, master the small.
—*Harry Beckwith*

W ITH THEIR UNINSPIRING MENUS, MEDIOCRE FOOD, and a décor that seems to spawn from a bad acid trip, why are fast food restaurants so popular? Yes, they are fast and cheap, and these factors count. But the number one reason is their overall consistency, and that matters more than most people think.

Harry Beckwith writes in *You Inc.,* that predictability is a source of comfort to customers. Even though the multinational burger chain menus are uninspiring, consumers have them memorized. Even though the food is mediocre, it's the same food you've been eating since you were a child, which can be the source of many fond memories. And even though the atmosphere is awful, a customer can be three thousand miles away from home and see the familiar.

The take-home message for your business is that people crave dependability. Consistency is often overlooked in the characteristics that define successful people. A client really wants someone she can count on. Or, when your boss e-mails you, he knows that he'll get a reply in a couple of hours, because that's what he's come to expect. If you can be viewed as dependable and consistent, you're off to take the world by storm, one returned phone call at a time.

SALES | THURSDAY

> Sharing food with another human
> being is an intimate act that should
> not be indulged in lightly.
>
> —*M.F.K. Fisher*

IN HER MORE THAN TWENTY BOOKS, SUCH AS *CONSIDER the Oyster* and *How to Cook a Wolf*, the brilliant food writer M.F.K. Fisher made the art of eating well part of American culture. From her years spent living abroad in France she learned that many aspects of interpersonal communication—class, education, grace, wit, and charm—are all transparently on display during a meal.

The importance of food-based communication in business cannot be underestimated. Business consultant Keith Ferrazzi titled his bestseller, *Never Eat Alone.* Talking about food is his personal strategy for establishing intimacy with clients because food is his chief passion. Sitting at a table in a good restaurant (which doesn't have to be four-star expensive—many ethnic restaurants offer incredible value), discussing what you're eating, or exchanging tales of food adventures is an ideal setting for firming up relationships or closing the deal.

In sales, never waste an opportunity to share food with a customer. But use discretion: don't opt for dining out with just anyone. Establish the food bond beforehand—and the cuisine the prospect favors before choosing to do business over the table. Then be wise about how much you drink—and, of course, always pick up the check.

LEADERSHIP | FRIDAY

> Like enemies, weaknesses are more
> dangerous when they are quietly
> corrupting your work and life.
> —*Marcus Buckingham*

NOBODY WANTS TO ADMIT HIS OR HER WEAKNESSES. It's painful. Intellectually, we know that weaknesses hold us back from achieving our fullest potential. But, we hide them, minimize them, pretend they don't exist, or feign ignorance when they are discovered. As a leader, evaluating them is not only necessary, it can be profitable.

When you acknowledge your weaknesses, you can manage them properly. If you have time management issues, solve them by getting a daily planner or setting your wristwatch ahead five minutes. If you refuse to admit that you're always late, you'll never be able to change this bad habit.

Conversely, Marcus Buckingham states that focusing on your strengths and putting your weaknesses "in a box" will marginalize the latter's impact on your day-to-day life. There's bound to be parts of your job that require you to do things that don't play to your strengths. Try to find co-workers who prefer these tasks and swap with them some duties that they don't like, but may be interesting and challenging for you. By swapping tasks and letting go of the parts of your job you hate, you'll increase your overall job satisfaction.

ENTREPRENEUR | SATURDAY

> To gain the edge, it's not enough
> just to be good at what you do:
> In today's fast-paced world, you
> have to be just as fast. —*Bo Dietl*

B O DIETL IS NO STRANGER TO THE FAST-PACED WORLD. As an New York City Police Department cop for more than sixteen years, Dietl learned early that you need to be fast to be a success. He knew acting quick was necessary to not only serve and protect, but to survive.

Two-hundred-plus years ago, everyday necessities (as well as people) came to the New World via ship, taking weeks to cross the Atlantic. Americans quickly began to make what they needed. To do that, they needed to get suppliers to provide them with raw ingredients faster. The pace of business has been accelerating year after year since.

The telephone gave business an exceptional boost in speed. Mailing an order was replaced or supplemented by picking up the phone if a customer had an established account.

Then the computer arrived, and in a flash every aspect of business stepped up in pace. If someone tries to order something and the process is too slow or too complex, or if the product is out of stock—click! A potential customer is off to a new site in a matter of seconds, spending his or her money elsewhere.

The faster the world moves, the faster customers expect it to move.

MANAGING PEOPLE | SUNDAY

> One of the most important ways to
> manifest integrity is to be loyal to those
> who are not present. In doing so, we
> build the trust of those who are present.
>
> —*Stephen R. Covey*

OFFICE GOSSIP SPREADS LIKE A VIRUS. USUALLY WITHIN a couple days, if not hours, employees reveal what they've heard about others. It could be work-centric: a hubbub about who will get promoted or let go. Or it could be personal: the latest on who's dating whom or who desperately needs a makeover. No matter the topic or the target, it's human nature to share this information. But the highly effective manager, the kind who lives and breathes Stephen Covey's *The Seven Habits of Highly Effective People*, should set an example of how decorum can affect office dynamics. Gaining employees' trust gives this manager real power to run a team, office, or organization.

Trust can't be earned if employees catch the manager talking negatively about others behind their backs. Quickly any loyalty, trust, or goodwill built up by the manager is gone.

Now contemplate the alternative: being a manager who speaks highly of workers who aren't present in the meeting, on the conference call, or at the proverbial water cooler. Everybody in the office is bound to feel more comfortable knowing the boss has their support. It's a good feeling, and it's a sign of a "virus-free" office.

MOTIVATION | MONDAY

Trust men and they will be true to you; treat them greatly, and they will show themselves great. —*Ralph Waldo Emerson*

ALTHOUGH MOTIVATIONAL WORDS NEVER HURT, sometimes you have to step back and realize that it's not just you who needs care and feeding in your daily work life. It might be time to start thinking about those you work with—your teammates, your staff, and your colleagues. You want to get the most you can from these people, because all of you want to deliver the best work possible.

Ralph Waldo Emerson believed that establishing trust in any relationship is the place to start. Getting others to trust you stems from your trust in them. This is the foundation of a good team. You can build on loyalty and trust and get spectacular dividends. Treat your colleagues to reflect your belief in them and their talents. Never miss an opportunity to tell them how great they are, and after a while, they'll not only believe it (because they are great), they'll prove themselves great.

Keep the team spirit high. You're the catalyst in this equation. It is your task to bring out the greatness in others by treating them as valued players in your mission. Inspire them by your example, and they will in turn inspire others. It's a winning formula.

TEAM-BUILDING | TUESDAY

> It is amazing what you can accomplish if
> you do not care who gets the credit.
> —*Harry S. Truman*

A REAL TEAM MEMBER IS NOT CONCERNED ABOUT INDIvidual credit. Like Harry Truman, she knows that she would not have deserved the credit without the other team members input. And she knows that the credit will come in the long run—that having been part of a successful team will put her in line to be on other successful teams, or earn a promotion, or simply make her more valuable when it comes to looking for a new job.

It's hard not to care who gets the credit. And even though it takes everyone's concentrated efforts to get the job done, you need to feel positive about your work even on those occasions when just a few get the credit that perhaps the whole team deserved.

A good team leader will make sure to credit the whole team. When announcing results of a team's efforts, the leader will emphasize how hard the team worked together, and what each employee contributed to the bigger effort. Don't worry about team members who didn't work as hard as they might have or that others might have wanted them to—they will be penalized when they are not picked for a new team. It doesn't matter once the team's work is done; it matters for the next time around.

CAREER | WEDNESDAY

A professional is someone who can do
his best work when he doesn't feel like it.

—*Alistair Cooke*

PLAIN AND SIMPLE, WORKING TAKES A LOT OUT OF YOU. With the amount of time and effort you put in, it's easy to see why people's efforts wane by the end of the week. Unfortunately, when you have a litany of excuses in your back pocket as to why your work isn't completed, it's a red flag to management and a sure-fire ticket to nowhere.

Alistair Cooke, the beloved British broadcaster, knew a thing or two about effort. He holds the record for the longest running broadcast radio show in history. He started *Letters from America* in 1946, and it continued until March, 2004. That's a fifty-year commitment that he made to entertaining and exciting his audience week after week.

Surely, there are days when you are not up to doing your best work. Whether you are a front desk manager or a stockroom employee, you are going to have good days and bad days. But with professionalism at an all-time low, now is the time for you to stand out. It's up to you to make the effort, even when you don't feel like it. Especially when you consider that your efforts now will pay off in raises and promotions later.

SALES | THURSDAY

*It is only the farmer who faithfully
plants seeds in the Spring, who reaps
a harvest in the Autumn. —B. C. Forbes*

BERTIE CHARLES FORBES, THE PATRIARCH OF THE FORBES business dynasty, planted his seeds early by beginning his career as a beat reporter in Scotland. After a few years, he moved to Johannesburg, South Africa, where he started up the *Rand Daily Mail.* Not content with the success of founding a newspaper, he immigrated to New York in 1904 and became a financial writer for Hearst. In 1917, he started *Forbes* magazine and happily remained editor-in-chief until his death in 1954.

Forbes certainly reaped a harvest in autumn from his seeds planted in spring. He had a plan, which was to be his own boss, doing what he did best—financial writing and editing. *Forbes* magazine was the realization of his dreams.

A career in sales may also take time, and it requires organization and commitment. Forbes was willing to do his apprenticeship, travel thousands of miles and move to foreign countries, and try new things to gain experience. It was hard work, but no plan is realized if it doesn't involve hard work. You may also have to realize that sometimes you will have to do the hard work at one point in the year to reap the sale later.

LEADERSHIP | FRIDAY

It would be a mistake—a tragic mistake, indeed—to think that the way you ignite a transition from good to great is by wantonly swinging the ax on vast numbers of hardworking people. Endless restructuring and mindless hacking were never part of the good-to-great model. —*Jim Collins*

JIM COLLINS, AUTHOR OF *GOOD TO GREAT*, DISCOVERED that most great companies do not resort to layoffs. Collins uses the illustration of "getting the right people on the bus" as part of the company having a "culture of discipline" philosophy. A culture of discipline demands that from the beginning, you hire extremely qualified people. Qualified people are most likely disciplined workers who don't need management holding their hands in order to get their job done. A culture of discipline also requires top management to take as much time as it needs to hire the right people for the job. Then, when the acquisition or merger eventually occurs, the company stands with its current workforce instead of cutting it.

Employees benefit from the company's commitment to them, adding a sense of security through tumultuous times. Even if you are just trying to pump up an underproducing division, people can be reassigned instead of fired. Good-to-great companies know the people are not the problem. Great leadership is about organizing the workforce and managing it effectively—not just swinging the ax.

ENTREPRENEUR | SATURDAY

It's kind of fun to do the impossible.
—*Walt Disney*

WALT DISNEY STARTED AN ANIMATION STUDIO AFTER working for the Red Cross in France in World War I. His first studio went bankrupt. Even an entrepreneurial genius like Walt Disney had to overcome failure. But Disney learned from his experience and went on to become known as the founding father of animation. He moved to Hollywood when he was twenty-two-years-old and began to produce animated films. In 1928, at age twenty-seven, he created his trademark character, Mickey Mouse.

The film *Snow White* was one of Disney's early visions called foolhardy by all those around him. He was so insistent on quality that he taught his staff of animators himself. He used his perfectionism to create a hugely popular long-format animated film at a time when movie houses were cutting back on showing short cartoons and going to double feature films instead. The rest is history. *Snow White* was a huge success. It allowed Disney the best of both worlds—animation at the full length of regular films.

But his vision for creating a huge amusement park is where Walt Disney excelled at doing the impossible. Disneyland in California opened in 1955. The vision was born of a desire to offer clean, safe entertainment for parents to enjoy with their children. And enjoy it they have!

MANAGING PEOPLE | SUNDAY

Keep your attention on your intention.

—*Pat Croce*

KNOWN AS A MASTER MOTIVATOR, PAT CROCE BELIEVES managers must ignite the passions of those beneath them. It's a laudable goal, but it occurs too seldom. Too often employees see inauthentic leaders above them who take more interest in their own careers than the fortunes of their subordinates. Croce would say these leaders are distracted, too busy with profit and loss statements, compliance issues, and marketing mumbo-jumbo to keep their attention on what really matters: inspiring the people around them. But when a manager's primary intention is to motivate, to cultivate excellence; and when that manager can delegate well, he will find plenty of time in the day to develop his employees.

While cynics might say that Croce is just another self-help guru, his career trajectory speaks volumes for the value of his advice. After launching into the sports medicine industry in the United States, he purchased the National Basketball Association's Philadelphia 76ers, then in last place, and within five years led the team to the NBA Finals while setting team records for attendance and revenue. He later found success as a TV commentator and today remains an entrepreneur, looking for new projects to launch into the stratosphere. There's no doubt that Croce rarely loses sight of his intention to succeed in any endeavor, whether he's managing people or projects. This is a fundamental rule from which any manager can learn.

MOTIVATION | MONDAY

First say to yourself what you would be;
and then do what you have to do.

—*Epictetus*

K NOW WHAT YOU WANT TO ACHIEVE. MAKE A LIST, IF you wish, of the qualities you want to have as a strong business leader. Believing in yourself, knowing who you want to be, is key to success.

Now, take it a step further. Beyond knowing what you want to be, you have to know which actions will take you there. Your actions have to reflect your confidence in yourself. To become a strong leader, you have to know what kind of leader you want to be and then know how to achieve your ends—produce results—staying true to that ideal.

Epictetus, who uttered his famous line in the first century BC, began his life as a Roman slave. But that didn't hinder him. He was determined to stand out from the crowd. He studied the Stoic philosophy and in a few years founded his own philosophical school in Greece, where he achieved fame. Epictetus believed that, despite adversity, you can be a master of your own life by harnessing strength of will and self-knowledge. Epictetus might very well have originated the familiar refrain we hear today: "Bite the bullet." Regardless of how it's said, you simply need to get the job done. Just do it.

TEAM-BUILDING | TUESDAY

*Some people are born on third base and
go through life thinking they hit a triple.*
—*Barry Switzer*

YOU ARE NOT AWARDED A "TRIPLE" IF YOU HIT A DOUBLE but later in the inning get moved to third base. Likewise, if you're "born" on third base, you didn't necessarily hit a triple.

Former football coach Barry Switzer's baseball analogy is an attempt to deal with difficult team members who believe that they deserve accolades even when they do nothing to earn them. They typically think they are more important to the team than they are. It's like the proverbial saying that a wealthy person was "born with a silver spoon in one's mouth." Many people don't think that the wealthy know what it is like to work hard to make money. They believe they are lazy because they didn't have to start from scratch. However, there are many wealthy individuals who didn't "start from scratch" yet still work hard and don't expect privileged treatment. In most cases, you wouldn't even know these people were born into money.

Don't assume that just because someone on your team was "born on third base" that she won't be able or willing to contribute to the team. Treat her like everyone else, and you will probably get the same hard work out of her as the person sitting next to her.

CAREER | WEDNESDAY

> The true test of any scholar's work is not what his contemporaries say, but what happens to his work in the next 25 or 50 years. —*Milton Friedman*

MILTON FRIEDMAN WAS NO ORDINARY ECONOMIST: his life's work was advancing new theories. Not only was he completely versed in his own and others' work, he was able to present his ideas in easily understood terms, which translated well to mainstream readership. Through his perseverance and unrivaled intellect, Friedman gained a large following among leading politicians of his time, both domestically and abroad.

When you are working in a field where your achievements can only be measured long after you are dead, it's difficult to judge the value of your contributions. Friedman was the first to realize that a lasting legacy would be his true achievement. Friedman made sure that he left no stone unturned. When adversaries challenged his theories, he met them with flawless logic and formidable knowledge.

Whether your job requires you to figure out spending less on copy paper or designing a prototype factory, learn all that you can about your field of business, including knowing what your detractors will say, so that your theories will be met with respect, not derision. By making sure that you are prepared, you will have a better chance at advancing your ideas or suggestions. And maybe they too will stand the test of time.

SALES | THURSDAY

You can't build a reputation on what you are going to do. —*Henry Ford*

B EAR IN MIND THAT YOUR REPUTATION IS NOT BASED on future goals. It's based on what you're delivering now. And equally important, your reputation is based on how your products or services stand up over the long haul.

When Henry Ford got into the auto business in 1905, there were on average fifty other start-ups a year—all trying to build a car for the wealthy. But Ford saw an entirely different market, smack in the midst of the workers who made the cars. Why shouldn't these workers have a car? After buying out his backers, Ford streamlined production by inventing the industrial assembly line. He also decided to pay his workers higher wages, so that they would deliver more cars in less time.

Ford built his reputation on devising methods that would quickly deliver quality vehicles to everyone. To do this, his genius came into play again and again. First with the assembly line, and then with the dealer-franchise system to sell and service cars. Then he worked to establish gas stations across the country to fill up those tanks he was putting on the road. These gas stations led to the building of better roads, and the beginnings of the Interstate Highway System.

Let your ideas flow freely. Don't wait to implement them later. Build your reputation on what you are doing now, with quality as your standard.

LEADERSHIP | FRIDAY

> I don't know the key to success, but the
> key to failure is trying to please everybody.
> —*Bill Cosby*

IN THE FICKLE WORLD OF ENTERTAINMENT, WHERE ACTOR/ comedian Bill Cosby plies his craft, studios make their products by relying on a collective process. Scripts usually have multiple rewrites with various screenwriters before they go to production. During production, various endings are routinely shot to target certain demographics. The rough cut, usually the director's choice of how she envisions the movie to be, is then dissected by the corporate "suits." Hand-picked audiences screen the final product and are polled for their opinion. As a result, too much input from too many "contributors" leads to the failure of many movies and TV shows.

This lack of a singular vision can wreak havoc on a business. From contradictory policies to divisions competing for the same resources, a leader understands the importance of decisiveness. By defining the company's purpose and focus on getting quality products distributed, a leader can maintain the company's vision. But what Bill Cosby is referring to is leadership by committee, and it's a recipe for disaster.

It's okay to consults others, but stay focused. If you don't, your business associates will sense your indecision and slant their advice toward meeting their own personal agendas. In this way, your indecision can be your worst enemy.

ENTREPRENEUR | SATURDAY

> The temptation in the existing business
> is always to feed yesterday and starve
> tomorrow. —*Peter Drucker*

PETER DRUCKER WAS KNOWN FOR HIS INTEREST IN simplicity. He could have been considered an early advocate for outsourcing as needed, instead of hiring numerous and perhaps unnecessary employees.

Drucker also fought our urge to hang our hats on "yesterday's successes," especially when they have outgrown their usefulness. Another way we tend to "feed yesterday" is with debt—debt service on money that has been spent robs the business we could be building if we had finances for new opportunities. Drucker's mantra was that a company's existence is to serve its customers—profits merely allowed the company to serve its customers better.

Focusing on customers seems like a lesson many businesses could use.

Restaurants are a place where a little attention goes a long way. If a customer is seated at a table, no matter how busy the staff is, someone should get that person a menu, and ask if he'd like something to drink—within three minutes of being seated. This simple gesture lets the customer know you value his business and respect his time. These simple solutions can mean the difference between a good experience and a bad one, and making a customer for life will ensure that you never starve tomorrow.

MANAGING PEOPLE | SUNDAY

> If you can't describe what you are
> doing as a process, you don't know
> what you're doing. —*W. Edwards Deming*

THE WORD "PROCESS" SUGGESTS THAT MANAGING people can be reduced to a simple 1-2-3 system of rules. But W. Edwards Deming's notion of a process is not that simple. Deming, who helped ignite Japan's postwar boom by pushing quality control at every turn, believed that an employee's success depends largely on the quality of the processes he uses at work and not simply on the quality of the person. That means companies can rely on all different types of personalities if their processes are precise.

During his career, Deming taught that an effective management "process" included skills training for employees and even the elimination of performance reviews that ranked one employee against another. The goal was to motivate employees so that they would feel joyful and committed to an organization's success instead of feeling like hired help.

Now think of a modern-day corporation in which disgruntled employees lack motivation and buy-in. Is it their fault? In some cases, yes, but Deming would say that ultimately it's the manager's responsibility. If she can improve both the process of producing widgets and the process of managing the people who produce the widgets, chances are most disgruntled employees will come around.

MOTIVATION | MONDAY

Attitude is the way you respond to
the situation, not the situation itself.
—*Jeffrey Gitomer*

MANY OF US HAVE HAD YEARS OF ATTITUDE TRAINING and experience—and the bottom line never changes. Act positive, maintain that "Yes!" attitude, as author Jeffrey Gitomer calls it, and you'll be a winner.

But life is not always going to present situations that are tailor made for the "can-do" and "I-love-it" attitude. Often in business you will be disappointed and run into situations that reek on every level. So how do you manage your cheerleader approach at these times?

You adapt. You keep your commitment and drive, but you change your response to the situation. Even if things look bad from every angle, use your proactive talents to find a way to make them appear differently. Nine-times-out-of-ten there won't be a way to make the situation better, or completely go away, but you'll be able to find a new approach to a heinous situation. It might mean bringing others in to help, it might mean new hires, and it might mean firing someone. So instead of complaining, the next time this happens find a solution where others may have met defeat. Then you'll really be the hero.

TEAM-BUILDING | TUESDAY

It is wrong to coerce people into opinions, but it is our duty to impel them into experiences. —*Kurt Hahn*

DON'T SHELTER THE PEOPLE WHO WORK FOR YOU. Get them out into the world so that they can experience life for themselves and form their own opinions. That way, they'll have more to contribute to the team. This is the premise of Kurt Hahn's organization, Outward Bound.

Encourage, teach, and model how people can use any experience from their lives to help the team solve the problem they are facing. Rock climbing, sailing, and quilting have lessons to be learned and applied to business. Someone who makes quilts knows about planning and the importance of precision. And anyone who participates in a traditional "quilting bee" certainly learns teamwork.

At one time, the workplace did not appreciate the experience of motherhood. But what great experience: taking care of children requires patience, the ability to juggle priorities, and the need to know a little about a lot, whether in education, nursing, or sports. Talk about multitasking!

Another underappreciated work experience is waiting on tables. Waiting on tables is the consummate lesson in customer service. You must be supremely conscientious if you intend to get great tips.

Bottom line: help your team to recognize the value and application of their outside-of-work experiences *inside* their jobs.

CAREER | WEDNESDAY

*The Internet is just a world passing
around notes in a classroom.*

—Jon Stewart

B EING ABLE TO COMPOSE AN E-MAIL MESSAGE QUICKLY
without offending the receiver has been elevated to an
art form. And, do you know what to do if your boss sends
you an e-mail "thank you"? Do you reply with an e-mail?
Such new dilemmas need a working knowledge of "neti-
quette" to maintain high standards for professional relationships—or in simpler terms, to stay out of trouble.

The Internet disseminates knowledge so fast that a
harmless comment about a co-worker's outfit will circulate
faster than a clothes-horse celebrity at a fashion show. Never
put disgruntled thoughts in an e-mail, and you never attach
your name to any inflammatory political or promiscuous
forwarding lists either. In addition to maintaining e-mail
decorum, knowing about viruses, hoaxes, spamming, flam-
ing, trolling, and an expanding set of acronyms (e.g., "IMO"
for "in my opionion" and "LOL" for "laughing out loud") is
crucial for today's worker.

While most businesses have developed company policies
to deal with interoffice Internet communications, common
sense will continue to serve you well in most situations.
Promptly return the most important e-mails, use proper
punctuation, and keep it professional—good rules to live by
on and off the Net.

SALES | THURSDAY

If you would persuade, you must
appeal to interest rather than intellect.
—*Benjamin Franklin*

ONE NORMALLY DOESN'T THINK OF BEN FRANKLIN AS a salesman, but selling is what he did as Minister to France during the Revolutionary War. At that time in his famously varied career, the future Founding Father was a diplomat, and diplomacy is all about persuasion. Franklin, more than anyone else, persuaded Europe to believe in what he was selling: an American nation. In particular, he sold France on why it should be interested in this new nation, thousands of miles across the Atlantic Ocean. He offered emotional reasons why America would be important to the French. In the end, without France's military and financial aid, England would have defeated the colonies in the War of Independence.

Persuasion always requires diplomacy. The best way to persuade your customer is to appeal to their interests first, and then be ready to remove any obstacles that might be in the way of the sale.

Some salespeople get sidetracked in their descriptions of all the bells-and-whistles or get bogged down in well-rehearsed technology lessons. They forget to say why the product or service is going to be great for the customer. They are forgetting that people buy for emotional reasons, and that sometimes TMI—Too Much Information— results in brain overload and no sale.

LEADERSHIP | FRIDAY

Leadership is communicating to people
their worth and potential so clearly that
they come to see it in themselves.
—*Stephen R. Covey*

T O SUCCEED IN BUSINESS, YOU NEED TO STAY MOTI-
vated and focused. But that is easier said than done.
Stephen Covey, who preaches self-reflection as a way to discover the unlimited power of your own potential, knows
that at some point everyone is going to hit a wall. That is
where a mentor can step in and help out. But, according to
Covey, finding a mentor takes more thought and effort that
most people realize.

A good place to start is to find someone whom you
admire who shows an avid interest in you. Don't prema-
turely choose your mentor. Get to know a variety of people
who can potentially mentor you, which will minimize the
chance of choosing someone for the wrong reasons. A mag-
netic personality is captivating, but too often, you can end
up becoming a groupie, basking in the glow of your mentor's superstar stature. It's better to pick someone whose
thought process and personality mesh with yours.

A mentor wants you to learn and adapt her philosophies
to become your own. A mentor should be available for
advice and feedback, but not babysitting your insecurities.
If you pick the right mentor, and you may have more than
one, it's usually the foundation for a lifelong friendship.

ENTREPRENEUR | SATURDAY

Some of the best lessons we ever learn are learned from past mistakes. The error of the past is the wisdom and success of the future. —*Dr. Dale E. Turner*

"THE VALUE OF FAILURE" AND LEARNING FROM MIStakes are common themes in the entrepreneurial world as well as the world of Dr. Dale E. Turner, who became famous taking on underdog causes throughout his life. If you try something, there is always the chance it isn't going to work out. And it does take some personal resistance to not be overwhelmed by what looks like failure. Yet some so-called mistakes turn out not to be mistakes at all. Sometimes the "mistake" comes in the marketing of an idea, and not the product or service itself. Or, perhaps the mistake occurred in the product packaging or distribution, or even in the product display in stores. Don't be afraid to go back to the drawing board and try again.

There is an old story about a young executive who made a mistake that cost a company a million dollars. He was called in to see the big boss, and the young executive immediately admitted that he knew he was about to be fired. The boss responded, "Are you kidding? Why would I fire you when I just spent a million dollars on your education?"

Don't throw away the money you've spent on your own education. Use your mistakes to your advantage!

MANAGING PEOPLE | SUNDAY

> So much of what we call management consists of making it difficult for people to work. —*Peter Drucker*

IT'S TEMPTING TO JUDGE EMPLOYEES AT EVERY TURN. Managers often feel they are not doing their job if they are not judging. But good judgments require sound foundations. In a changing economy where knowledgeable workers now play the most important roles, Drucker believed that employees should be treated as well as you would treat volunteers, because they can take their knowledge and go elsewhere anytime they want.

But too often, employees are treated like possessions that can be stockpiled or discarded at management's whim. To keep them and help them thrive, Drucker said, management needs to appeal to their interests. They will stay—and produce—when they have a clear understanding of what an organization is trying to accomplish, when they have responsibility for results, and when they feel they're gaining more of the one thing no one can take away: knowledge. Anytime management makes it difficult for an employee to understand the mission (by not sharing it), to be accountable (by failing to give consistent feedback), or to gain new skills (by ignoring the importance of training), an organization suffers. The employees might be blamed in these circumstances, but Drucker would say management needs to look in the mirror and judge itself first.

MOTIVATION | MONDAY

If we're stubborn and opinionated at work, what are the odds we become excessively open-minded when we get home? —*Marshall Goldsmith*

HAVE YOU EVER WONDERED HOW YOU'RE PERCEIVED by your colleagues? If you have the money—say, about $250,000—executive coach Marshall Goldsmith will give you a rundown on your weaknesses and show you how to fix them.

Barring that option, you have two choices: ask around and see what your co-workers say about your negative traits (many might be too eager to volunteer), or if that sounds too intimidating, take stock of yourself. Listen to yourself through the course of the day. Anything stand out that might be categorized as, uh, "negative"?

What? You heard yourself talking negatively about the new guy because you thought your idea was better than his? Whoa!—later that day you did the same thing to someone else? Could you be... stubborn and opinionated?

The true laboratory for discovering negative traits, however, is the domestic front. The odds are stacked that you're going to exhibit the same stubbornness at home as you do in your workplace. If you're not open to suggestion within the family group, always demanding the last word, you're not going to be open-minded in your job.

You want success in your home and office life. Take stock, isolate the problem, and work to change yourself.

TEAM-BUILDING | TUESDAY

*Never hire the first person who
walks in the door.* —*Martha Stewart*

THE FIRST PERSON WHO WALKS IN THE DOOR MAY BE perfect. She may possess all the qualities you are looking for in the position you are trying to fill. And she may be the person you end up hiring. But as Martha Stewart says, don't hire her without interviewing several candidates. You have no idea what the next person might be like if you don't check out everyone.

Hiring is a tricky business. Just the hiring process itself represents a large investment of time and money. And actually hiring someone is further investment. You don't want to take on this job cavalierly.

Interview several candidates. Ask them open-ended questions that encourage them to do the talking. The most important information about an interviewee comes out during more casual conversation.

Use the interview to assess what kind of person the interviewee is. If you are concerned with his experience and work history, look at his resume, and call a few references and only talk with the person for a few minutes. Make sure you are hiring the best person for the job as well as the one who is going to be a good fit with the rest of the team.

Don't interview in a vacuum. Make sure the team members meet the new hire and ask their own questions. The rest of the team should not wonder who you are bringing on; they should be part of the process.

CAREER | WEDNESDAY

> You can make more friends in two
> months by becoming interested in
> other people than you can in two
> years by trying to get other people
> interested in you. —*Dale Carnegie*

IF YOU WANT TO CREATE SATISFYING, INTERESTING BUSI-
ness relationships, you are going to have to start listening
to others. All of us have surely been involved in a conversation that suddenly takes a turn for the worse. One person
starts with a challenge about "who knows who" or "I did
that, too," and then you realize that nobody is listening.

It's time to break the chain. If you ask a question, you'll
get a lot more out of it if you listen to the answer. By asking
people questions about themselves and sitting back to actually listen, you are conveying a clear message that you are
interested in who they are, what they think, and what's
important to them. Most of the time, they, in turn, will have
kind feelings toward you and be inclined to reciprocate.

Unfortunately, this will backfire on occasion. Once in a
while you will get into a conversation with someone who
seems completely self-centered. He or she will hog the floor,
railing on and on with no indication of letting you get a
word in edgewise. Instead of getting frustrated, pay close
attention to your inner reaction. Then remember what you
felt the next time you want to do all the talking.

SALES | THURSDAY

Your most unhappy customers are your greatest source of learning. —Bill Gates

THE GENIUS OF BILL GATES LIES NOT SO MUCH IN HIS ability to create new technology—after all, he bought, not invented, the programming language BASIC, which begat DOS, which begat Windows. Rather, his genius is his sales and marketing skills. By closing the deal and getting his newborn operating system inside an IBM computer in 1980, he beat out the competing operating systems that were vying for the same honor, and he positioned Microsoft to become the software technology leader of the world.

Bill Gates has also been concerned about listening to the customer and learning about the customer's needs. When something doesn't work for the customer, Microsoft marshals the brainpower of thousands of programmers to fix it. (Granted, they don't always get it right the first time, but they keep trying until they do and send out millions of patches in the meantime.)

Picking the brains of your unhappy—hopefully, not angry—customers can be the most potent tool you have for improving your own products and sales. Knowing how to gather that information, how to manage it, and how to use it is your mission. If you're not learning from your customers now, start tomorrow. Their input is invaluable.

LEADERSHIP | FRIDAY

> Managers do things right;
> leaders do the right thing.
> —*Pat Croce*

I F BEING A GREAT LEADER REQUIRES MANAGEMENT EXPERT-
ise and being a great manager requires leadership expertise, are the two positions interchangeable? Not so fast, Pat
Croce writes in his book, *Lead Or Get Off the Pot.* Although
both positions are important in terms of guiding the company to success, crucial differences set managers and leaders
apart. Managers do their jobs by making sure that workers
follow rules, but leaders change the rules to make the system work better.

Pat Croce went from being a physical therapist to creating
a multimillion dollar chain of freestanding physical therapy
centers. He realized that a leader is unique from everyone else
because he must supply the vision and motivation for the rest
of the organization. Looking for a new challenge, he saw
potential in the Philadelphia 76ers, an underperforming basketball team mired in unhappy organization. He realized
quickly that current ticket policies were not fan friendly, pre-
venting the 76ers from building a large following. He thought
that he could be an effective leader and bought the team.

One change he made allowed fans to receive their season
ticket deposits back if the next season's prices went up. He
personally handled the most difficult customers, showing his
employees exactly how it's done. By setting the tone, Pat
Croce led by example and his employees followed suit.

ENTREPRENEUR | SATURDAY

To invent, you need a good imagination and a pile of junk. —*Thomas A. Edison*

I F YOU WANT TO MAKE A SCULPTURE, TAKE A BLOCK OF stone and carve away what doesn't need to be there. With inventing, it is the opposite—take pieces and put them together to create a completely new and useful thing.

Inventing is the purest form of entrepreneurship. Yet many good ideas for inventions are never completed because people are intimidated by the process: not only must your idea come to fruition, you also need to patent it, make it in large numbers, and sell it. Sometimes it's just simpler to cash out: sell your design to someone else to produce and sell your vision.

If you want to hold onto all of the profits, you will have to go through the complicated patent process yourself. You would be wise to hire a patent attorney.

Those who persevere through the patenting process can realize substantial rewards. Dean Kamen, the inventor of the Segway personal transport, holds over 440 U.S. and foreign patents. He was already the inventor of the infusion pump used for insulin and chemotherapy delivery before inventing the Segway, and Kamen is now referred to as an "inventrepreneur."

MANAGING PEOPLE | SUNDAY

> Effectiveness comes about through
> enabling others to reach their potential—
> both their personal potential and then
> corporate or institutional potential.
>
> —*Max Depree*

W HAT WORKS FOR THE HERMAN MILLER FURNITURE company could work for you. According to Max Depree in his book, *Leadership Is An Art,* his father, D.J. Depree, founded Herman Miller Furniture determined to produce a quality product within a quality working environment. That was in 1923, when touchy-feely ideas like "improving corporate culture" didn't exist.

Flash forward to the 1960s. Max and his brother Hugh took over their dad's company and instituted the Scanlon plan, which focuses on managing people through incentives. Today, under Max's continued reign, Herman Miller consistently wins a spot in Forbes' Best Companies to work for poll.

Depree recognizes that the work environment plays a large part in employee satisfaction. At the Greenhouse, one of their facilities, the building's glass enclosed structure mingles individual departments, bringing together employees from marketing, sales, and design into one dynamic think tank. If a salesperson has a question about a new product, he can walk over and talk to the engineer who designed it. Small touches make a difference, and nurturing the spirits of your employees helps you manage them effectively.

MOTIVATION | MONDAY

Remember that nobody will ever get
ahead of you as long as he is kicking
you in the seat of the pants.

—*Walter Winchell*

A S A FEDORA-WEARING CITY REPORTER OF THE 1920S,
Walter Winchell invented the gossip column. In the
next decade, though unseen by his radio broadcast audience,
he still wore the fedora, and went on to alter journalism by
developing his gossip into the culture of celebrity that has
become an industry today.

Winchell once offered the famous piece of advice quoted
above to a victim of slander whose name was in the headlines, thanks to Winchell. Immersed as he was in reporting
on and/or attacking public figures, Walter Winchell knew
criticism. He was always embroiled in one sensational battle or another. He knew how to roll with the punches and
make good copy out of it.

Criticism isn't always a bad thing if you put it into perspective. Sometimes you need to make it work for you. If
people are trying to keep you down, "kicking you in the seat
of your pants," according to Winchell's inimitable phrasing,
that's good news. It means they're spending far too much
time on you instead of tending to their own careers. In the
meantime, you should keep doing what you're doing, as long
as you believe in it. Use their criticism to fuel your determination. It's very likely you're right and they're wrong.

TEAM-BUILDING | TUESDAY

You cannot run away from a weakness;
you must sometimes fight it out or perish.
—*Robert Louis Stevenson*

EVERYONE HAS WEAKNESSES. EVEN THOSE WHO HAVE developed an outstanding and unique legacy prove to have faults. Thomas Jefferson, Martin Luther King, Jr., and even Mother Theresa had to deal with their weaknesses. No one can be good at everything; it's just not realistic. And remember, we are not striving for perfection, at least not all the time.

There are two basic ways to overcome a weakness. Famed novelist Robert Louis Stevenson believed that one way is to eliminate the weakness by becoming better at what is holding you back—learn more about business finance, or take a course in closing sales. Better yet, find a mentor who can give you the tools that you don't possess.

The other way is to hire around your weakness. If you are a poor writer, hire a team member who is a strong writer to take on your writing tasks. If you are not a people person, hire a second-in-command who can be your personnel contact.

Lastly, don't avoid confronting your weaknesses. Don't be ashamed of them. How you deal with them makes the difference between success and failure. So, what are you waiting for? There is no better time than now to change something about yourself that isn't working.

CAREER | WEDNESDAY

Where you start is not as important as where you finish. —*Zig Ziglar*

EVERY SUMMER, MILLIONS OF COLLEGE FOOTBALL FANS across America eagerly await the preseason polls. If your team happens to be ranked in the top ten, it's a time for celebration. If your team happens to be the preseason number one, though, it's a time for mourning. Having the number one ranking before a ball is ever snapped is practically the kiss of death. Very rarely does a team get through an entire season on top and capture the coveted national championship title.

It's easy to fall into the trap of assuming that because you didn't have the opportunity to attend Harvard Business School, you're starting at a disadvantage. Zig Ziglar suggests that these types of "disadvantages" are an illusion. Our lives do not depend on the past—but rather on what we learn from the past and how we apply it toward a better future. If you are having a hard time visualizing a successful path, write down some of the things that have happened in your life and how you overcame them. Write down all of the things that you do well, because this will show you the skills you already have to move forward. Then, write down all of the great people in your life and how they can help you. Visualizing a future is simply letting go of the past and accepting your personal path to greatness. Being focused on success will guarantee your place on top in the future, no matter where you came from.

SALES | THURSDAY

> If you would like to fill your corporate
> bank accounts, refocus and redouble
> your efforts on the people that fill them
> first: your present customers.
>
> —*Jeffrey Gitomer*

TAKE A LOOK AT YOUR SALES FIGURES AND SEE WHO your biggest customers are. Then calculate what percentage of business comes from those customers. The typical finding is that in a successful business, 80 percent of revenue comes from 20 percent of the customer base. With figures like these, it's easy to see that customer loyalty is key.

To keep your customer base steady and profitable, repeat business is crucial. The first sale is often costly for your company and requires a lot of hard work. And once you reap the rewards, the hard work isn't over. Every time you land a new customer, you have to redouble your efforts. Keep the lines of communication open with your steady customers. Always be available to them, and always be ready to take that extra step to satisfy their needs. Your job is to anticipate their needs. Establish a rapport so you can contact them any time with new ideas and so that they feel free to call on you whenever they need anything. Knowing you'll be there for them is the secret of a great sales relationship—and that relationship is the foundation for loyalty.

Redoubling customer service adds value to your products and services. If you focus your efforts on your present customers, they'll keep coming back.

LEADERSHIP | FRIDAY

A benevolent monopolist cuts his prices
before a competitor can cut them.

—Peter Drucker

S TAYING AHEAD OF THE COMPETITION IS PARAMOUNT
for success. Peter Drucker's book, *Innovation and Entre-preneurship*, uses the term "benevolent monopolist" to describe the method by which a corporation fights off encroachment. According to Drucker, the father of modern management theory, there is no need to fight dirty. If leaders focus on bringing products and services to the market quickly, they will be ready to defend against the advances of other companies. In essence, you must do anything and everything that is aligned with your company's purpose, mission, and values to maintain your market share.

To do this successfully, you must first know who your competitors are. Second, you must have a continuous source of product or services to introduce as old products/services lose ground. Third, time the introduction of new products or services to hit the market before your competitors do—this will deflate their splash on the scene and keep you in the game. Thinking about Microsoft's failure with the Zune MP3 player is all the motivation you need to get to the market first.

Nobody likes someone who beats them at his or her own game, but in business, like baseball, it's best to pitch a shut-out.

ENTREPRENEUR | SATURDAY

When you're the first person whose beliefs are different from what everyone else believes, you're basically saying, "I'm right, and everyone else is wrong." That's a very unpleasant position to be in. It's at once exhilarating and at the same time an invitation to be attacked. *—Larry Ellison*

L ARRY ELLISON IS ANOTHER ENTREPRENEUR WHO MADE his fame and fortune through computer technology. Ellison is the founder of the software company Oracle. He knows a lot about being attacked. He is one of the wealthiest people in the world, lives a somewhat extravagant lifestyle, and doesn't seem to hold back his opinions.

Expressing a different belief is almost always controversial. But the reaction to saying you are "right" and everyone else is "wrong" depends a lot on how you present your message. Some people can say something negative to others and have them receive it as a compliment. If you are coming on strong, you have to be sure to have the facts to support what you are saying. Then you can make your point and people will listen.

If you want people to accept your beliefs, you need to present them in a way that makes your audience relate to them in the same way you do. The most persuasive approach is to focus on proving yourself right, rather that proving others wrong.

MANAGING PEOPLE | SUNDAY

Positional bargaining puts relationship and substance in conflict. —*Roger Fisher*

M ANAGERS ROUTINELY ASSUME THAT THEIR AUTHORITY gives them the power to make people do whatever they ask them to do. In the end, this kind of manager ultimately fails because the art of negotiation is never learned. Roger Fisher's business classic, *Getting to Yes*, is one book every manager needs to master.

When you take a position that seems immovable, it's called positional bargaining. Unfortunately, if you use positional bargaining too often, you'll develop a reputation for pig-headed stubbornness. Your single-minded attitude will not only cause hard feelings, but it rarely reflects what you actually believe. Usually, stubbornness is simply a knee-jerk reaction.

Negotiating should result in both parties feeling they are getting something out of the deal. The way to avoid positional bargaining is to avoid stating your position too early in the negotiation. Not only do you back yourself into a corner, you put the other party in a defensive position. Instead, invite a discussion about why the other person wants something and then find a way to achieve it. If your employee wants a day off but you need him in Chicago, maybe you can let him take his wife and stay the weekend on the company. In this instance, everyone wins.

MOTIVATION | MONDAY

> Great ability develops and reveals itself increasingly with every new assignment. —*Baltasar Gracian*

BALTASAR GRACIAN WAS NOT A BUSINESSMAN; HE WAS a Jesuit priest in the early seventeenth century. He acquired fame as a preacher and wrote *The Criticon,* an allegorical novel. In the story, Critilo, a man of the world, is shipwrecked and meets Andrenio, a man who has grown up away from civilization. An unlikely pair, the two travel the world together seeking answers.

On their journey, many disappointments and surprises come their way, and many life lessons are learned. Each day is a new "assignment" for the two men, and gradually they realize that each event changes them, makes them grow in their abilities, and helps them with their goal of reaching immortality.

While reaching immortality is probably not your goal, you need to adopt Gracian's attitude with each new assignment. See if you can identify new revelations about your abilities. Let yourself learn and develop your potential with every new challenge. Your experiences will uncover your many abilities as your career unfolds.

Gracian's writings later influenced the nineteenth-century philosopher Schopenhauer, whom Winston Churchill was said to have read on a ship that took him to the Boer Wars. By adopting the tenets of Gracian's philosophy, you will be in good company.

TEAM-BUILDING | TUESDAY

*If you have great confidence in your
lure, you'll fish with confidence.*
—*Thomas J. Stanley*

WHEN FISHING FOR HIGH-QUALITY TEAM MEMBERS, your company needs to be your lure. Construct a great company, and you will be able to fish the employee pool with confidence that your company can attract the best. In his bestselling book, *The Millionaire Mind*, Stanley argues that the wealthiest Americans spend the least amount of time collecting high-status objects. The same principle holds true for most businesses. Most companies can draw good employees without fancy gadgets or the latest desktop computers. They just need to be people oriented.

Create a place where your employees brag to others about where they work. Make sure your company is family-friendly and allows workers to design flexible schedules to meet childcare needs. Until health care stops being job dependent, offer the best health care options you can afford. If your company is too small to pay for complete health care, find a way to get the best group plans you can. Find other ways to reward and compensate, like flexible spending accounts or group-plan pet insurance.

There are many ways to be creative to make your company a great lure to the workforce so that you can go fishing with confidence—and one of the greatest lures of all is to have a great group of people working at your company.

CAREER | WEDNESDAY

It takes twenty years to build a reputation and five minutes to ruin it. —Warren Buffett

I T ONLY TAKES AN INSTANT TO RUIN A LIFETIME OF HARD work. When quarterback Michael Vick's dog-fighting allegations surfaced, young boys across the country were shocked. Not only was their idol in trouble, but being cruel to animals took routine "bad boy" behavior to another level. This one horrific-act headline sank his reputation.

Whether it's deserved or not, your reputation will stick with you for a long time, especially if it's related to bad news. And in business, your reputation is often all you have. People want to know that they can count on you personally and professionally. If you make a customer angry because you are having a bad day, it can affect your business in serious ways. People like to talk about good experiences, but they love to talk about the bad ones.

Professionalism means maintaining a sterling demeanor when dealing with customers or clients. Avoid office gossip, and minimize displaying negative personal feelings to colleagues. Cutting corners or making unscrupulous deals will definitely ruin your company's reputation, as well as your own.

SALES | THURSDAY

*Give them quality. That's the best
kind of advertising.* —*Milton Hershey*

H AVE YOU EVER HAD A BAD HERSHEY'S KISS? OR,
have you ever seen anyone turn one down? The Hershey
Company chocolate empire was built on the quality of its
products—with a little addictiveness thrown in. With a
product that reliable, who needs more advertising?

It's hard to imagine, but when Milton Hershey started
his company in 1903, milk chocolate didn't even exist in
America. It was a Swiss luxury product. But Hershey, already
in the confection business, saw a future in chocolate. After a
lot of research and development, he created his own formula,
using fresh milk from local dairies near Lancaster, Pennsyl-
vania. He built a factory designed to manufacture chocolate
with state-of-the-art mass production. Meanwhile, he kept
experimenting and perfecting the process. A high level of
quality was assured by Hershey's proximity to dairy farms—
and by his demanding standards for excellence. Soon enough,
Hershey was able to change the American palate to yearn for
a product they had never even known they were missing.

In sales, quality is paramount, and will always translate
into better relationships with your customers. If your product or service is excellent, it represents honesty and integrity,
which will generate great buzz: the best (and cheapest) kind
of advertising.

LEADERSHIP | FRIDAY

> A sense of humor is part of the art of leadership, of getting along with people, of getting things done.
> —*Dwight D. Eisenhower*

WHEN PRESIDENT DWIGHT D. EISENHOWER WAS A cadet at West Point Military Academy, he abhorred the rules and regulations that restricted the students' lives. Once he was so fed up by an order from an upperclassman to appear in "full-dress coat," that he showed up wearing neither trousers or underwear.

Early on Ike learned the power of a sense of humor, which helped get him through tough situations in years to come.

As president, Ike found that running the government was a different sort of challenge. On paper, the hierarchy and structure were similar enough to the army to give him confidence to lead the nation. However, the differences caused him frustration. Not used to having his opinions challenged, the former general had to find a way to get his point across without seeming like a dictator. Once again, he handled many situations, including his many press conferences, with humor and a touch of grace.

If you are a serious business leader with a ton of responsibility on your shoulders, try handling stress with humor. People like to laugh, and they always like those that make them laugh.

ENTREPRENEUR | SATURDAY

> In many ways a lot of what's involved in business planning is like physical exercise. It's really no good for you if you don't do it yourself. —*Tim Berry*

M ANY FIRST-TIME ENTREPRENEURS WANT TO OPEN A business without going to the trouble of creating a formal business plan. But, as business plan writer Tim Berry knows, you just have to do it, for myriad reasons, not the least is the bank. A business plan should include an overview of the business you intend to open, biographical info about yourself, your qualifications for starting this particular business, an analysis of the market in the area in which you are opening, an evaluation of the competition, your marketing plans to promote your business and bring in customers, and of course, financial projections.

A formal business plan will give you the following assistance:

- Help you secure start-up money
- Determine the start-up supplies you will need
- Give you an outline to fall back on if you feel you are growing confused about your business's direction, and most of all,
- Provide a guiding framework for your business, both present and future.

Don't avoid doing a business plan because you don't want to be locked in. Instead, do your homework, create a business plan, and see where it leads.

MANAGING PEOPLE | SUNDAY

A company's culture is really the behavior of its people. And leaders get the behavior they tolerate. —*Dick Brown*

WHEN DICK BROWN INHERITED ROSS PEROT'S FORmer company, Electronic Data Systems (EDS), it was a bloated corporate structure being crushed by younger, hipper, competition including Razorfish and Viant. When he went to make a call from a top management office, he found that the phone didn't work because it had been cut off so the manager wouldn't have to answer calls. Talk about being disconnected. The corporate culture at EDS, a premier computer technology company, was completely dysfunctional, with problems running all the way from the top down.

Dick Brown had a few tricks up his sleeve to change the complacent behavior of bureaucracy. He reorganized the structure to be more client centered. Each month, the top 125 leaders had to attend a conference call where everyone discussed their numbers. A byproduct of the conference call was that these same leaders worked harder to solve any existing problems before this monthly call. He implemented a quality control program called Dashboard, in which clients gave feedback on performances. If a client posted negative feedback, any leader with answers could immediately join to solve the problem. He also brought back performance-based financial incentives. Those who produced more money, received more money. Brown says the real key is that immediate feedback is imperative to correct problems.

MOTIVATION | MONDAY

Eighty percent of success is showing up.
—*Woody Allen*

A LLEN SOUNDS HUMOROUSLY CYNICAL, BUT AS WITH all great comic lines there's wisdom embedded in his punch line. Indeed, this line could well be Allen's own time-tested formula for success.

It's stunning how often people don't follow through with their intentions or promises. How many times have you heard, "I'll have that report for you next week, I promise!" and it runs into two weeks, three weeks? Or how many times have you used excuses to postpone projects, even though you present those excuses in the most maddeningly sincere way imaginable. Showing up—delivering—is essential to success. Establishing yourself as a responsible person is actually a good deal more than eighty percent of success.

So what's the other twenty percent in Allen's equation? Perhaps it's being a creative talent with driving ambition, just as he is. Several times in his career, after receiving substantial negative publicity, everyone thought he was finished. But Allen knows how to make compromises, new deals, and, most important, he knows how to deliver within budget and on deadline. That's why he's still churning out a new film every year. That's why he is a success.

Showing up is about doing. Completing your projects, adhering to deadlines, and knowing that you came through as you promised are major achievements.

TEAM-BUILDING | TUESDAY

When you sit in judgment of others,
you're likely to be wrong about them.
—*Arnold L. and Clifton N. Lazarus*

I T IS HARD NOT TO BE JUDGMENTAL, AND RARELY WILL anyone succeed in avoiding it altogether. However, rash judgments are usually wrong. Think about the last time you heard someone talking about a person you know, while knowing that what you were hearing was either wrong or misinterpreted.

Psychologists Arnold and Clifton Lazarus point out that when someone starts being judgmental, it may be best to walk away from the conversation. If you can legitimately come to someone's defense, that is certainly a good thing to do. But when people are judgmental, it is unlikely that they will listen to anyone anyway, so you may be wasting your breath.

If a team discussion devolves into judgmental talk—about someone, another company or another company's product or service—it's your obligation to redirect the conversation because the discussion is wasting everyone's time.

On the other hand, there are times when discussing the qualities of another company's product or service is important. But the conversation should stick to the facts—such as the color of the competing company's product and how it affects its ability to be kept clean. In this way, being critical is also being constructive, so that choosing the color of your product becomes an informed decision.

CAREER | WEDNESDAY

We run our schools like factories. We line kids up in straight rows, put them in batches (called grades), and work very hard to make sure there are no defective parts. Nobody standing out, falling behind, running ahead, making a ruckus. —*Seth Godin*

WHILE LEARNING THE BASICS IS IMPORTANT, IT'S JUST as important to discover new and creative ways of doing the same old things. The real route to success is a combination of learning and creative thinking—not by conforming to the norm.

In his book, *Purple Cow*, Godin's message is simple: be remarkable. A purple cow is something counterintuitive, phenomenal, and exciting. His lesson is to put a purple cow into your business thinking, whether you are in marketing, production, or sales, so that you will attract the attention you deserve.

If you always follow the manual, it's time to change your mindset. Creativity needs to be nurtured, and it's hard to do so in an environment saturated by business-as-usual politics, as well as the disruptions of streaming e-mails and phone calls. To put yourself in a mindset that will encourage you to think outside the box, make an effort to tune out the outside world. And instead of just doing your job, give some thought on how you can do it differently. This way you just may change your company, product, or service in a way that nobody ever thought before.

SALES | THURSDAY

Work for the fun of it, and the money will arrive some day. — *Ronnie Milsap*

THERE ARE INEVITABLY GOING TO BE DAYS WHEN YOU question what you're doing in this business. You may be going through a dry spell, or maybe you lost an account and your bills are piling up, waiting to be paid. You're left wondering how long until you can coast into a smooth landing.

Country star Ronnie Milsap was born blind into bleak Appalachian poverty and given away to his grandmother after his mother decided that his handicap was a punishment from God. He was sent to the state school for the blind in Raleigh, North Carolina where he was subject to brutal discipline. Fortunately, Ronnie had a radio. Music became his salvation. He took such joy in music that a spark of optimism was all he needed to keep his spirits alive.

Milsap released his first single at age twenty, but he had to put in years of hard work before he found success. Even so, he had fun the entire time because he was in the music business—something he always dreamed of. Milsap went on to win seven Grammy Awards and countless country music awards and to record multiple number one hits.

You can learn to adapt to any situation by following Ronnie Milsap's example. Use your creativity to transition from a low point to a high. Energy and enthusiasm will pull you out of the black hole you think you're in and fuel a new start. If you enjoy what you're doing, the money will come.

LEADERSHIP | FRIDAY

If you're going to be a leader, you have to undertake the difficult things (the things that are arduous to do) because you want the organization and the people within it to be successful. —*Herb Kelleher*

HERB KELLEHER IS NO STRANGER TO HARD WORK. HE did practically everything for Southwest Airlines Co. when it started. No task was ever beneath him or too miniscule to undertake because somebody had to do it to get the organization off the ground. There's no doubt that because of Kellaher's attention, Southwest Airlines has been one of the best-run airlines since its inception. His leadership style and magnanimous personality continue to inspire the employees today. One Southwest employee recorded this observation: "Herb has a way of making you feel like an old friend every time you see him by calling you by name and recalling the funny thing you said to him when you last met."

Combine those observations with numerous customer service awards, thirty-plus years of profitability, and a consistent product, and you've got Kelleher's formula for success. From day one, Herb Kelleher insisted that customers came second, and taking care of his employees came first. Nobody believed that would make the airline great, but he proved everyone wrong.

As a leader, set the example. And if that means doing the small stuff, you can't be too big for the job.

ENTREPRENEUR | SATURDAY

The new law of evolution in corporate America seems to be survival of the unfittest. Well, in my book you either do it right or you get eliminated. In the last seven deals that I've been involved with, there were 2.5 million stockholders who have made a pretax profit of 12 billion dollars. Thank you. I am not a destroyer of companies. I am a liberator of them! The point is, ladies and gentleman, that greed, for lack of a better word, is good. —*Gordon Gekko*, Wall Street *(1987)*

THE CHARACTER, GORDON GEKKO, PLAYED BY MICHAEL Douglas in the movie, *Wall Street,* was roughly based on real-life financial character Ivan Boesky. His name, like Gekko's, became synonymous with corporate greed within the 1980s investment banking industry.

Boesky became famous when he was indicted for participating in a Wall Street insider trading scandal in the mid-1980s. He was prosecuted for making investments based on tips he received from those inside corporations in which he invested. Boesky was jailed and banned from ever working in the securities business again.

Underhanded business dealings rarely go unpunished. Keep your business on the up and up, and there's no reason to ever compromise your integrity.

MANAGING PEOPLE | SUNDAY

Most managers are "gunnysack" discipliners.
—*Ken Blanchard*

T HE WILD POPULARITY OF THE WORKPLACE PARODY, *The Office,* is infinitely revealing. Millions of TV viewers also feel that their bosses are incompetent, cruel, or purely motivated by self-interest—so laughing at caricatures of their bosses never fails to satisfy.

Not all bosses fit the mold, but the exceptions may be few. More than twenty-five years ago, world-renowned business consultant Ken Blanchard pointed to an epidemic of bad management in his now-classic book, *The One Minute Manager.* Blanchard noted that most managers use "gunnysack" discipliners: they store up examples of an employee's poor performance in a figurative gunny sack, never bothering to tell the employee what's wrong, and then they fire away during annual reviews or when they're having a bad day. The employee is left to wonder where she went wrong and why her boss never gave her a chance to correct any of these problems.

Managers who use this technique are lazy and childish. Worse, they undercut their real goal: getting the best from employees. No one working for you can fix what's wrong without knowing something is wrong. Blanchard's solution? One minute reprimands. If a worker's performance slips, you intervene immediately. Explain what's not right, ask for an explanation, and work together to correct the problem.

MOTIVATION | MONDAY

> Failure is nature's plan to prepare you
> for great responsibilities. —*Napoleon Hill*

NAPOLEON HILL WAS A PIONEER IN THE GENRE OF books on business success. His most famous book, *Think and Grow Rich,* is still one of the bestsellers of all time.

Hill believed that having a purpose or a plan is essential to attaining success. He advised readers to think their way through a failure, to view failure as a small part of a plan that will ultimately benefit them. If you analyze a failure—see it as a plan with a purpose it will prepare you for bigger challenges. In this way failure can only make you better because it prepares you for greater responsibilities.

Hill's official biography says he was born in a two-room cabin into wretched poverty. He began working at age thirteen as a reporter for small-town newspapers in rural Virginia. He later put himself through college. Meeting the powerful industrialist Andrew Carnegie and hearing his ideas led to Hill's lifelong project, interviewing the most famous and wealthy men of the time. What Hill learned from these men became the basis of his successful books.

An amazing fact is that Hill never mentioned the word "achievement" in *Think and Grow Rich*—he felt that readers would benefit most by discovering the keys to achieving their goals themselves as the result of his winning philosophy.

TEAM-BUILDING | TUESDAY

> Politics is when people choose their
> words and actions based on how they
> want others to react rather than based
> on what they really think. —*Patrick Lencioni*

C ORPORATE TEAMS CERTAINLY OPERATE IN THE REALM of office politics. But everyone benefits if team members don't play politics among themselves, says business writer Patrick Lencioni.

In order for a team to work together successfully, everyone needs to be apolitical, and there needs to be a transparency about the work and how the work is going to get done. Transparency is not an invitation to be mean-spirited or rude. But a team is not going to be truly effective unless everything is out in the open. Political double-talk has no place on a team.

When the team leader presents the team's research or findings or intentions to the larger world, some spin—or carefully chosen words—may be needed to highlight the efforts made. However, try not to coerce or dupe anyone to accept your efforts. The worst scenario would be to get a project green-lighted that no one really wants but was conned into.

Don't hide your true agenda and direct people's thinking. Say what you really think, act in a way that is true to your thinking, and you will gain respect.

CAREER | WEDNESDAY

Confession is good for the soul
but bad for the career. —*Anonymous*

JOKING WITH CO-WORKERS ABOUT YOUR LACK OF SOCIAL
life or troubles with the in-laws may seem self-effacing,
yet natural. After all, theses are the people with whom you
spend most of your waking hours. But sharing confidences
can come at a cost. People have their own goals and interests in mind at the office. Someone who may appear to be
a good friend can turn on you if the situation benefits him.
If you aren't sure that someone can be trusted with your
personal information, then it's better to err on the side of
caution.

Here's a test you can perform to decide whether or not
to confide in someone at work. Ask yourself if you no longer
worked with this person, would you still try to maintain
close contact after you leave. If not, and most people will fall
into this category, its better to keep your thoughts to yourself. Hire a therapist or go to the gym to vent your frustrations, but don't let it all hang out at work.

SALES | THURSDAY

*Success seems to be connected with
action. Successful people keep moving.
They make mistakes, but they don't quit.*

—*Conrad Hilton*

THE HOTEL BUSINESS IS SYNONYMOUS WITH THE NAME Hilton, a chain whose success was predicated on action. Conrad Hilton started out in 1919 with one hotel—the Mobley—in the dusty town of Cisco, Texas. He started putting his own name on hotels in 1925, in Dallas, and launched his first high-rise Hilton, in El Paso, in 1930. America's first hotel chain was in full swing by 1943. Hilton made his international move in 1954, buying the Statler Hotel chain, and kept on leaving his mark on every continent.

During the Depression no one could afford to travel, and Hilton lost several of his hotels to the stagnant economy. He tried to keep as many open as possible, running his business on credit and good will. Years later, he was able to buy back his hotels. He repaid his debts, and learned from the hospitality and charity he was shown by others during these bad financial times. Hilton became determined to show the same qualities in his hotels, and his success enabled him to pursue his own philanthropic interests, including the establishment of the Conrad N. Hilton Foundation.

The Hilton hotel empire is a monument to Conrad Hilton's perseverance. His formula for success is a testament to hard work and an undying spirit.

LEADERSHIP | FRIDAY

*Better beggar woman and single than
Queen and married.* —*Elizabeth I*

ENGLAND'S QUEEN ELIZABETH I WAS A POWERFUL
leader, but she wasn't perfect. She was sometimes seen
as independent to a fault, relying on her own judgment
rather than the counsel of others. Elizabeth fiercely desired
freedom from any political alliances that might threaten
her country's sovereignty. But, in 1578, England watched
in horror as Spain began a campaign to expand its empire.
Rich from its exploration of the new world, Spain set out to
conquer the Netherlands. For England, this was geographi-
cally too close for comfort. Queen Elizabeth began serious
engagement negotiations with the French prince, Francis,
Duke of Anjou, in hopes of forming an alliance with France.

Unexpectedly she fell in love with him. Elizabeth continued the courtship, but her Protestant subjects detested
Francis, for he was a Catholic. After much debate, a dejected
Elizabeth stopped the engagement and made a vow of
chastity. In the end, her loyalty was to the sovereignty and
the people of England.

Sometimes a leader must choose between personal feelings and what is best for the company. Whether it's firing a
relative for poor performance or telling a friend that you
can't do business anymore, a leader must always do the right
thing, despite the pain. When it comes to the good of the
company, consider your alliances and make them without
compromising your company or your values.

ENTREPRENEUR | SATURDAY

> Your present reputation determines
> your future fate. —*Jeffrey Gitomer*

YOUR REPUTATION IS YOURS TO BUILD OR DESTROY. Someone else can try to smear your good name by saying negative things about you, but if you have built your reputation with a solid foundation, it is hard to destroy.

The way to build that foundation is by never deviating from your core principles. Those principles need to include honesty and trustworthiness. Never play the other person's game, always play your own.

No matter how tempting, don't retaliate with negative comments about your opponent. Instead, let your reputation save you. If a competitor accuses you of underhanded business practices, remind people of the things you have done that have built your reputation—quality products, excellent service, a customer-based approach to business, and "open-book" policy of your finances and donations to local and global causes. These are not the common activities of one who cheats.

Maintaining a solid reputation is a full-time job, and often you need to defend it with actions, not words. You can tell people "I am a good person," or "My business is reliable." But unless you give them concrete reasons that support your claims, they will never agree with you.

MANAGING PEOPLE | SUNDAY

You build step by step, whether
it's friendships or opportunities.
—*Barbara Bush*

MOST MANAGERS FAIL BECAUSE THE EXPECTATIONS they have for their employees and themselves don't match reality. Making friendships and building relationships take time. Managers and workers all take shortcuts, regularly stereotyping each other based on shallow interactions. Former First Lady Barbara Bush's pearl of wisdom can put it into perspective for you. Whether you are a new manager or have been doing it for twenty years, remember that any successful venture requires a serious time commitment, and the ability to set aside hastily made judgments.

Consider it a privilege to lead your employees on their career journey, instead of focusing on their day-to-day tasks. Since a great company invests in its people, providing your employees with opportunities to build their careers should seem obvious. But many companies don't take an active role in managing their managers, and, as a result, these managers start to look out only for themselves. At this point, asking them to take an interest in their employees, beyond whether they show up on time and do their job, seems ridiculous.

Managing people takes a combination of people skills, intuition, and maturity. If you are a manager, become a sincere career advisor to your employees. Be a member of their life team, and you will earn back loyalty and performance.

MOTIVATION | MONDAY

> If we were always guided by other
> people's thoughts, what's the point
> in having our own? —*Oscar Wilde*

THE BRILLIANT OSCAR WILDE HAS HIS HEROINE, ERLYNGER, speak this line in his play, *Lady Windermere's Fan.* Erlynger is trying to convince Stella, Lady Windermere, that she must remain strong and true even though society may be against her.

No one ever accused Wilde of being guided by other people's thoughts. Indeed, he might as well have played Stella himself. Among countless memorable lines he wrote, the one above stands out as the motto of his life. He never lost sight of his goal of becoming a famous writer. This goal determined his every thought and belief in himself—he truly believed that it was ridiculous to ever consider being guided by others.

The line in Wilde's play flies by as witty repartee when performed, but it continues to resonate in present-day social relations as well as the marketplace. Indeed, Oscar Wilde resembles Jack Welch and Lee Iacocca when it comes to leadership style.

Your goal is to be a leader, not a follower. You've worked and studied hard to get where you are—or at least know where you want your career to lead—and you believe in yourself. Your ideas are your own—they will determine your life. Be fearless like Oscar Wilde: let your ideas guide you, and don't be swayed by others.

TEAM-BUILDING | TUESDAY

> Whatever you are by nature, keep to
> it; never desert your line of talent.
> Be what nature intended you for and
> you will succeed. —*Sydney Smith*

BRITISH ADMIRAL SIR SYDNEY SMITH BELIEVED THAT talent should be nurtured. Our culture widely admires artistic, musical, and other creative talents. But talent is a wide-ranging concept. Business talents can include being good with people, being good with numbers, or being good at thinking innovatively.

As a team leader, choose members with diverse talents. Don't stick with the obvious—there are many talents that aren't good fits on a project but that end up becoming useful. For example, musical talent may not seem like something handy on a business team. But a classical musician's (or rock musician's) disciplined focus, or ability to recognize complex and harmonious patterns, might have a calming influence on others when the team begins to spin out of control. Or, a rock musician might be just what you need to rev up the team when morale seems at a low. And any musician who plays in a group will help a team be successful because of their ability to work cooperatively for a common purpose without hogging the spotlight.

Find out what talents your team members are proud of outside of the office, and use their seemingly nonrelated strengths to bolster the entire group. It will help your team succeed.

CAREER | WEDNESDAY

Successful people are incredibly delusional about their achievements. —*Marshall Goldsmith*

HUMANS LEARN THROUGH YEARS OF TRIAL AND ERROR, positive reinforcement, and behavioral modification. But, if you ask people to tell you how they became successful, they will most likely rattle off the typical characteristics that define successful people—a take-charge attitude, the ability to follow through, and perseverance in the face of disaster. There is an underlying assumption that these people naturally possess more of these characteristics and act this way because they are born this way. Not so! While leadership characteristics can help you get further in your career, people underestimate all the other factors that come into play.

Marshall Goldsmith is reminding you not to forget about everything else that went into your success. Don't forget about your co-workers who watch your back when you need them; the former boss you leaned on for advice when you found yourself in a difficult situation; or even your spouse who takes care of the kids and/or your home so that you can work late and stay focused. More important, don't forget the long hours you've already put in that taught you the intricacies of your business so that you know how to do your job better than anyone else. Like any professional sport, the team on top is usually the one that's worked harder, worked together, and practiced the most.

SALES | THURSDAY

A fly, Sir, may sting a stately horse
and make him wince; but one is but
an insect, and the other a horse still.
—*Samuel Johnson*

LOSING A SALE CAN STING. YET, AS SAMUEL JOHNSON, one of England's most famous writers, said, you have to keep your bites in perspective. You worked hard and long but something happened; somewhere the deal jumped ship. Now it's your job to assess the situation. It would be wise to learn from this mistake and put what you learn into your sales strategy database (or your head) for future reference.

Where did your communication with the customer break down? Pinpoint it. Did you fully understand the goals of your customer? Is there anything you might have overlooked? If you're still coming up empty, consider bouncing your once-bitten tale off someone else. Bring the case history to one of the more seasoned veterans in your company—or a veteran at an outside company, as long as it's not the competition—and ask what a pro would have done differently in your shoes. Don't be embarrassed—it's never too late to ask for mentoring.

There's strength to be found in discovering the solution to any problem or setback. To find the solution, you have to understand the problem so that you can figure out what exactly bit you.

LEADERSHIP | FRIDAY

> Don't be too timid and squeamish about your actions. All life is an experiment. The more experiments you make the better.
>
> —*Ralph Waldo Emerson*

IN THE 1830s, PROGRESSIVE THINKING WAS UNFAMILIAR territory amongst America's elite. Most intellectuals were members of social clubs where they forged their political, religious, and business alliances.

Having just published *Nature,* Ralph Waldo Emerson was emerging as a serious literary figure. Disgusted with the state of intellectualism, he and his contemporaries, including Henry David Thoreau, Margaret Fuller, and Bronson Alcott, formed the Transcendental Club in Cambridge, Massachusetts, in 1836.

Talk about experimenting. The group met sporadically and kept out those who excluded any topic from examination. From morality to mysticism, the members explored new thoughts, ideas, and concepts previously uncharted. Emerson emerged as a great public speaker whose strong personal belief system gave him the courage to buck popular trends. As a result, he was well rewarded in a career that indulged his passion for provocative thought.

As a leader, you need to envision the future and experiment as much as possible. You just might find the answers you are looking for.

ENTREPRENEUR | SATURDAY

> We live in a world that assumes that
> the quality of a decision is directly
> related to the time and effort that went
> into making it. —*Malcolm Gladwell*

EXPERIENCED ENTREPRENEURS HAVE THE ABILITY TO MAKE what may seem like "snap" decisions. But all decisions are made based on prior experience and personal history, even if it seems that the decision has been made on the fly. As Malcolm Gladwell, the author of *Blink: The Power of Thinking Without Thinking,* states, popular perception is that well-thought out decisions are often the best decisions. The truth is, "snap" decisions may produce better results.

The veteran entrepreneur can assess the difference in circumstances. Does the product have a part that is going to be more difficult to get? Does the economy show the same all-around factors that led to a shortage seven years ago? Or, is there a difference that would make a shortage unlikely?

The savvy entrepreneur is constantly up-to-date with the state of his or her market. Is there an impending strike that might put the workforce onto the picket line just after you agreed to take on a big job? Is there a paper shortage predicted in three months, just a month before your project is scheduled to go to press?

There are always possibilities of unknown factors. But rarely is an entrepreneur making a snap decision, even if it may appear that way from the outside.

MANAGING PEOPLE | SUNDAY

A slip of the foot you may soon recover, but a slip of the tongue you may never get over. —Benjamin Franklin

STATESMAN BEN FRANKLIN IS THE ONLY PERSON WHO signed all of the following: the Declaration of Independence (1776); France's Treaty of Alliance, Amity, and Commerce (1778); the Treaty of Peace between England, France, and the United States (1782); and the Constitution (1787). He also helped create both the Declaration of Independence and the Constitution. Franklin was keenly aware that he couldn't have negotiated these historic agreements— and helped create the United States—without mastering the use of clear, convincing, and cooperative language. He knew that insulting, disrespectful, or overly pedestrian speech would sink his grand plans.

Now fast forward to the twenty-first century, a time when business leaders, managers, and employees communicate only occasionally in person but more often by e-mail. It's far too easy to make a mistake using this technology. A little caution can ensure this never happens: double check everything you write, including the address fields; use the spell checker; and keep the sarcasm, anger, and giddiness out of sight. For that matter, use the same approach in person, whether you're speaking to customers or colleagues. If keeping it short and sweet was good enough for the birth of a nation, it should work for your business as well.

MOTIVATION | MONDAY

It's a lot better to initiate change while you can than it is to try to react and adjust to it. —*Spencer Johnson, M.D.*

MANY OF US RESIST CHANGE. YOU MAY FEEL THAT you lack the skills to adapt, or maybe it's just the old attitude, "If it ain't broke, don't fix it." But this attitude doesn't play well in today's modern business world. In fact, it never did.

The title of Dr. Spencer Johnson's bestselling book, *Who Moved My Cheese?*, comes from a small, yet life-changing incident. Hungry at home one day, Johnson went looking for cheese, only to find it had been moved from its usual place. What did he do? He gave up, saw the situation as hopeless and settled for gnawing hunger. He passively tried to adjust to a blatantly simple change (the missing cheese), rather than do something about it (go out and get more cheese, or even choose something else to eat).

Of course, Dr. Johnson quickly came to his senses, but in that moment he realized he was dealing with a much larger concept. He understood it is crazy to wait for a situation to be hopeless (dying of hunger!) before you act. He recognized that change requires you to be proactive. So, in your business, watch out for signs that change is coming. Then be the first to fashion a brand new solution to turn change to your advantage.

TEAM-BUILDING | TUESDAY

It had long since come to my attention that people of accomplishment rarely sat back and let things happen to them. They went out and happened to things.

—*Elinor Smith*

YOU WANT TO BE A PERSON WHO MAKES THINGS HAPpen, just like famed aviatrix, Elinor Smith. Otherwise, life takes control of you instead of you taking control of your life. Think of the people you know who live in what can only be described as "full-crisis mode." They call or e-mail you with one personal or job-related crisis after the next. These bad times happen to everyone, but these people wait for something to happen and then they react.

Proactive people, on the other hand, try to prevent crises from controlling their lives. They work hard at their jobs, try to stay healthy, and keep their personal lives under control so that work and home life enhance each other instead of interfering with each other.

And when bad things happen to those who live proactively—which they do—they just work hard at making things right again, and then they move on. They don't dwell on the crisis and bring everyone they know into it.

Always hire people for your team who go out and make things happen.

CAREER | WEDNESDAY

> Public speaking is a form of empowerment. It can—and often does—make a difference in things people care about very much. —*Stephen E. Lucas*

S URVEYS AND ANECDOTES REVEAL THAT PEOPLE ARE more afraid of public speaking than they are of dying. Yet making presentations is a skill most professionals need. Stephen Lucas teaches in his book, *The Art of Public Speaking,* that there are a variety of small steps you can take to ensure that your next speech will be your best.

First, write a speech that delivers on its promise. Go for drama rather than perfect delivery. Enliven your message with real-life stories and anecdotes. Most important, be yourself: if you aren't great at cracking jokes, then don't start with one.

To craft a speech that will be well received, find out who will be in your audience, and tailor your talk to their interests. Avoid rattling off statistics, technical jargon, and whittle your data to two or three main points. Giving a speech that is interesting, concise, and to the point should be your goal.

Lastly, stop putting incredible pressure upon yourself to create a flawless performance. Achieving a certain amount of competence is important, but be realistic. However, if you don't practice the piano, you won't be a playing a concerto anytime soon. Practice your speech until you feel comfortable with the material. When the big day comes, if you're prepared, you are sure to be effective.

SALES | THURSDAY

20% of what we do leads to 80% of the results.
—*Richard Koch*

IN 1897, THE ITALIAN ECONOMIST VILFREDO PARETO observed a pattern of how wealth and income was distributed in Europe. Naturally, it wasn't balanced equally, but the results were still startling. In Italy, 80 percent of income went to 20 percent of the population. The pattern extended to every other country he studied.

Pareto's Principle has become known as the 80/20 rule. Richard Koch has written several books connecting this rule to various models, including business management, production quality control, computer science, and even social relations. Indeed, the 80/20 rule is behind Woody Allen's famous line, quoted in this book, "Eighty percent of success is showing up!"

In sales, you've probably already seen that 80 percent of your business comes from 20 percent of your customers. The lesson inherent in this is to focus on your repeat customers and nurture your relationships with them. Growing loyalty is just as important to your bottom line as growing your business.

But, that's not to say you should ignore the other 80 percent of your customers. Analyze what you're doing right, and apply it to these accounts. Why are some customers loyal to you and your product or services? Knowing what drives your repeat customer base is a valuable tool for increasing your profits and your effectiveness in sales.

LEADERSHIP | FRIDAY

> There are two types of people, people worthy of respect who try to resist explaining things, and people who cannot resist explaining things. —*Nassim Nicholas Taleb*

URING HURRICANE SEASON, THE SO-CALLED EXPERTS track tropical storms trying to predict their routes. To cover their bases, they make every coastal town a potential target and end up scaring more people than necessary. Nassim Nicholas Taleb, author of *The Black Swan: The Impact of the Highly Improbable* and *Fooled By Randomness: The Hidden Role of Chance in Life and the Marketplace,* wishes these weather forecasters would admit they don't know where or when the storm will hit.

Taleb calls this kind of thinking epistemic arrogance—that if asked, most people will attempt to answer a question, whether they know the answer or not. He first experienced epistemic arrogance while working on Wall Street. According to Taleb, there's very little difference between the skills of a professional trader and the average person off the street. If you let one thousand random people trade stocks, a certain percentage would become instant junior Warren Buffets, their success due to random probability.

If your company routinely relies on economic indicators and financial forecasting to make decisions, you must decide whether these indicators are fact or fiction. Taleb challenges us to research the forecaster's average rate of error before acting on his "expert" opinion.

ENTREPRENEUR | SATURDAY

Today, the one sure way to fail is to
be boring. Your one chance for success
is to be remarkable. —*Seth Godin*

S ETH GODIN BECAME REMARKABLE BY TAKING A CLEAR
look at the age of technology and assessing exactly what
was going on. Then he was able to make sweeping statements about how businesses had to think about this new
world, not only to succeed but to stand out. Godin was a
small business owner who has churned out books that have
made him a big success. Try adding these Godin concepts
into your entrepreneurial mix:

The Dip: A Little Book That Teaches You When to Quit—
Godin promotes the theory that there is a dip in the road
that is either the entrance to superstardom or the signal you
are hitting a dead end.

Small Is the New Big—Godin discusses the backlash
against bigness after several pivotal events, including the
Enron debacle. He talks about how "small" can move faster
than "big" and how that can mean the difference between
success or not.

All Marketers Are Liars—Godin gives countless examples
of marketing people "stretching the truth." But he makes
one thing clear: "Your story won't spread [which is the
whole principle of marketing] if the facts don't back it up."

Survival Is Not Enough—Successful entrepreneurs
embrace change—and change is only happening faster with
the Internet age.

MANAGING PEOPLE | SUNDAY

> Knowing others is intelligence, knowing
> yourself is wisdom. Mastering others is
> strength, mastering yourself is true power.
> —*Lao Tzu*

CONFUCIUS DEVELOPED A SIZEABLE FOLLOWING BY THE time he was still a young philosopher. According to legend, to measure himself against the formidable philosopher, Lao Tzu, Confucius set off to meet the great spiritual leader. Imagine his dismay when Lao Tzu told Confucius that he was too proud, conceited, and worried about ambition to matter to anyone.

If Confucius didn't merit a compliment from the "Old Master," there doesn't seem to be much hope for the rest of us ordinary working stiffs. Yet Lao Tzu's teachings show us that the opinions of others really don't matter, but that we should only concern ourselves with our own actions.

Lao Tzu's advice works for anyone whose job is managing other people's work. Since supervisory positions require being a good judge of people, it makes sense that you can't be a good judge of others unless you are comfortable with who you are. If you lose your temper when you get frustrated, you can't very well reprimand an employee for flying off the handle. According to Lao Tzu, knowing yourself allows you to find the inner strength that will make it easier to handle whatever you encounter.

MOTIVATION | MONDAY

Champions keep playing until they get it right.
—*Billie Jean King*

BILLIE JEAN KING CERTAINLY GOT IT RIGHT! SHE WON twelve Grand Slam singles titles, sixteen Grand Slam doubles titles, and eleven Grand Slam mixed doubles titles. It is easy to see why she's considered one of the greatest female tennis players—and athletes—in sports history.

But sports is not all that King triumphed in. She was the first to speak out for women in sports and their right to earn as much as men. In 1972, she won the US Open but got $15,000 less than the men's champion, Ilie Nastase. She was outraged, declaring that if equal payment wasn't offered she would never play in the tournament again. She stood her ground, and the US Open organization recognized that she was right. From then on, equal prize money was offered to both sexes.

It was not just tennis this champion kept playing till she got it right. She started the first pro women's tour, called the Virginia Slims Tour, sponsored by Philip Morris; founded a women's players union; and started a magazine, *womenSports*. She's still active in tennis competition as a coach, and she is on the boards of many sports-related organizations.

Billie Jean King has the champion spirit. She has never stopped playing, both in sports and in business, finding new challenges and ceaselessly striving to get it right. If you follow Billie Jean King's lead you will likewise be successful in business and life.

TEAM-BUILDING | TUESDAY

We judge ourselves by what we feel capable of doing, while others judge us by what we have already done.
—*Henry Wadsworth Longfellow*

A SOLID TEAM THAT HAS BEEN SUCCESSFUL ON A PROJ- ect or, even more important, several projects, can be a useful marketing tool to get more business. The same is true of the whole team. If a certain configuration of talents has created a successful product, use the team again, and promote them. That's why Hollywood films often say, "From the director of..." or "From the folks that brought you..." They are allowing the viewing public to determine competence based on previous success, just as Longfellow said almost two hundred years ago.

Law firms have also learned this technique and know how to make use of this experience. They collect people with specific experience and proven skills, which make them valuable for the next similar case. Legal teams—as opposed to a single attorney—allow for many aspects of the case to be investigated at the same time. After a while, the firm becomes known to specialize in one area because they have the best team to get that particular job done.

Internally, when a team works well, figure out how to use it again. It may not be in the exact configuration—the new project may need people with skill sets the old project didn't—but don't waste all that learning experience and talent that was developed by recreating the wheel.

CAREER | WEDNESDAY

A fat purse quickly empties if there be no golden stream to refill it. —*George S. Clason*

I N CLASON'S CLASSIC, *THE RICHEST MAN IN BABYLON,* Arkad was the son of a humble middle-class family merchant who didn't inherit wealth, didn't have the opportunity for scholastic learning, and wasn't the smartest guy on the block. But, he had determination and wanted to become rich. So he sought advice from a wealthy old man, who advised him that one must learn and observe the laws that "govern the building of wealth." Arkad applied these principles and went on to become the richest man in Babylon.

What can we learn of prosperity from a common merchant in an ancient civilization? Plenty. People want to believe that wealthy people are smarter than everyone else. But that is not the case. They are usually just more disciplined.

Whether you are a rug maker in ancient Babylon, an entrepreneur in Idaho, or a boat builder in a beach town, the basic financial lessons for building wealth remain the same. If you make money and don't pay yourself first, you will have worked for nothing. If you hoard your wealth and worry about it, then you will not be able to reap the benefits, so be generous. If you did nothing to earn your wealth, unless you learn to manage it, you will lose it.

Your career will be marked by years when you might be the richest man in Babylon, as well as years when you struggle. But if you remember these lessons, you'll always feel in control of your destiny.

SALES | THURSDAY

The first thing you have to sell is yourself.
—*Ray Kroc*

R AY KROC'S HISTORY AS A SALESMAN BEGAN WITH SELL-ing coffee beans door-to-door. After that, he sold rib-bon novelties. Driven by ambition, he made people believe in his product, no matter what he was selling. When he signed on with the Lily Tulip Cup Company, he already had a wife and family, and he was determined to devote every ounce of energy to selling for them.

Kroc spent seventeen years selling paper cups for Lily Cup. He was their top salesman, constantly thinking of new ways to sell product and on the lookout for the potential to grow his business. He frequently dropped in at soda foun-tains to sell his wares and spotted a new automatic milk-shake machine that he thought had potential. In short order, he began selling the Multimixer, which could make five milkshakes at once.

That's how Kroc heard about the McDonald brothers in San Bernardino, California. They already owned a Multi-mixer—in fact, they owned eight of them. That was a sizable capital investment at the time. Kroc drove to San Bernardino, bought the company, and the rest is Golden Arches history.

Kroc sold the McDonald brothers on the idea of selling their business to him because he radiated confidence. Believing in your ideas, knowing what you want and who you are, makes a great salesperson. Sell yourself first, and then sell your product.

LEADERSHIP | FRIDAY

> An effective leader has an empathic
> imagination and is willing to give it
> free rein. —*Alan Axelrod*

MAKING DECISIONS OFTEN REQUIRES A LEADER TO evaluate other points of view. Alan Axelrod makes this point clear in his book, *When the Buck Stops with You: Harry S. Truman on Leadership.*

President Truman was respected for his integrity and principles. He decided that the segregation of the armed forces disgraced the country. When Truman promoted a young African American captain to head the largest ship in the Navy, the decision ruffled many feathers. It fell to Admiral Robert L. Dennison to convince Truman to rescind the order. Admiral Dennison convinced Truman that without earning the position, the young captain wouldn't garner the respect of the sailors. President Truman, heeding the good advice, abandoned his plans, but he did not abandon his vision. Since he knew Congress would circumvent any proposed legislation, he issued Executive Order 9981 causing the immediate desegregation of the military.

True leadership requires individual conviction. Being in charge requires a steadfast belief in a set of principles and acting upon them. If you stand up for your principles, you'll command respect, and your goals will be easier to achieve.

ENTREPRENEUR | SATURDAY

*I don't look to jump over 7-foot bars;
I look around for 1-foot bars that I can
step over.* —*Warren Buffett*

O NE OF THE BEST WAYS TO OVERCOME A LARGE HURDLE is to break it down into manageable pieces. Look for the one-foot bars. Often you'll find that as you eliminate each smaller hurdle, the one you thought was so large will have disappeared. Better still, subsequent problems will be easier to get over.

For instance, perhaps you have the chance to land a big, long-term gig for your company. But the workload would be such that you would need to hire six new employees and purchase a large piece of equipment. That sounds daunting! The job, however, is the perfect growth opportunity you've been looking for. Where do you begin?

If you try the "break it down into manageable pieces" approach, you might begin by searching for one of the six employees—the key person to focus on this job. Perhaps you will give this person a "manager" title, and then give her the responsibility of hiring the rest of her team. Now all you have to do is focus on purchasing the equipment. Perhaps the new manager will know where you might lease equipment you need, or where a used machine might be for sale.

Breaking down something that seems complex may mean the difference between taking your business to the next level, or running in place.

MANAGING PEOPLE | SUNDAY

> Inculcating values throughout an
> organization starts with the leader,
> who sets the standard of behavior for
> everyone in the organization.
>
> —*Bill George*

I N HIS BOOK, *AUTHENTIC LEADERSHIP,* BILL GEORGE recounts a story that made him realize that just stating values isn't enough to make employees buy into them. As CEO of Medtronic, a medical device company, he routinely watched medical operations to get an idea of how Medtronic equipment performed. When he saw a Medronic catheter fall apart during one operation, he had to duck when the physician threw it at him in disgust. Afterwards, he found out that the sales rep for this device had repeatedly reported defects to the company but never received any feedback. To add insult to injury, the engineers denied their culpability in the faulty design. The engineers were too far removed from the customers to care, no matter how much cheerleading management did about putting the customer first. George insisted that the engineers see their products working in the field. Once that happened, the engineers became much more engaged in making products that served the customers well.

Make sure that all employees see how their work makes a difference. Whatever your mission statement is, make sure that each employee can live by it and understands how it applies to his or her specific job.

MOTIVATION | MONDAY

What would life be if we had no courage to attempt anything? —*Vincent van Gogh*

THE NUMBING BIOGRAPHICAL FACT ABOUT VINCENT van Gogh is that he sold only one painting during his lifetime. He was sanguine about his lack of financial success: "I can't change the fact that my paintings don't sell. But the time will come when people will recognize that they are worth more than the value of the paints used in the picture."

Van Gogh was not financially successful because his paintings were not the norm. His spirit to try new things began when he was a lay preacher in the mining region of Belgium. He began to do charcoal drawings at this time— wonderful, earthy presentations of the miners at work and in their homes. The drawings were so good that his devoted brother, Theo, convinced him to stop preaching and take up painting.

Vincent was twenty-seven when he first picked up the brush. He lived only another ten years and filled those years painting. With each new place he moved to, he learned more about his craft and kept changing his style.

What would his life have been if he had not had the courage to attempt to be a painter? (And what would our lives be without him?) Van Gogh knew what his work was worth. He had total confidence in it, and that confidence gave him the courage to try new things. If you value your efforts, you will also be able to create your own masterpiece.

TEAM-BUILDING | TUESDAY

*Meetings are indispensable when you
don't want to do anything.* —*Vince Lombardi*

M EETINGS ARE UBIQUITOUS. EVEN VINCE LOMBARDI
had to suffer through team meetings. No doubt he
had to hold many as well.

Do everything you can to make meetings productive. If
your team knows your meeting will follow these rules, they
will look forward to them rather than dread them.

MEETING RULES

- *Have one very specific goal for each meeting.* Don't try to cover
  every concern in one meeting.
- *Stick to your goal.* Don't get sidetracked talking about
  things everyone wants to talk about and don't let other
  participants move the meeting off-topic.
- *Insist on punctuality.* Lead by example.
- *Be organized.* Make sure everything is done prior to the
  meeting.
- *Give everyone a chance to speak.*
- *Set a timeframe for the meeting and stick to it.* If you said the
  meeting will go from 1:00 to 2:30, don't pretend to be
  oblivious that it is almost 3:00.
- *Be aware of the schedules of attendees.* If three of the people
  you need in your meeting have two other meetings that
  day, find another day to meet.
- *If you are not the right person to be the leader of the meeting, pick
  the right person and let that person take over.* Teach your team
  how to lead meetings, and insist that they do.

CAREER | WEDNESDAY

> To love what you do and feel
> that it matters—how could anything
> be more fun? —*Katharine Graham*

"LOVE WHAT YOU DO" IS THE CATCH PHRASE IN BUSI-ness today. It's an outgrowth of the work-life balance movement that is forcing employers to come up with job-tailoring strategies that meet the needs of their employees, who, in turn, are seeking and demanding new ways to make their jobs more fulfilling. "Love what you do" is a key component of self-actualization, a term coined by the famous German psychologist, Kurt Goldstein, and made popular by Abraham Maslow, who placed self-actualization at the top of his famous hierarchy-of-needs pyramid theory. As people are spending more and more time at work, that seems to be the place where they expect self-fulfillment to happen.

Katherine Graham didn't have a profound love of journalism when she took over *The Washington Post.* She was thrust into the leadership role with the passing of her husband, the *Post*'s previous publisher, and had to learn by doing, since daily pressing matters didn't afford her the luxury of learning the business slowly. But, as she focused her efforts on running the paper, she found that the job gave her great personal satisfaction and a life purpose that she hadn't ever felt before.

Ask yourself if your job is life affirming. If not, it might be time to find a different path.

SALES | THURSDAY

Touch your customer, and you're halfway there. —*Estée Lauder*

ESTÉE LAUDER TURNED BEAUTY PRODUCTS INTO BIG business. As a young woman, she started selling her uncle's skin potions at local beauty shops in Queens, New York. But her goal was to get out of the boroughs and into a Manhattan department store. When Saks Fifth Avenue finally gave her a space to set up shop in 1948, her personal selling approach blossomed.

Giving out samples by her always flattering sales staff was the innovative hallmark of her personal touch. The customer appreciated the free gift, and immediately felt a bond and became brand loyal. (Estée Lauder was the first to devise the promotion of the free gift.) Look at the cosmetics industry now and her legacy is legion—no counter is without a complimentary sample, and no aisle without attractive women (and men) offering spritzes of new and inviting fragrances.

Another personal touch was her brilliant packaging. Estée's products were contained in beautifully designed boxes or ceramic and glass jars in classic exotic patterns based on her own art collection. Her customers felt beautiful just looking at the packaging.

Lauder focused on a personal approach with a demand for quality that reflected her world view. Think of how you can take her lessons and apply them to your business. Make sure that your production people are asking for your input, and let them know what you think will sell best.

LEADERSHIP | FRIDAY

To deal with men by force is as impractical
as to deal with nature by persuasion.

—*Ayn Rand*

FEAR OF THE UNKNOWN OFTEN MAKES PEOPLE BELIEVE in far-fetched premises. For example, despite the sophisticated level of the arts and sciences in Ancient Greece, people believed twelve gods ruled the earth from a mountain in the heavens known as Olympus. Such fear of the unknown and the lack of scientific knowledge led to the rise of most world religions. Even Native American cultures that did not proscribe to a specific deity believed that they could persuade Mother Nature to make it pour with a rain dance.

Ayn Rand, ever the practical philosopher, likens humans' attempt to dominate one another by force similar to the American Indians' rain dance—a futile effort. In business, her observations have a ring of truth. When a belligerent boss bullies his employees regularly, the effect may be temporary but the damage is forever. A leader can't force his employees to achieve great things. He can only motivate them to achieve greatness.

Make sure you have people who want to make a contribution and work toward company goals. How they actually accomplish their goals is up to them. After all, you can't be caught doing rain dances in your office when profits fall.

ENTREPRENEUR | SATURDAY

> Business is a lot like a game of tennis—
> those who serve well usually end up
> winning. —*Anonymous*

A BASEBALL GAME IS OFTEN WON OR LOST ON THE pitcher's mound. How the horses come out of the starting gate says a lot about how the race will go. The jump ball in basketball and the face-off in hockey determine who gets control. But in tennis, the game goes to the person who controls the ball, especially if you have a killer serve.

Setting your business up with a solid foundation puts you in control from the very start. How you present your new business to your customers influences whether or not they become loyal customers who give you repeat business.

If you open a new restaurant, each customer's first visit will determine whether or not she comes back. She might forgive slow service on a busy opening night, but the food must be excellent and the atmosphere inviting to draw her back again.

Be in command when you launch your venture. Even if you have butterflies in your stomach, serve up a confident demeanor to the world. People believe in people who seem self-assured.

Preparation, like practice, is the key to a smooth start-up. Think about your own experiences as a customer—if you walk by a shop or even a trade show booth that seems unorganized and not ready to do business, you don't go in. Serve up the best you have right from the beginning.

MANAGING PEOPLE | SUNDAY

> The power of knowing, in that first two seconds, is not a gift given magically to a fortunate few. It is an ability that we can all cultivate for ourselves. —*Malcolm Gladwell*

I N HIS BOOK, *BLINK: THE POWER OF THINKING WITHOUT Thinking,* Malcolm Gladwell surmises that in high-stakes decision making most people inaccurately access situations and can't rely on intuition to save them.

Even after thousands of years of running from tigers and battling rival clans, the human brain is programmed to release endorphins that cause blood to leave the brain and flow to our hands and feet. As a result, during times of stress higher-level thinking diminishes, clouding our judgment. The upswing is, you can curse like a truck driver, sprint for a departing flight, and strangle your lawyer—all without a second thought. The downside is that none of those will help you clinch a deal.

Malcolm Gladwell believes it's possible for us to harness the power of our endorphins. The trick is to slow down the endorphins that are hampering our ability to use our full senses. Remaining calm in the face of danger can be learned. Before your next power meeting, get a co-worker to practice various scenarios with you so you will be calmer during a difficult confrontation. Your decisions will be much more effective if you have the ability to leverage the nuance of the situation.

MOTIVATION | MONDAY

Control your destiny or someone else will.
—*Jack Welch*

A S CEO OF GENERAL ELECTRIC CO., JACK WELCH'S innovative management strategies and brilliant leadership style made him a business legend. He was dubbed *Fortune*'s 1999 Manager of the Century—no mean feat.

Welch had a flamboyant, highly individual style both in and outside the office. He once declared, "The only thing a mentor is good for is to show you where the coffee and where the lunchroom is." Instead of a mentor, he preferred getting advice and following the lead of a variety of people. He believed he remained in control using this approach as he wasn't bound or indebted to one person.

The aforementioned quote is his number one rule for successful leadership. Welch believed the essential dynamic of great leadership begins by knowing your destiny, possessing the energy to execute that vision, and setting out directions for others to follow as you lead. All three components are vital to ensure success.

Vision without action and follow-up means nothing. Before you know it, someone is going to come along and either take your idea or take the lead. Remain on top of your vision. Keep your visions alive with tremendous energy, and get others to follow your lead. You will prosper if you follow these steps.

TEAM-BUILDING | TUESDAY

> There is no other way of guarding one-self against flattery than by letting men understand that they will not offend you by speaking the truth; but when everyone can tell you the truth, you lose their respect. —*Niccolo Machiavelli*

TRUTH IS A TWO-WAY STREET. IN ORDER FOR YOUR TEAM to feel comfortable telling you the truth, they must feel you always share the truth with them.

This does not mean you have to tell them everything. And, as Machiavelli says, it does not mean that every individual on the team needs to be comfortable blurting out his innermost feelings. Some professional distance usually provides a certain amount of respect.

But in order for a team to operate successfully, they need to believe they are not being lied to and that they don't need to lie themselves. If, say, the team project is in jeopardy, telling this news to the team may be motivating or it may kill motivation. If the project is going to be phased out but top management doesn't want the competition to know, then not telling the team may be necessary. Not telling and lying, though, are two different things.

Be prepared, however, for the conversation that follows after you haven't completely divulged everything, but the information has gotten out in some other way. You will need to explain yourself without losing credibility.

CAREER | WEDNESDAY

No person, no matter how wealthy
or prominent, stands above the law.
—*Federal Judge John M. Walker*

T HE LATE, INFAMOUS HOTELIER LEONA HELMSLEY, NICKnamed "the Queen of Mean," was brought to trial for tax evasion in 1989. However, her court appearance quickly became a media circus as a parade of witnesses came before the jury to describe the utter contempt that Leona Helmsley held toward others. Witness after witness spoke of people she had lied to, stolen from, or cheated in the course of doing business. Federal Judge John M. Walker had heard enough. From the bench, he concluded that her "conduct was the product of naked greed. Throughout its course you persisted in the arrogant belief that you were above the law."

What led to Leona Helmsley's undoing? A gifted business woman who frequently donated to charity, she nevertheless will be remembered for her temper tantrums, abusive behavior toward employees, and cheating on her income taxes. Cleary, Leona Helmsley felt beyond approach.

Many a titan has fallen with this attitude. Don't be tempted to do the wrong thing when doing the right thing is well within your grasp. The written and unwritten rules of your business have governed your industry for years. Your job is not to break these rules.

SALES | THURSDAY

> Personality can open doors, but only
> character can keep them open.
> —*Elmer G. Leterman*

E LMER G. LETERMAN WAS, IN DALE CARNEGIE'S WORDS, "the greatest insurance salesman in the United States." His career spanned over forty years, beginning in 1925, at a succession of firms that he founded (the last, Leterman-Gortz, is still in business). He was also a bestselling author of *The Sale Begins When the Customer Says No* (1953), *The New Art of Selling* (1957), and *How Showmanship Sells* (1965).

Dale Carnegie used him as an example in his lectures because Leterman certainly knew how to "win friends and influence people." Leterman was known for turning every opportunity into a sale. He had his teeth cleaned by seven dentists a year. Eventually he'd talk insurance with each dentist. He rode horseback in Central Park for recreation and gifted each of the patrol cops $1,000 policies. Later, when those cops were promoted, Leterman was a crony of a number of city officials.

Leterman definitely had the colorful personality to open doors, and he was well aware that his largesse would get him sales, but what kept those customers loyal and got them to refer him to others was his honesty and integrity.

Character keeps the door open for everything in life, but especially in sales.

LEADERSHIP | FRIDAY

> The criterion for measuring the success of our leaders should be how well they serve everyone that has a vested interest in the success of the enterprise. —*Bill George*

LOSING WEIGHT IS HARD TO ACCOMPLISH BECAUSE MANY people focus on the wrong goal. Most weight loss experts say it is the day-to-day execution of a plan that gets results, not the need to lose ten pounds in two days.

Running a business is no different. Focusing on short-term profits can undermine a leader's ability to achieve long-term growth. With the media constantly buzzing about quarterly expectations and corporate raiders stalking them from the shadows, it's no wonder that most companies are feeling the pressure to boost their stock prices. Bill George writes in *Authentic Leadership* that focusing on short-term profits of rising stock prices does more harm than good. "It may sound old fashioned, but I believe the time has come to get back to financial fundamentals as the primary measure."

A leader needs to know three important financial indicators. First, a company needs to serve its customers. Second, it needs to increase its market share. Third, it needs to develop and nurture relationships with its employees, suppliers, and government. When each of these components is operating smoothly, not only will the company's profits grow, but so will your reputation as a great leader.

ENTREPRENEUR | SATURDAY

If I were in this business only for the
business, I wouldn't be in this business.
—*Samuel Goldwyn*

B USINESS CAN BE ANYTHING—IT CERTAINLY DOESN'T
have to be as complex and expensive as the film industry in which Samuel Goldwyn was an instrumental player. If
you are going into business just because you love conducting
business, you might as well find something less complicated
than making Hollywood blockbusters.

If you simply like business, and you've started a few
yourself, you might consider being a business start-up consultant. That would allow you to tinker around with the
strictly business side of things without being concerned
about the specifics. Finance, marketing, and employee concerns are generally the same whether you are selling bras,
wood stoves, or Tiffany lamps.

Think long and hard about the business you intend to be
in. Talk with as many people as you can to gain a strong
sense of everything you will need to know and everything
you will encounter along the way. A friend once got a degree
in surveying, thinking that was an industry he could be in
that would allow him to spend time outdoors. But he discovered that a surveyor spends a lot of time in front of a
computer—exactly what he did not want to do!

MANAGING PEOPLE | SUNDAY

People with tact have less to retract.
—Arnold H. Glasgow

NOBODY'S PERFECT. EVERY MANAGER PUTS HIS FOOT in his mouth once in a while. But when it happens more than once, at least more than once in the memory of employees, respect is quickly lost, and a manager begins paving his own road to ruin.

This can happen quickly when managers get too chummy. Maybe you want to talk about a movie you just saw or regale a colleague with a funny vacation story—everyday conversation shows your human side. That's all well and good, until you slip into discussing a risky topic like the attractiveness of a particular actor or his shenanigans at the ski resort's ice bar. Now the conversation includes potentially offensive material, the kind sure to be repeated by those listening or others within earshot. Soon you develop a reputation you don't want.

Don't use tact solely when you deal with clients or customers. Show discretion during all professional conversations. Given the choice to berate an employee for a big mistake or build him back up now that the mistake is old news, you may well feel it's within his job description to punish as a means toward correction. By taking your frustrations out on your employees you will undoubtedly get in hot water with human resources, or worse. And that's a cold place to be.

MOTIVATION | MONDAY

No problem can stand the assault
of sustained thinking. —*Voltaire*

VOLTAIRE, THE FRENCH PHILOSOPHER AND WIT, WAS A champion of rational principles. He lived during the era of the Enlightenment, a divergent time in which the prevailing philosophy was all about using reason as one's guiding authority. Solutions to humanity's greatest problems could be found using sound logic, instead of counting on divine intervention. The American Founding Fathers were greatly influenced by these ideas, which are reflected most famously in our Bill of Rights.

Three hundred years later, reason is still the best way to approach a problem. But thinking about a problem too much can often get you nowhere. You have to avoid the all-too-common mistake of thinking too much without acting. Examining every detail of a problem again and again, speculating on what went wrong, and plotting out what-if scenarios are all a big waste of time. The more you dwell on a problem, the greater your chances are of getting stuck.

Move forward instead of just treading water. Worrying wastes your resources and, subsequently, the company's resources as well. If you can't find a reasonable solution within a reasonable amount of time, maybe it's time to drop the problem. Plot your next move, but be rational.

TEAM-BUILDING | TUESDAY

> A team should never practice on a field
> that is not lined. Your players have to
> become aware of the field's boundaries.
>
> *—John Madden*

S ET UP PARAMETERS FOR THE TEAM'S GOAL—THE DEAD-lines for when things need to be done, budgets that the project needs to stay within, and resources that can or can't be used. Parameters are useful and followed when all of the players are made aware of the "field's boundaries." Don't withhold information from your team.

The value of good communication cannot be underestimated. Figure out the best way to communicate to the team and use it judiciously. Don't be afraid to hold meetings as often as you need to, but be sure you actually need to. Make sure the meetings are effective and that the team gets crucial information as a result of the meetings, or you will waste everyone's time and build resentment.

Use e-mail if it is the best way to communicate with the whole team. Think, however, about how your whole team works and whether e-mail really is the best way to communicate. Does your team consist of a few people who don't use a computer every day? Those people are not going to benefit from e-mail as an effective communication tool.

When everyone is on the same field, you can lay out these boundaries and everyone will understand where they are and what they mean.

CAREER | WEDNESDAY

You can't connect the dots looking forward; you can only connect them looking backwards. So you have to trust that the dots will somehow connect in your future. —*Steve Jobs*

S TEVE JOBS'S WENT FROM BUILDING THE FIRST APPLE computer in his garage to a billion-dollar publicly traded company, to being ousted from it a year later, and then returning to bring his tarnished company back to its former glory. As Apple Inc. blazed through the electronic industry's uncharted territory, Steve Jobs made decisions that were so radical (and much criticized) that he had no way of knowing whether they would be successful or not. In a *Washington Post* interview in 1992, Jobs said, "If you look at my life, I've never gotten it right the first time. It always takes me twice."

Learning on the job has been Jobs's mantra. He continually uses the past to figure out how to minimize the possibility of disaster even in an unpredictable future. As inconsistent as Jobs has been in keeping his career going, his one unfailing consistency has been his faith that he would figure out things as he went along.

Sometimes it takes a leap of faith to launch a vision or project. However, a creative, innovative person who wants to make changes has to believe it will all work out at the end, and be ready to strap in for a wild ride.

SALES | THURSDAY

Always bear in mind that your own resolution to succeed is more important than any other one thing. —Abraham Lincoln

EVERY AMERICAN KNOWS THE STORY OF LINCOLN'S birth in a one-room log cabin, the son of two uneducated farmers. In total, he had eighteen months of formal schooling; the balance of his education was self-taught. His resolve to educate himself was just the beginning of an extraordinary life. He refused to be daunted, no matter what adversity he faced, because of his steadfast resolution to succeed.

You may well have experienced the terrible sinking feeling when a deal you've been working on for months falls apart. Or how about that presentation you stayed up nights writing only to get the news that your contact at the prospect's firm left for another job, closing down the entire department.

Stuff happens. Especially in sales. And when it does, you have to put everything in perspective and resolve to succeed the next time. It's a monumental effort, but when the chips are down you must review your goals and your desire to succeed. Chalk up the losing deals to experience, and use them as learning tools.

Abraham Lincoln also suffered from great depression. Despite this, he kept his eyes on the prize, and let only a few people know of his torments. That's resolve.

LEADERSHIP | FRIDAY

The importance of the morning meeting cannot be underestimated.—Rudolph Giuliani

I N HIS BOOK, *LEADERSHIP,* RUDOLPH GIULIANI WRITES that it's important to keep current with all aspects of your organization. When he was mayor of New York City, his team always knew were they could find him. They also continually apprised him of what was happening in the city. By getting the information firsthand, he was able to prioritize his time to deal with the most pressing issues of the day. Giuliani noted that when 9/11 occurred, the camaraderie between departments helped ease many tensions during the following weeks when resources were taxed.

A morning meeting is a great way to establish leadership with your team. Instead of impromptu meetings that no one can prepare for, or a two-hour weekly meeting that carves out too much of the day, a short morning meeting works most efficiently for everybody. Such meetings allow each member of the team a chance to be heard, give advice, or take advice. The meetings also reinforce the message that the departments must work together to promote smooth operations. If a turf war develops, the meeting serves as an immediate forum to work out conflicts.

If you feel disconnected from the inner workings of your business, a quick morning meeting might just be the instrument to get everyone back up to speed. This way, business will not suffer.

ENTREPRENEUR | SATURDAY

> Lack of money is no obstacle. Lack of
> an idea is an obstacle. —*Ken Hakuta*

THERE ARE GOOD IDEAS AND BAD IDEAS. KEN HAKUTA should know. He is known as Dr. Fad, and he made a name for himself when he introduced the Wacky Wall-Walker to the U.S. market. One of the best-selling fad toys of all time. Hakuta earned $20 million while selling 250 million copies of a rubber spider over a period of six years.

Hakuta can also attest that what may seem like a bad idea to someone may be viewed as an awesome idea by someone else. Everyone knows of an idea they heard about and thought was not going to go anywhere and then, voilá—five years later the company not only succeeded, but the idea spawned other related ideas and the business grew exponentially. Think of the Pet Rock, Chia Pet, and any sort of stress management desk toy.

Be on the lookout for new ideas that appeal to the masses. As you go about your daily life, look with different eyes at the jobs people are doing all around you. Are there ways of doing those jobs more easily? Are there aspects of an industry that intrigue you? Do you find yourself attracted to businesses that help people? That involve the elderly? Do you see something that can make these people's lives easier? By answering these questions, you may be able to come up with something unique that the market will respond to positively.

MANAGING PEOPLE | SUNDAY

> There's nothing sophisticated about the process of getting the right people in the right jobs. It's a matter of being systematic and consistent in interviewing and appraising people and developing them through useful feedback.
>
> —*Larry Bossidy and Ram Charan*

DELEGATING IS SOMETHING MANY MANAGERS COULD do in their sleep. Unfortunately, according to Larry Bossidy and Ram Charan, delegating the choice of a new hire can create huge headaches down the road. In their book, *Execution: The Discipline of Getting Things Done,* the pair write that one of the most important tasks managers face is hiring the right people.

Bossidy and Charan claim that managers routinely assume that human resources screen each candidate's references. The reality is that most of the time they perform a perfunctory cull through the resume pile and pass it along. If you become more involved, then you're guaranteed to hire the right person. Once the right people are in place, productivity and effectiveness skyrocket.

The second important lesson is to have frequent, yet candid appraisals of your team and your business. You have to give your employees the truth about their performance and help them get better in their jobs.

MOTIVATION | MONDAY

The difference between the impossible
and the possible lies in a person's
determination. —*Tommy Lasorda*

W HAT COULD BE A SIMPLER FORMULA FOR SUCCESS
than Tommy Lasorda's? The colorful longtime manager of the L.A. Dodgers had a passion for his job that translated into fiery determination.

Love for any job translates into success. No one will ever
forget Tommy Lasorda and his on-and-off-field rants that
became baseball classics. Love for the game of baseball was
his guiding spirit, and it took his team to two World Series
championships, four pennants, and eight division titles. In
1997, the first year he was eligible, he was voted into the
Baseball Hall of Fame. The impossible seems to disappear
when you truly enjoy what you are doing every single day.

What's more, everything becomes a possibility when
you are determined to win. The second part of his success
was his enormous dedication to his Dodgers. He had an
unshakable faith in what his team stood for and what they
were doing on the ball field.

Lasorda's determination was contagious. He believed in
his Dodgers like no one else, and his players responded in
kind. As a manager, he inspired others to do their personal
best—and the players delivered. Because of his winning
results, Lasorda will always be remembered as a legendary
baseball leader who bled Dodger Blue.

TEAM-BUILDING | TUESDAY

> You lose the respect of the best when
> you don't deal properly with the worst.
> —*John C. Maxwell*

D ON'T LET AN UNPRODUCTIVE, RUDE, OR UNQUALIFIED team member drag the rest of the team down. Boost morale by dealing with bad behavior swiftly.

The first way to assess a bad performance is to sit in on some team meetings. Your presence will initially change the dynamics (everyone will be on good behavior), but after a few meetings you will begin to melt into the background and you will get a true sense of the situation.

Once you have first-hand knowledge of the situation, talk to your most trusted team member and get her take on the situation. Then, start to formulate some ideas on how to take action. Talk to the person in question. Get the team to talk together. Perhaps there is a way for everyone to feel good about keeping the person on board once his inappropriate behavior is publicly addressed.

Don't get rid of people because someone else says to. You are setting up yourself for a discrimination suit somewhere down the road if you don't have documentation of an employee's poor performance. And remember, everyone's perception of a given situation is different. It may be that once out in the open, the problem can be addressed simply without altering the dynamic of the team.

CAREER | WEDNESDAY

Money was never a big motivation for me,
except as a way to keep score. The real
excitement is playing the game.

—Donald Trump

DONALD TRUMP, KNOWN FOR HIS HIGH STAKES wheeling-and-dealing, makes mind-boggling amounts of money. So when he tells you that it's not about the money, you have to wonder what it is about for him. For "The Donald," real satisfaction comes during the emotional roller coaster that precludes every big deal he makes. For him, playing the game means challenging his intellectual abilities, figuring out strategies, and negotiating terms—all the elements required to make a big deal happen.

In the 1950s the psychologist Frederic Herzberg discovered the Two-Factor theory, a widely accepted concept about job satisfaction. He divided up the requirements into hygiene factors and motivational factors. The hygiene factors must satisfy a person's standards for quality working conditions, effective management, safety and salary. If you're office is a pit and your boss is a jerk, you aren't going to be happy, no matter how much money you make. The second part, the motivational factors, includes personal growth, advancement, achievement, and recognition. When you enjoy what you are doing, excelling and getting accolades can mean just as much to you as a raise. If you had to choose a career, a career that excites you is the best kind. For a career to be rewarding, it can't just be about the money.

SALES | THURSDAY

> When a deal you get works for you,
> don't try pushing a single into a double.
> A hit is a hit. —*James A. Randel*

J AMES RANDEL DIDN'T START OUT SELLING REAL ESTATE; he made his fortune buying properties as investments. In the process he became a broker and honed and developed dynamic sales strategies. In his book, *Confessions of a Real Estate Entrepreneur,* Randel says that his success was based on "a function of hard work, perseverance, and integrity."

But Randel's road to success was not always smooth. Many times, things went awry, and luckily for us, he's been willing to talk about some of his mistakes. On some of his deals, he extended himself too much: trying to hit a home run, instead of settling for a single. He learned the hard way that misjudging a pitch is like misjudging people: it can ruin your at-bat, just as easily as it can ruin a sale.

Passion for what you're doing is necessary in sales, but it can get in the way. Zeal, if not harnessed, can grow out of control. You have to become adept at risk-reward analysis. Don't risk a nice commission for a couple more dollars. Stick with the deal that works for you and your customer. Even in the big leagues, a walk's as good as a hit.

LEADERSHIP | FRIDAY

Just as people tend to overestimate their strengths, they also overrate their weaknesses. —*Marshall Goldsmith*

A CCORDING TO MARSHALL GOLDSMITH IN HIS BOOK, *What Got You There Won't Get You Here,* most successful people reach a point in their career when their weaknesses become the primary issue holding them back from success. Goldsmith notes that what people think is holding them back and what is really holding them back can sometimes be completely different. In fact, the parts of your personality that you think might be holding you back might not matter at all.

For example, Goldsmith tells the story of an employee at a large corporation who took a leadership course that was offered to potential senior managers and was amazed at the feedback from his peers. He assumed his time management skills were a real problem for his co-workers. However, his time management skills were consistently praised as one of his greater strengths. He generally prided himself in being an eloquent debater. In fact, his colleagues consistently criticized him for his inability to concede his point of view in staff meetings.

Since you rely on your employees to help you get your job done, it's important to have an understanding of how others view you, and how your strengths and weaknesses affect them. If you are open to advice, you might find out some very interesting things about yourself you didn't know.

ENTREPRENEUR | SATURDAY

> In this new wave of technology,
> you can't do it all yourself, you have
> to form alliances. —*Carlos Slim Helu*

TELECOMMUNICATIONS BILLIONAIRE CARLOS SLIM HELU learned early in his career that money partnering is critical to helping ensure success. While Helu made his money creating Mexico's first privately owned telecom company, Telemex, he had to partner with French and American telecom companies in order to take his native Mexico's phone service away from the government.

Today, partnering opportunities exist everywhere, especially on the Internet. Common partnerships used to be geared around hyperlinks and banner ads. Today, social networking sites like Linkedin and Twitter have created a virtual "six degrees of separation," where you can connect with your associates—or your friends—and make business contacts in minutes.

The Web continues to morph as we get our minds around the technology that is available to us. You don't have to be a multinational corporation to take advantage of the Internet, or any other type of business partnerships: synergy exists on every level and is there for the taking.

MANAGING PEOPLE | SUNDAY

> Remember that unjust criticism is often
> a disguised compliment. —*Dale Carnegie*

M ANAGERS WHO DON'T THINK SOMEONE IS WORTH their efforts won't bother to correct them. Lost causes don't merit feedback; they usually get fired instead.

In Dale Carnegie's famous book, *How to Stop Worrying and Start Living,* he states that criticism from above is often a signal that you have been noticed, or that you've made your mark on the company. You may consistently make big contributions that are followed by a minor transgression, or perhaps you are threatening others or arousing jealousy. So go ahead—pat yourself on the back for being noticed.

But be prepared to defend yourself when the feedback gets fiercely critical. If you can do so objectively, closely analyze the criticism. If it seems unjust, then take the pot-shots as a compliment. Deflect the criticism, knowing you're doing the job right. If it has some merit, change your behavior so that you'll go back to being the wunderkind once again.

Managing down to your staff presents a different challenge. If your bosses tend to deliver unjust criticism (why else would Carnegie have said this in the first place?), managers must decide whether to model this behavior or concentrate on delivering constructive feedback. The right choice, of course, comes straight from these other Carnegie principles: "Don't criticize, condemn, or complain;" "Use encouragement;" and, "Make the fault seem easy to correct."

MOTIVATION | MONDAY

We didn't lose the game;
we just ran out of time.
—*Vince Lombardi*

IT'S ALMOST A LAW THAT THE WORD "LEGENDARY" PRE-
cede the name of Vince Lombardi. As head coach of the
Green Bay Packers, Lombardi essentially placed the National
Football League into the American consciousness. In nine
years, his Packers won five NFL championships—including
three consecutively—and went on to win the first two Super
Bowls. This is the stuff of which legends are made.

Lombardi's management style was successful because his
players were completely devoted to him. This was because
he treated them fairly and with respect. His devotion to
hard work and his commitment to winning inspired them
on and off the playing field. Intrinsic to his success was his
gift for communication. In brilliantly articulated motivational speeches, he skillfully conveyed his philosophy on
winning to his team game after game. Many of Lombardi's
lines, like the classic quote above, are still repeated widely
today.

Even though the Packers lost the particular game referred
to in Lombardi's comment, he was able to put a positive spin
on it. The underlying message was that his team couldn't
"lose" because they were inherently winners. He believed
that a winning attitude will work even when the chips are
down—and he was right.

TEAM-BUILDING | TUESDAY

You never really hear the truth from your
subordinates until after 10 in the evening.
—*Jurgen Schrempp*

J URGEN SCHREMPP WAS ONCE THE CEO OF DAIMLER-Chrysler AG so he knows the difficulty for anyone at the upper echelons of a corporation to learn much about the people who work for them. Schrempp's point is that getting together with coworkers outside of the office environment can allow people to learn a lot about each other that might help build them into a better team during the workday.

The work week represents many hours, and it would be nice if the long hours included some fun. This isn't to say people need to "yuk it up" six out of eight hours a day. But, there is no reason the workday can't be entertaining.

You can promote a more lighthearted atmosphere in your office by having colleagues learn about each other after hours. Trade shows and other work travel experiences are often a place where people get to know more about each other. Business travel throws people together during non-work hours, forcing them to have meals together and form relationships with others they know little about. Business people who have traveled together bring their experiences back to the office and often become better work associates because of it—partly due to the shared travel adventures they can laugh about.

CAREER | WEDNESDAY

The rich don't work for money.
—*Robert Kiyosaki*

THERE IS A BIG DIFFERENCE IN KNOWING ABOUT LIFE and implementing that knowledge successfully. Many people incorrectly assume that once they have graduated from college and land a well-paying job they are on their way to being wealthy. Getting a job and working is the way to start, but it's the right job that matters. Often, it's not the one that pays the most. Robert Kiyosaki's theory, explained in his book, *Rich Dad, Poor Dad,* is that if you wanted to own a fast-food franchise, a "Poor Dad" would tell you to get a degree in hospitality management and then work for a corporation. The "Rich Dad" would tell you to start washing dishes at your favorite restaurant. "Rich Dad" wouldn't worry that his son was a dishwasher and not making much money, but rather he would take pride in knowing you're gaining invaluable experience in learning every aspect of the business. This is why he says that the rich don't always work for money: sometimes they work just for the experience.

Don't be afraid to apply this theory to your own career path. As you work your way up, the ins and outs of the business will unfold around you as well as many nuanced real-life situations that you won't encounter in a classroom.

SALES | THURSDAY

> Our real capacity far exceeds the average
> expectations other have for us.
> —*Harvey Mackay*

I N HIS BOOK, *Swim With the Sharks Without Being Eaten Alive,* Harvey Mackay tells the story of a stonecutter who hammered a rock a hundred times and it wouldn't split, but then wham!—it finally splits. The stonecutter knew it was not the 101st blow that cracked the rock, but all the blows that came before it.

The stonecutter has the confidence to know what he's capable of and the patience to work hard to achieve his goal. It's the same in sales—you have to know what you're capable of. It doesn't matter if your competition thinks your product isn't as good as theirs—that's the sales game. The "sharks" in Mackay's book title are, guess what?—other businesspeople. The warning is, don't let them eat you alive—a bit of hyperbole, but more completely phrased as, don't quit. Believe in your own capacity to succeed, and there's nothing you can't accomplish.

How do you know your capacity? Challenge yourself. Set goals. Mackay suggests goals like improving your sales ranking in one quarter, or adding X more accounts, Y more income, and Z more total sales. The goals can be simple and uncomplicated, but you have to set them, and then you have to develop a plan to achieve them.

Know your real capacity for achievement and leave the naysayers in your wake.

LEADERSHIP | FRIDAY

It is what we learn after we think we know it all that counts. —John Wooden

AFTER LONG HOURS AND HARD WORK, IT'S EXHILARATing to bask in the glory of our accomplishments, especially ones that exceeded our expectations. Career kudos translate into monetary value, such as raises and promotions. But, you must be careful if you think your past victories guarantee you a spot in the winner's circle. Just like a company's balance sheet, it's important to take frequent stock of your personal assets and liabilities that add or subtract from your professional career goals.

According to John Wooden, famed basketball coach for the University of California, Los Angeles (UCLA), resting on your laurels is a recipe for disaster. He made it a personal priority to review meticulously every detail after each game in order to continue improving as head coach. Wooden was just as interested in improving his performance when he was winning as when he was losing. His outstanding results prove his theory correct.

When you stop trying to improve, you do a disservice to yourself. Focus on what you can do to learn from yesterday and apply it today. Even if you've just landed a big account or made a substantial profit that raises your profile at the office, there's still room to be better.

ENTREPRENEUR | SATURDAY

> There are one-story intellects, two-story
> intellects, and three-story intellects with
> skylights. All fact collectors with no aim
> beyond their facts are one-story men. Two-
> story men compare reason and generalize,
> using labors of the fact collectors as well as
> their own. Three-story men idealize, imag-
> ine, and predict. Their best illuminations
> come from above through the skylight.
> —*Oliver Wendell Holmes*

THE ABOVE QUOTE IS A COMPLICATED WAY OF SAYING people have different levels of complexity. The simplest thinker is the one who bases everything on straight facts.

The next level of complexity is the person who takes those facts and figures, compares their thinking with others, uses information about the economy or the market, and comes up with what to do next.

The third type Holmes describes—"three-story men"— use all of the same info as the two-story and one-story men, but they use it to decide what to do for the future. They have the benefit of being on the top floor where their imaginations have room to spread beyond the skylights. They are the ones who say, "If widgets sales are on the rise, then we should make 40 percent more widgets this month than the last two and encourage more people to buy widgets."

Bottom line: you need all three kinds of people for your business to become a real success.

MANAGING PEOPLE | SUNDAY

Only knowledge put to use can create capital.
—*Mikel Harry and Richard Schroeder*

SUCCESSFULLY MANAGING PEOPLE CAN FEEL LIKE A magic act. You see it happening right in front of you, but you can't quite figure out how they do it. According to the authors of *Six Sigma,* Mikel Harry and Richard Schroeder, true problems are hard to spot because people won't admit to them. Invariably, businesses look to blame a particular person for mistakes, but doing so often buries the problem. Then, to make matters worse, managers implement rashly conceived ideas to solve problems, only to cause even more problems.

The Six Sigma strategy encourages you to analyze the company's processes and use the data to standardize any discrepancies. Whether you are managing six people stuffing envelopes or six hundred on the floor of a factory, the answer to any problem lies in finding the truth. By using employee knowledge and feedback to gain an accurate picture of what is happening in your company, you'll be better off. But getting employees to buy into the oversight of the processes is difficult when in the past management has always blamed the people. The true cost of doing business is directly related to how interested you are in getting to the truth and how well you respond to that knowledge.

MOTIVATION | MONDAY

Passion is a catalyst. Use it to your advantage and you can start achieving tremendous things. —*Donald Trump*

N O ONE CAN PROMOTE A DONALD TRUMP PROJECT better than Donald Trump. When he talks about a new hotel or his latest television show, you can bet that a superlative is going to be in the first sentence—and virtually every one after that. For Trump, everything is the most "important/colossal/stupendous/marvelous" project in the history of real estate/resorts/reality television. You may not be enamored with his idea for a backstage at the Miss Universe reality TV show, but you will be impressed by his grand-scale delivery about how great it's going to be. His passion is contagious, which is exactly what he wants it to be. He has the ability to turn the hum-drum into fabulous just by sounding passionate.

Trump even makes a Trumpism out of the word "passion"—while the rest of us mortals usually term it "enthusiasm." He believes the stronger your enthusiasm, the more it will "trump" any obstacles in your path to realizing your dream. Enthusiasm or passion, however you want to say it, is essential to loving what you do and exciting those around you to buy into your ideas. Use your passion to your advantage.

TEAM-BUILDING | TUESDAY

> Good people are good because they've
> come to wisdom through failure.
> —*William Saroyan*

LEARNING THROUGH FAILURE IS NOTHING TO BE ashamed of, according to famed Armenian American writer William Saroyan. You tried something and it didn't work out, big deal. But failing a second or third time because of repeating the same mistake is not wisdom. You need to learn from failure in order to not repeat it.

Great teams cannot afford to dwell on failure. They don't consider failing a negative act, so they don't mope about it. Instead, they review the facts, figure out what didn't work, and move on to the next task at hand. In short, they get on with their lives. Successful people are already looking for the next opportunity instead of reliving the past.

Even the most respected, well-funded, and well-resourced companies have experienced failure and grown from it. Take NASA, for example. If the U.S. space program did not use the wisdom gleaned from the *Challenger* and *Columbia* space shuttle disasters, space exploration would have come to a permanent halt. Although NASA seemed to be in temporary hiatus while they regrouped and worked through every detail of what caused these catastrophes, they used what they found to make changes. Now the shuttle program is more successful than ever.

CAREER | WEDNESDAY

Getting fired is nature's way of telling you that you had the wrong job in the first place. —*Hal Lancaster*

THERE IS NO WAY TO PROCESS THE GAMUT OF EMOTIONS that run through your brain like an electric shock when you hear the words, "You're fired." You might feel anger, resentment, fear, sadness, or relief. Whatever the case, you need to control your emotions so that you can bounce back quickly.

Despite the sudden urge to join the National Rifle Association (NRA), stay calm and remain professional. Whether you were fired as the result of a company-wide downsizing or because of a performance issue, remain professional while you wrap up matters. First, visit the human resources department to make sure your firing was handled within company guidelines. Ask if you can offer your resignation instead of being fired and how that would affect any severance package that you might receive.

Keep in mind most people can look back at the experience and tell you that, "It was the best thing that ever happened to them." It may take getting fired for you to sit back and ponder how you perceived yourself in your job and whether it was truly a good fit. By turning the experience into an exercise in self-reflection, you can use the new information you have to find a better job and even a more suitable career path.

SALES | THURSDAY

> You can get everything in life you want
> if you will just help enough other people
> get what they want. —*Zig Ziglar*

HELPING OTHER PEOPLE SOUNDS LIKE CHARITY, BUT not in the sales department. By solving your customers' problems, you're helping them get what they want. Helping other people is the value you bring to negotiation in sales. Unless you want to come off as a high-pressure salesperson, you're not going to close a deal before you clearly establish you're interested in your customer, and not just interested in yourself.

Plotting the potential client's present and future needs is an exhausting task but a rewarding one. But you will establish your value to the prospect, and she will appreciate your help. Even if the prospect doesn't buy in the end, you're on the right path.

Many little things happen on the way to determining sales results. Some of those things—a thank-you e-mail sent after your first meeting, bringing lattes to everyone at a presentation, and your design of an organizational chart for all—communicate that you believe in what you're doing.

The time you invest on the way to closing a deal by helping the customer is going to make a big difference in the long run. Success will be yours when you help others and your customers get what they want.

LEADERSHIP | FRIDAY

> Although the one-eyed man in the land of the blind has a distinct advantage, he'd be foolish to pass up the opportunity to see with both eyes. —*Mikel Harry and Richard Schroeder*

IT'S HUMAN NATURE TO BASK IN THE GLORY OF YOUR accomplishments. Go ahead and congratulate yourself, say Mikel Harry and Richard Schroeder, authors of *Six Sigma*. Give yourself a quick pat on the back, but then get back to work. While you might be at the head of the pack right now, there's no guarantee you will stay ahead of your competition.

Even in high-performing companies, there's always room for improvement. While most good companies operate at a three or four sigma, the goal should be six sigma. Six sigma requires a company to benchmark itself to the competition, analyze processes to pinpoint problems, and reduce the amount of defective products that a company makes. This will result in everything from better customer satisfaction to increased market share. From the amount of time it takes to deliver an invoice, return a phone call to a client, or ship a container half-way around the world, time is money, and seconds can cost millions of dollars in profits.

To find out where the problems are—to see with both eyes, if you will—is the goal even if you're already meeting your greatest expectations. Living in your glory is like seeing with only one eye.

ENTREPRENEUR | SATURDAY

Designing your product for monetization first, and people second will probably leave you with neither. —*Tara Hunt*

I F ACQUIRING MONEY IS AT THE TOP OF YOUR LIST, SOME-thing else eventually suffers. This statement has proved to be true for centuries and was recently mentioned by well-known blogger Tara Hunt. That is certainly the case when, as an animal or pet becomes a profit center, the animal's natural instincts are hampered. For example, horses who naturally love to roam for miles and eat all day get locked in stalls twenty-three hours a day so they don't get injured or use up their energy frolicking in a field. Dogs get bathed religiously yet aren't allowed the rough-and-tumble play they like because they need to have a show coat. And even when winning a competition seems more important than earning money, the two go hand in hand when a winner can demand higher prices for puppies or stud fees.

In your business, think about your customers first—they are the ones handing over the money. Keep in mind the old adage that says that if someone has a good experience, they tell one person; if they have a bad experience, they tell a dozen. And it's not just customers you need to consider. Don't place money over employees either—you will definitely have fewer revenues if your employees aren't emotionally or monetarily invested in your products or services.

MANAGING PEOPLE | SUNDAY

Speak clearly, if you speak at all;
carve every word before you let it fall.
—*Oliver Wendell Holmes*

"THE CHAMBERED NAUTILUS", A FAMOUS POEM BY Oliver Wendell Holmes, refers to the beauty of a particular shell with its perfect spiral. As the mollusk grows, it closes one section and builds another to live in. It is one of the few mollusks that never outgrows its shell since the shell grows with it. Holmes wrote the poem as a metaphor for the pursuit of intellectual growth. "Growing with your shell" can only happen if you have an open mind to pursue knowledge throughout your life.

When Oliver Wendell Holmes talks about learning for the sake of learning, it's not only about acquiring all the knowledge you can, but learning when and how to share that knowledge. You need to choose your words carefully and understand the significance of how they affect circumstances when speaking with others. Too many times, people, especially those in authority, speak without thinking. That's a recipe for disaster in the work place.

If you manage many different people, practice different ways of communicating with each employee so that each individual understands exactly what you expect from him or her. It might take a lifetime to learn how to do this, but the effort will endear you to employees.

MOTIVATION | MONDAY

> Getting ahead in a difficult profession
> requires avid faith in yourself. That is why
> some people with mediocre talent, but
> with great inner drive, go much further
> than people with vastly superior talent.
>
> —*Sophia Loren*

SOPHIA LOREN IS TALKING ABOUT ACTING, BUT SHOW-biz is a business, like any other, and the same rules apply.

How many people have impressed you in your business life who, you discover later, got where they are today on a wing and a prayer? No MBA, no special appointments or promotions through family ties, maybe no more than a GED high school diploma or a stint in the army. Yet he got to where he is, hopping over fully qualified types who have the degrees and the connections because he showed that priceless quality: driving ambition.

Determination and faith in yourself can never be under-estimated in any recipe for success. An unshakable inner drive that works overtime often means much more than a brain-busting IQ or fancy business school degree.

TEAM-BUILDING | TUESDAY

While meetings are essential to the decision-making process, they are not the best forum for decision making.
—*Mark H. McCormack*

H OW MANY MEETINGS HAVE YOU ATTENDED WHERE the discussion goes round and round and no decision is made? It's infuriating. Yet meetings that are conducted in a positive way can result in great decision making—if you encourage that outcome.

Mark McCormack, sports marketing legend and founder of International Marketing Group (IMG), knew the importance of Team-Building during negotiations. He believed the first way to guarantee a decision-oriented meeting is to be sure the right people are in attendance. In our attempts to create a democratic workplace, we often try to include everyone in the process. A great management trick is to include everyone in the process leading up to the actual decision, then limit the actual decision making to the few people who really need to be involved. That way, no one feels left out, and you've also given everyone the opportunity to share their thoughts.

CAREER | WEDNESDAY

*Better to remain silent and be thought
a fool than to speak out and remove
all doubt.* —*Abraham Lincoln*

I T TAKES A CERTAIN AMOUNT OF BUSINESS SAVVY TO know when and where to keep your mouth shut. Take a piece of advice from Honest Abe: don't underestimate the power of silence.

In any business setting, being silent doesn't mean you should be afraid to say what you think. Listen to what everyone else in the room has to say before you make your comments. If you think what you have to say will still contribute value to the conversation, then have the confidence to bring it up. Before speaking, though, think about whether your thoughts will make a difference in the outcome of the situation. If you aren't sure, it might be best to keep listening.

If you add your two cents but find that your opinion isn't well received or is not taken under advisement, then it's time to reassess what you want to get across and change your approach. If your coworkers don't get your point, don't insist on being right. Instead, let them suffer the consequences as you quietly watch the rest of the conversation unfold. Remember, if they don't listen to your advice, and their ideas don't pan out, you can always remind them of your thoughts the next time around.

SALES | THURSDAY

When you hug often enough, you
find that your customers hug back.
—*Jack Mitchell*

DON'T BE PUT OFF BY THE HUGS PERMEATING THIS quote. Though it might sound a tad too warm and fuzzy, "hug" used here is simply a euphemism for putting the personal into your sales pitch.

Hugging your customers means showing constant expressions of gratitude for their business. You can say thank you in a variety of ways whether it be a call, an e-mail, a note, or a gift.

In his upscale clothing stores, Mitchells and Richards, Jack Mitchell outfits CEOs. The business was started by his father. Jack has not only inherited his dad's sales principles but has taken it a step further, writing a book about them, titled *Hug Your Customers.*

Jack has such a sunny outlook that he won't even use the word "problem." He sees everything as an opportunity or a challenge. No surprise that he also shuns the word "no." It's always, "Yes, of course." The "of course" is mandatory. Whatever the customer wants, the response by him or any staff member is prefaced by, "of course": "Of course I'll get your order out two weeks earlier than we planned."

Personalize your sales and you'll get repeat customers. According to Jack Mitchell's experience, it costs six times more to get a customer back than it does to keep a customer in the first place.

LEADERSHIP | FRIDAY

> We have to let go of this notion that for Apple to win, Microsoft has to lose. We have to embrace a notion that for Apple to win, Apple needs to do a really good job. And if others are going to help us that's great, because we need all the help we can get, and if we screw up and don't do a good job, it's not somebody else's fault, it's our fault. —*Steve Jobs*

WHEN APPLE ANNOUNCED IT WAS FORMING A PART-nership with Microsoft, Mac devotees went ballistic in chat rooms everywhere. This was the ultimate betrayal to Apple fans. Bill Gates, who they routinely cast as Satan, was frequently held responsible for Apple's profitability problems.

Steve Jobs, never one to ponder his popularity for long, did think long and hard before committing to this partner-ship. After analyzing the company's viability, he realized that Apple needed help. Jobs knew that sometimes you have to embrace an imperfect solution to a problem. He realized that snubbing Microsoft's offer was like refusing a life vest as the ship sinks. Apple was able to turn the company around and become profitable again by partnering with Microsoft.

When the chips are down, a leader must put aside ego and make the best decision for the company, even if it means embracing a partnership with its sworn enemy.

ENTREPRENEUR | SATURDAY

Trouble is only opportunity in work clothes.
—Henry J. Kaiser

WHILE TROUBLE SEEMS MORE INNOCUOUS THAN FAIL-ure, a business person may look at them in the same light. But just like failure, you can't have success without some trouble along the way. American industrialist Henry Kaiser knew it's how you react to the trouble that matters.

Sports teams deal with trouble, or inconveniences, all season long. The Boston Red Sox had their share of trouble in the 2007 season. One of their star players, Manny Ramirez, was sidelined with a muscle injury for about three weeks in the summer. A young player, Jacoby Ellsbury, was brought up from a minor league team to play while Ramirez recovered. Ellsbury proved to be such a good player that manager Terry Francona found a way to keep him in the line-up even after Ramirez returned from his injury. Ellsbury went on to play throughout the rest of the season, which culminated in a World Series Championship for the Red Sox.

For the business owner, trouble may come in the form of a manufacturing glitch, an unexpected time delay, or an act of God like a fire or flood—or perhaps even a disgruntled employee. The key to your success will be how you deal with these inconveniences. For example, use the manufacturing glitch as a chance to strengthen your relationship with your key manufacturer or to find a new manufacturer.

Show your business acumen by responding well to so-called "trouble."

MANAGING PEOPLE | SUNDAY

> There are times when even the best
> manager is like the little boy with the
> big dog waiting to see where the dog
> wants to go so he can take him there.
>
> —*Lee Iacocca*

T HE MAN WHO FATHERED THE FORD MUSTANG AND resurrected Chrysler from financial oblivion wasn't born knowing how to pull off those magic acts. At Ford he initiated careful research about how American demographics and the financial wherewithal of consumers would change during the 1960s. He listened to smart people tell him what the country needed, and he delivered a classic automobile.

Years later at Chrysler, Iacocca landed at a corporation in turmoil. Careful analysis showed that the company was in such dire straits that extreme measures would have to be taken to save it. Iacocca ended up needing loans from the government to keep Chrysler afloat. But once he got the money, he revived the company.

In each case the "big dogs" for Iacocca were the demands of the business: the need for new thinking at Ford and absolute need for a survival plan at Chrysler. These dogs forced Iacocca to listen to them, follow them, and ultimately steer him in directions that would benefit both companies.

Managers who wag the dog make decisions without letting the facts tell them what's right. Managers who take the opposite approach usually get the treats.

MOTIVATION | MONDAY

> People have just two choices when it
> comes to their emotions: they can
> master their emotions or be mastered
> by them. —*John C. Maxwell*

J OHN MAXWELL IS A BUSINESS BOOK GURU WITH MORE
than fifty books to his credit. His book, *The 17 Essential
Qualities of a Team Player,* provides characteristics of a good
team player. He believes that team members need to be
intentional (focused on the big picture), relational (focused
on others), selfless (willing to take a backseat for the good of
the team), and tenacious (works hard to overcome obstacles),
among others.

Maxwell also knows that being a good team player on
the job isn't always easy. Personal traits you once took pride
in can seriously get in the way. Your competitiveness, for
example, is a plus when you're working solo, but can work
against you on a team where everyone shares a common
goal. And, if you did work solo before, adapting to a team,
subordinating your role, and sharing your insights and
progress can be a major challenge.

On a team you can find yourself dealing with issues you
thought you had gotten over in high school or therapy, and
suddenly your emotions get in the way of work. Maxwell
recommends that either you master your emotions, or be
mastered by them. For the good of the team, try the former,
at least until your deadline has passed and/or the project is
handed in.

TEAM-BUILDING | TUESDAY

*Incompetents invariably make trouble
for people other than themselves.*

—*Larry McMurtry*

INCOMPETENT PEOPLE ARE RARELY AWARE THAT THEY ARE hopelessly useless and inept. It seems as if they are blindly moving through the day, getting little accomplished. Or what they do get accomplished just makes more work for everyone else. Incompetent people simply do not get the work done. They may not know how to research something or do whatever it is they were asked to do. And so they slow up the rest of the team, or require someone else to cover for them.

Novelist Larry McMurtry often wrote American westerns that were filled with incompetent characters. In his books these characters were usually killed off so that the hero could prevail. The same strategy holds true in business, except in most cases you don't bring your Smith & Wesson to the job.

Sometimes people are incompetent at a particular task. In this situation you have two choices. Either remove them from the team and the project and put them on another task that better uses the skills they have. Or, you can get them the tools or education they need to become competent. This is often the better choice, affording you a small investment which can pay off in the long run.

CAREER | WEDNESDAY

The best people are always underpaid
and the worst people overpaid.
—*Richard Koch*

M ANY PEOPLE SETTLE FOR BEING MEDIOCRE AT THEIR
jobs. According to Richard Koch, author of *The
80/20 Principle,* mediocrity is rampant. The 80/20 principle
is based on statistical analysis that you can measure anything and find that 80 percent of the results are produced by
20 percent of the effort.

Look around your office and observe who is or isn't
pulling their weight. If 80 percent of the work is being done
by 20 percent of the people, what can you do about it? If
you are one of the 20 percent, chances are you are being
underpaid. If this is the case, learn as much as possible in
your job and start looking to move on. If you aren't enjoying your job enough to provide the company with real
value, chances are you are in the nonproductive, unhappy
part of the 80/20 equation. In this case, it might also make
sense to look elsewhere for work.

Apply the 80/20 principle to your workforce if you are a
business owner. Determine who are the 20 percent "star
employees" and compensate them by giving out bonuses for
productivity. Productive employees will feel grateful that
their performance was acknowledged. If you don't, someone
else will. Next, cut through the 80 percent that are overpaid
and don't pull their weight. The entire value of your business
will grow exponentially.

SALES | THURSDAY

Under promise; over deliver.
—*Tom Peters*

TOM PETERS, THE AUTHOR OF WHAT MANY CONSIDER the greatest business book of all time, *In Search of Excellence,* doesn't mince words. This statement is simple, but it is awesome advice, and it applies to every avenue in business.

Look at it in the context of sales. Customers want two things: they're looking for solutions to a specific problem, and they want to feel good about the sale. In your creative role as salesperson you are supposed to find those solutions. The trick is to never promise anything you can't deliver— yet, you still need to exceed your customer's expectations. That's the way to wow in sales.

If customers have questions or complaints, get back to them in twenty-four hours. Don't make them wait or sweat out your response. If you set a price, maintain it. Even if costs go over, the small loss in profit will be boosted by the high marks your reputation earns. These little extras are what customers remember, and what keep them coming back.

Just don't promise the moon before you deliver it, and sprinkle a few stars along the way to make the customer feel great. Your confidence in yourself and in the quality of what you're selling will move the product. Your creativity and enthusiasm will deliver the extras.

LEADERSHIP | FRIDAY

> Character is more like a bundle of habits
> and tendencies and interests, loosely
> bound together and dependent, at certain
> times, on circumstance or context.
>
> —*Malcom Gladwell*

W HEN IT CAME TO MARKETING ITS NEW GAME CON-
sole, Wii, Nintendo decided to spurn traditional
marketing techniques of commercials and print advertise-
ments. Instead, they gave the new game to a select group of
"Alpha Moms," a term used to describe highly influential
mothers, or what Malcom Gladwell calls "connectors" in his
book, *The Tipping Point*. These trend-setting moms made the
Wii the "gotta have it" item. One mom's e-mail resulted in
200 other moms buying Wiis based on her single recommendation. It didn't matter that they had never heard of the game
or it was too expensive. Word-of-mouth from the right person was all that it took to create a tipping point, resulting in
a mass product shortage and hysterical parents everywhere.

Gladwell surmises that "behavior is contagious." Learning that a person's behavior is directly influenced by the
context of his surroundings will give you a better understanding on how to influence your consumers. You'll also
come to understand why it's important for your clients to
garner tickets to Lakers games and lunches at the Four Sea-
sons. When you figure out who the connectors are within
your client base, you will be able to create circumstances
that affect behavior and ultimately improve your business.

ENTREPRENEUR | SATURDAY

> When it comes to money, most people want to play it safe and feel secure. So passion does not direct them. Fear does.
> —*Robert T. Kiyosaki*

CONTEMPORARY PERSONAL FINANCE GURUS TALK A LOT about two fundamental money-related topics: understanding your own attitude toward money and learning to respect money.

If you ever took formal driving lessons, especially learning to drive a motorcycle, you are taught to always look for an escape route. If you come around a corner and there is a log across the road, where can you head the car or bike to escape a collision with the log? If you are driving down a two-lane highway and an oncoming car has poorly judged the distance needed to pass, where is your opening to avoid a head-on collision?

You will also need to plan an escape route in case your business doesn't work out and you have to call it quits, at least for a while. The best way to have a financial escape route is to have a backup—a savings account of some kind, an asset you could sell if you absolutely had to, a line of credit, or even a business relationship strong enough to help you in a pinch. Look for your financial escape routes so you can follow your passion and feel more secure about taking well-thought-out business risks.

MANAGING PEOPLE | SUNDAY

> You can do so much in 10 minutes' time.
> Ten minutes, once gone, are gone for
> good. Divide your life into 10-minute units
> and sacrifice as few of them as possible in
> meaningless activity. —*Ingvar Kamprad*

TIME MANAGEMENT IS A CONCEPT THAT ALL OF US grasp, but few of us truly live up to. With relentless e-mails and cell phone calls competing with our to do lists, it's no wonder that over-achievers regularly amaze us. Ingvar Kamprad, the visionary founder of IKEA Systems B.V., believes in not wasting a moment of the day being unproductive. Being hardworking and frugal to the extreme, the billionaire frequently eats an inexpensive lunch in the IKEA cafeteria, which also saves him time because he isn't driving anywhere.

If you are a manager who wants to get the most out of his people, design products that eliminate waste, cut costs, and work well. Products built around these principles will make a happy, productive workforce. As IKEA became a global employer, the corporate philosophy spread easily throughout the IKEA empire. Managers efficiently run their teams and are justly rewarded. On the eve of the millennium for instance, all IKEA workers, from cooks to accountants, split the day's profits from the stores around the world. This amounted to a month's salary for some. It's no wonder, that Kamprad wants people to get back to work. He doesn't want them to waste a second of their time.

MOTIVATION | MONDAY

You win a few, you lose a few. Some get rained out. But you got to dress for all of them. —Satchel Paige

L EGENDARY HALL OF FAME PITCHER SATCHEL PAIGE WAS a unique sideline philosopher while he was playing baseball, and his savvy, homespun insights live on. He was true to his word each day of his life, and never stopped using his talents under any circumstances. In 1965 when Paige was sixty years old, he took the mound for the last time, throwing three shutout innings for the Kansas City Athletics.

The game of business has a lot in common with baseball. You can't win every game—some of your plans may be out-and-out failures, others may just fizzle and die, and others you'd rather forget they ever happened. Even in business it can't be about winning all of the time.

Paige's sage advice is this: when it's not going your way, maintain your best intentions. Stay focused and always be ready to try again. Don't get misled from your future path by thinking about what went wrong in the past. Bad days are going to happen. Plans go awry or just plain go missing. Focus on your potential instead of the misses. Stay in that "will to win" mode.

Enthusiasm plays a major role in this kind of determination. Use it to nurture your love for your job, your career, or your industry. If you work to preserve your enthusiasm, your determination will stay intact. In other words, you'll be dressed and ready to play everyday.

TEAM-BUILDING | TUESDAY

A man always has two reasons for doing anything—a good reason and the real reason. —*J.P. Morgan*

J. P. MORGAN, A LEGENDARY EARLY-TWENTIETH-CENTURY American financier, knew that closing deals successfully often requires more than a sound business argument. After all, the nature of business means that there's no such thing as a sure thing. For every good reason why a particular action makes sense, there's always an equally good reason, sometimes several, why the risk outweighs the potential gain. This means that at some point you're asking the person with whom you're negotiating to take a leap of faith. To make this happen, you need to know your opponent's real, often unspoken, motivations.

Is your business rival looking for money, respect, or the chance to be seen as shrewd by her superiors? Is it more important for her to offer a quick deal that makes the next quarterly report; or a cheaper one that improves her department's fiscal bottom line?

Assume your competitors make as equally good business arguments as yours, then look beyond those to find less obvious factors that might influence the outcome. If you've done your research—about the industry as well as the company and person you're approaching—you'll have an idea of where to look for such make-or-break motivators. If not, develop a flexible pitch or presentation style that helps you gather a broad range of information.

CAREER | WEDNESDAY

> What people say and do in the most
> innocent situations can speak volumes
> about their real selves. —*Mark H. McCormack*

WHETHER IT'S CLINCHING A DEAL, LANDING A JOB, or selling market share, there is always a need to collect information that will increase your position, thus improving the outcome of your business dealings. One of the most important sources of information is being able to read people. Legendary sports agent Mark McCormack believes that "Most business situations provide all sorts of tangible evidence that allow you to see beneath the surface." He insists clues for insight abound, to be used by anyone who is tuned into them.

Words account for only 7 percent of the total message when people are talking, leaving you with 93 percent in nonverbal actions to decipher. Be ready to read the clues people give you, and don't forget the clues you are giving them. The next time you are in a conversation, focus on the other person's body language, and see if the message he is sending with his body matches what is coming out of his mouth.

You can also learn about a person during seemingly inconsequential situations. Let's say you're introduced to a person who seems genuinely nice, but has a reputation of being self-centered. When the two of you approach the door to a building, wait and see if she will open the door for you. You might be pushed aside as she walks in, or you might be given the proper respect and allowed to enter first.

SALES | THURSDAY

> Too often, everyday throwaways
> amount to easy fortunes lost.
> —*Dennis L. Prince*

E BAY HAS MADE SELLERS OUT OF MILLIONS OF PEOPLE worldwide who have never uttered terms like sales strategy or marketing advantage in their lives. Yet these amateurs have learned a lot about sales techniques by osmosis. Chief among these methods of eBay selling is finding new markets for their wares.

Dennis Prince cites the day he collected two bags of old videotapes to take to the dump in his book, *101 Ways to Boost Your Fortune on eBay.* Then he reconsidered—might someone be interested in the original *The Wicker Man* on VHS, or a vintage version of *Jaws*? He turned around and put them up for sale on eBay and netted $500 for what he had previous thought of as junk.

Use this lesson to look at your product from a new perspective. What if there's a market out there for which it wasn't originally intended? Are you limiting yourself by adhering to what the conventional strategists say is your market segment? And look at your current customers—is there another product or service in your line that could open a new revenue stream?

There are plenty of growth opportunities if you have a growth mentality. Don't throw sales opportunities away, assuming they might be a dead end. You may be throwing away a fortune.

LEADERSHIP | FRIDAY

The respect that leaders need to have for the people with whom (and through whom) they want to get something done has to be huge, and the people have to recognize it. It's all about loving your people. If you love your people, you'll do things that will help them to succeed.

—*Hyrum Smith*

GETTING SOMEONE TO DO WHAT YOU WANT NEEDN'T involve guilt or fear, according to Hyrum Smith, who founded Franklin Quest in the basement of his house. His company started with just twenty people and quickly grew to four thousand, ultimately merging with Steven Covey's Leadership Centers to form FranklinCovey.

Smith found leadership challenging at first. As his company grew bigger, Hyrum spent more and more time away from the office. He had to rely on employees completing their work without his personal supervision. He asked himself, "How do I create an atmosphere that says, 'Do it because you want to and not because you have to.'" He realized when people were emotionally committed to their job, they became self-motivated. To make his employees buy into the mission of FranklinCovey, Hyrum believed he had to be humble, show a bit of humor, and appreciate his employees. When people sense you genuinely care about them, they are more willing to go the extra mile for you. Guilt and fear don't have a chance against love.

ENTREPRENEUR | SATURDAY

A real entrepreneur is somebody who
has no safety net underneath them.
—*Henry Kravis*

HAVING A SAFETY NET IS NOT A BAD THING. IF YOU can afford one, you certainly should have one. But a true entrepreneur will follow through on a business idea even if there is no safety net. And, it is rare that the security of a safety net will always be present, or will always work when you need it.

Doing business without a safety net is actually the opposite of being more risky. Entrepreneurs often prepare much more thoroughly, thus decreasing the likelihood their business will take a face plant. They use their business planning and overall acumen as their safety net, instead of relying on money in their bank accounts.

Henry Kravis also brings to mind the idea that everyone approaches life in his or her own way. You don't need to apologize for doing whatever works best for you. Maybe your best friend does everything without a safety net—and she is successful at most everything she does. If you feel nervous or anxious without that safety net—go ahead and prepare yourself for a safer, softer landing. Neither way is wrong, but the right way is the one that works for you.

MANAGING PEOPLE | SUNDAY

> A problem well stated is a problem
> half solved. —*Charles F. Kettering*

CHARLES KETTERING, FOUNDER OF KETTERING UNIVERsity, knew a thing or two about solving problems. Before he came along, people started their cars with hand cranks and then sweated even more once inside their automobiles, which lacked air conditioning. Kettering helped fix those problems by inventing electric starters for cars and coolants for their air conditioners in the early twentieth century. He also patented an automobile lighting system, a device that treated sexually transmitted diseases, and an incubator for premature infants, among hundreds of other inventions.

Kettering was a practical visionary—and any manager worth his salary can learn from him. Leading a team or an organization requires foresight and goal setting. Achieving these goals starts with stating them clearly, Kettering would say. Explain exactly where you are heading and what the company expects of all employees. Use practical examples, not broad generalizations. When questions arise, find out what instigated these inquiries. When members of your organization identify real problems, applaud their assertiveness and stress to everyone that goals to be reached are, in essence, problems to be solved. This pragmatic approach simultaneously keeps everyone in your organization focused on the finish line.

MOTIVATION | MONDAY

> People often say that motivation doesn't last. Well, neither does bathing—that's why we recommend it daily. —*Zig Ziglar*

Z IG ZIGLAR HAD A HARDSCRABBLE CHILDHOOD GROWing up during the Depression as one of eleven children raised by a widowed mother in rural Alabama. His main focus during his early years was having enough food to eat. After serving in the Navy during WWII, he sold kitchenware door-to-door. After scraping by for a couple of years an executive took him aside and told him if he would only recognize his ability, he could become "a great one."

That was all Ziglar needed to hear. Soon he was the number two salesman at Wearever Aluminum. In fact, he was so successful as a salesman that eventually he took his new skills, not his pots, on the road. He became a full-time speaker and best-selling writer who trained other salesmen in the techniques he developed.

One of Ziglar's essential lessons is that it takes daily commitment to remain motivated. It's easy to achieve the early burst of enthusiasm, but later it's important to remind yourself why you're doing what you're doing and why you want to win. Bottom line: motivation will last indefinitely as long as you renew it regularly.

TEAM-BUILDING | TUESDAY

*A good plan, violently executed now,
is better than a perfect plan next week.*
—*Gen. George S. Patton*

G EN. GEORGE PATTON KNEW PLENTY ABOUT EXECUT-
ing a plan. He knew that during war, you may not be
around next week to execute a more perfect plan, so you
might as well go with a relatively good one as soon as possible. Still, the plans he executed tended to get the job done.
His staff was handpicked and, with their help, his military
prowess became legendary.

Patton's toughness led most outsiders to believe that his
subordinates despised him. His gruff exterior and macho
displays fueled the stereotype of a general on the edge of
sanity and on the edge of losing his troops.

But while Patton was tops in his field by all accounts, he
also had his faults. He was heavy handed with his militia: in
a time before Post Traumatic Stress Syndrome had been diag-
nosed, Patton was reprimanded for roughing up two soldiers
in a military hospital when he believed they were faking ill-
ness and displaying cowardice.

But upon his death in 1945 at age sixty from injuries
attained in an auto accident, almost twenty thousand soldiers
volunteered to serve as pallbearers for his casket. This genuine outpouring of admiration and respect proved Patton left
an impression on his soldiers that extended well beyond the
battlefield.

CAREER | WEDNESDAY

> Denial is one of the biggest reasons it's
> so difficult to motivate other people to
> change. We think we can enlighten them
> by telling them the facts, but they're in
> denial because they've already confronted
> the facts and they can't handle the facts.
>
> —*Alan Deutschman*

DENIAL IS A POWERFUL DEFENSE MECHANISM THAT THE brain uses to cope with unmanageable stress, or things out of your control, like global warming or nuclear holocaust. Denial, though, becomes harmful when we use it to gloss over very real personal problems, such as anger issues. In his book, *Change or Die,* author Alan Deutschman notes that it's impossible to be objective about what we are denying. "The reality is that even the smartest of us—the ones with the best educations, the sharpest, quickest minds, and the greatest abilities for digesting and analyzing loads of complex information—are likely to act this way."

Blowing up at underperforming employees might seem appropriate to you, but it is rarely an effective method to achieve higher productivity. Unfortunately, rationalizing bad behavior like this can cause real headaches for you. It's important to make sure that you are managing your stress so it won't become an issue holding you back from your career goals.

SALES | THURSDAY

For brands, like people, there is a time to live and a time to die. —*Al and Laura Ries*

"MARKETING IS BUILDING A BRAND IN THE MIND OF the prospect," Al Ries and his marketing firm partner (and daughter) Laura Ries write in their book, *The 22 Immutable Laws of Branding*. "If you can build a powerful brand you will have a powerful marketing program. If you can't, then all the advertising, fancy packaging, sales promotion and public relations in the world won't help you achieve your objective."

Powerful brands are all about emotion—what the customer or prospect feels about the brand—and no amount of sales skill is going to sell a brand if you have lost the customer's trust. Salespeople live and breathe their brand and integrate its spirit and value proposition into their presentation. But it's a mistake to step back and let your brand do the talking for you. Satisfaction and price are other integral elements in building a strong customer relationship.

Public fascination or fickleness will make or break your brand. Even if your product is a well-known part of the lexicon—like Xerox, Kleenex, Band-Aid, Jell-O, Q-Tip, Saran Wrap—it's your task to keep your approach fresh and put some zest back in your brand.

LEADERSHIP | FRIDAY

Nearly all men can stand adversity,
but if you want to test a man's character,
give him power. —*Abraham Lincoln*

WATCHING A TEMPER TANTRUM BY A TWO-YEAR-OLD is amusing for everyone but the child's parents. Drunk with power, toddlers abuse their parents with laser-sharp focus. Because they are unsure of how to get what they want, they routinely test the boundaries set for them. Some adults, unfortunately, never learned this lesson, choosing instead to abuse their position of authority for personal gain.

Abraham Lincoln earned the nickname "Honest Abe" because he possessed a high moral character, which fueled his commitment to ending slavery. Unfortunately, his life ended tragically because of his crusade.

Standing up for your beliefs against the tide of public opinion can be costly. Character is the motivation to do the right thing, even when nobody is watching. People constantly pressure leadership to make decisions where they must choose between exercising their power or behaving in an ethical way. When the news is full of business leaders routinely fudging profit reports and stealing from employee pension funds, it makes you wonder whether you can trust anyone. But if you let your strong moral compass guide you, you'll refrain from abusing your position of authority.

ENTREPRENEUR | SATURDAY

Nothing succeeds like the appearance
of success. —*Christopher Lasch*

WHO WOULD YOU BE MORE INCLINED TO DO BUSI-
ness with—the business that appears successful or
the one that looks like it's about to close up shop? Most consumers tend to go with a name brand or a sure thing when
all other things are equal. But as social critic Christopher
Lasch points out, unless a company is publicly traded, the
average consumer would have a hard time knowing whether
a company was in dire financial straits. How many times
have you let out a little gasp of surprise when you read a
headline about some huge company filing for bankruptcy or
laying off thousands of employees? To the average consumer,
these companies have always appeared successful. Yet, what
they were hiding was completely the opposite.

Sports coaches often encourage their players to act like
winners. Career coaches tell their clients to go to an interview dressed like they are ready to step into the job. People
who work at home are advised not to make important calls
dressed in their pajamas—dressing for success will make the
call more likely to result in a sale.

The psychological benefit of feeling successful is enormous. And who's to say you're not? Give yourself every edge
you can. And if things are going really badly, don't broadcast
your situation until you are ready to give up, and have a plan
in place to take care of your customers once you close shop.

MANAGING PEOPLE | SUNDAY

Nobody will ever win the battle of the sexes. There's just too much fraternizing with the enemy. —*Henry Kissinger*

YOU DON'T HAVE TO BE AN INTERNATIONAL STATESman like Henry Kissinger to understand the warning behind these words. In the corporate world, men and women work side by side every day. Managers, either men or women, who believe they are in any way superior to members of the opposite sex will quickly find out how limiting this idea can be.

Even managers cannot always help themselves when it comes to the simple laws of sexual attraction. If they know what's good for them, they'll separate those feelings from their professional responsibilities. Fraternizing, flirting, smiling, or joking may all be reasonable behaviors at happy hour, but they aren't always welcome on the job. In some cases, office romances are the awkward result. In other cases, fraternizing can be used to your advantage and help build strong working relationships. Try to assess the social climate in your office before you bring out your "fun side" in full force. And remember, the law says to treat everyone equally.

MOTIVATION | MONDAY

> How you think about a problem is more important than the problem itself—so always think positively. —*Norman Vincent Peale*

NORMAN VINCENT PEALE'S *POWER OF POSITIVE Thinking* was an instant bestseller when it was published in 1952 and has sold twenty-two million copies to date. Dr. Peale formulated a three-step process for positive thinking: the first step involves prescribed exercises, the second attaining divine power, and the last urges to eliminate negativity in your life.

When faced with a problem, it's natural for most of us to feel defeated or to feel negative. Problems inherently breed negativity. But unless you just arrived from Pluto, you've already heard that a negative attitude will never be compatible with attaining happiness and success. Get stuck in a negative groove, and negativity will radiate into everything you do.

Peale believed how you think about a problem is more important than the problem itself. Today, his philosophy has been translated into "thinking outside the box," which is nothing more than looking at things from a unique perspective. When you're able to do that, you can find new ways to resolve your problem. And, at the same time, your enthusiasm and positive attitude toward your job are reinvigorated. It speaks to your faith in yourself. If you're able to think positively—and eliminate negativity—good things are going to happen to you.

TEAM-BUILDING | TUESDAY

> Building a sense of community helps overcome the pervasive sense of alienation and distrust so prevalent in contemporary workplaces.
>
> —*Jeffrey Pfeffer*

T HE CONTEMPORARY WORKPLACE CAN BE A HOTBED OF deceit, lies, and negative energy. This leads to lots of wasted time as people sequester themselves in each other's offices and talk about the pitfalls of the company.

On the other hand, there is a positive, palpable dynamic when you walk into a company where the employees feel invested. One way to accomplish this is to communicate to all employees what is going on in the company.

Stanford University professor Jeff Pfeffer teaches that when bad things happen to your business, you are best to get one step ahead of the rumor mill. Don't deceive yourself into thinking that gossip isn't happening in your company—it is! Instead, stay ahead of the gossip mill by revealing what you can to as many people as possible. If there are things you can't reveal, say so—"This is what I can tell you. There is more to it than that, and I hope you will trust that I will tell you more when I can."

The main thing is to make people feel like their time and their life is of value to the company. When you feel like you are on the inside, you aren't as distrusting because you feel like you know what is going on.

CAREER | WEDNESDAY

$6,000 and it isn't even leather.
—*Cyn to Tess McGill,* Working Girl *(1988)*

B REAKING INTO A FIELD THAT REQUIRES SOCIAL SKILLS to match your business acumen is a great responsibility when you are starting out. From what to wear to what to order on a business lunch, it can all affect the speed it will take to move up the corporate ladder. Usually, that's where a mentor comes into play.

Tess McGill (played by Melanie Griffith in the movie *Working Girl*), with big hair and blue-collar friends (like Joan Cusack's Cyn, quoted above), could have used a playbook to fit in at her Wall Street job. After seeing a dress in her boss's closet for $6000, Tess realizes that moving up the ladder would mean more than a drastic make-over. As she transformed tacky into tailored, she alienated her old friends and family who thought she was "putting on airs."

While nobody recommends Tess McGill's drastic methods for career advancement that ensue as the plot unfolds, her willingness to makeover her wardrobe and hairstyle demonstrate that appearance does matter in the world of business. Analyze your self-image and make sure that it is in line with your company's culture. But take care not to overspend on a new wardrobe or change so much that your own mother might not recognize you.

SALES | THURSDAY

You don't get paid for the hour. You get paid for the value you bring to the hour.
—*Jim Rohn*

JIM ROHN MADE HIS FORTUNE IN DIRECT SALES AND became a millionaire at age thirty-one. He's since become a business coach and motivational speaker. His number one lesson for salespeople is that time is valuable.

Good salespeople have to develop perfect timing. Every phase of the sales process is important and in presenting each phase, time is of the essence. Perhaps the most blatant and anxiety-producing disruption of timing is when you offer an appointment and the prospect hesitates, saying something such as: "Listen, I don't want to waste your time or mine." Rapid-fire calculations on your part necessarily follow: Is the prospect really not interested or is he holding back because he thinks he can't afford it?

Moments like these are when you have to compute every formula you've ever learned about sales techniques. Should you pretend you didn't hear the prospect's protest and just go ahead with your pitch, or do you alter your offer on the spot, adjusting the terms to make it more attractive?

This is when you need to push forward into the "value" phase of your pitch. You have to be totally effective in this phase in order to save the sale. Later, you'll close the deal—but don't think about that now. Concentrate on the moment and use your well-honed techniques to maximize the opportunity.

LEADERSHIP | FRIDAY

In the world of work, concern that propels us to take responsibility for what needs doing translates into good organizational citizenship. —*Daniel Goleman*

P SYCHOLOGIST DANIEL GOLEMAN, AUTHOR OF *SOCIAL Intelligence: The New Science of Human Relationships,* knows that empathy, or concern for others, is a manifestation of social intelligence. If your company has a reputation as being "cut throat," it does not value empathy. For example, certain companies use layoffs to increase the price of the stock for the stockholders. Unfortunately, this comes at the expense of the workforce. The underlying message from leadership suggests that the company values the shareholders over the employees. This is never a good message—ultimately morale is affected, and productivity suffers.

Since people do not operate in a vacuum but take their lead from others, goodwill must come from the top echelons. You must promote empathy as a core value and not just some promotional stunt to foster a better public image when you are a company leader. Leaders who demonstrate integrity in their personal behavior and corporate actions promote goodwill among the rank and file. If you haven't been clear about your company values, now is the time to make an action plan. First, address past actions, and then slowly make changes. It all starts with you at the top—then others will get the message and follow your lead.

ENTREPRENEUR | SATURDAY

Respecting your relationship with
money, you see, is the key not only to
your security and independence, but
to your happiness as well. —*Suze Orman*

SUZE ORMAN HAS CERTAINLY LEARNED TO RESPECT HER
relationship with money—and she has made lots of it
advising others to do the same in books like her bestselling
9 Steps to Financial Freedom. She tells future entrepreneurs
that they have to have respect for money before they open a
business.

One time-tested way to see where you stand with money
is to track your spending every day for a month. Don't do
anything different from what you usually do—buy that $4
latte or the expensive jacket you have your eyes on—and see
just how careful or carefree you are with the money you've
worked so hard to earn.

At the end of a month, figure out all those things that
you could easily have done without. Then multiply that
times twelve to calculate roughly what you "waste" over a
year. Then divide that by your hourly wage and figure out
how many hours you would need to work to buy things that
are not exactly essential.

Starting up a business is not for the faint of financial
heart. Lack of operating capital is one of the main reasons a
start-up business fails within its first year or two. If you can
get your personal spending reigned in, your business will
surely fair better.

MANAGING PEOPLE | SUNDAY

> We haven't had big companies before
> that had that kind of ethic. I think we
> can be a positive force. —*Larry Page*

W HILE MANY COMPANIES ARE CUTTING POSITIONS
and removing coffee makers to save money, Google™
has done the opposite. In addition to the widely dispersed
$1,000,000/year compensation packages, the company offers
free gourmet lunches and lets people play volleyball, get a
massage, or take yoga.

If this sounds like a far-fetched plot from the movie,
Pleasantville, it isn't. Larry Page and his partner, Sergey Brin,
are determined to make corporate life at Google™ not only
profitable, but interesting. They have figured out how to
make employees happy. From the beginning, Page and Brin
felt strongly that a value-centered company would be a better place to work.

Creating a value-centered company that produces real
profits is a challenge in any era. Many people don't believe
that Google™ can sustain their corporate culture if they
grow too big. Page and Brin have wondered that themselves. Still, their plan is to nurture their people and continue to make Google™ a great place to work. By doing
that, they'll attract the brightest minds and make technological leaps in the industry. When it comes to managing
their people, Google™ has made a huge commitment to
enhancing the careers of their employees.

MOTIVATION | MONDAY

What is defeat? Nothing but education; nothing but the first step to something better. —*Wendell Phillips*

WENDELL PHILLIPS, BORN IN BOSTON IN 1811, WAS an American abolitionist who stopped practicing law to fight for human rights. His oratorical abilities were so convincing that he was known as "Abolition's Golden Trumpet." When the Civil War ended and African Americans finally gained the right to vote in 1870, Phillips did not return to his career. Instead, he shifted his attention to Native American and women's rights. He worked tirelessly to educate others and undoubtedly helped make this country a better place.

Wendell Phillips could not afford to dwell on defeats during his turbulent times, and he suffered many intellectual blows. Focusing on his goals, he did not brood over his mistakes or failures. Instead Phillips was wise enough—and strong enough—to view each setback as valuable educational experience that would help bring him a step toward achieving goals.

If you, too, can learn to turn your mistakes into life lessons, they'll benefit you in the long run. It takes a strong character to admit to mistakes, but mistakes make you who you are, and the more you know yourself, the closer you'll be to success and happiness.

TEAM-BUILDING | TUESDAY

> Look for intelligence and judgment and, most critically, a capacity to anticipate, to see around corners. Also look for loyalty, integrity, a high energy drive, a balanced ego and the drive to get things done.
>
> *—Gen. Colin Powell*

THE MORE TRAITS SUCH AS THOSE MENTIONED ABOVE that your team members possess, the better your team will be.

Intelligence and judgment are necessary for the ability to "see around corners." While you don't want someone always looking for the worst to happen, you do want your team members to be on the lookout for signs of trouble.

Loyalty almost goes without saying. Integrity is critical to the world's view of your company. Every single member of your team should work—and, indeed, live—with integrity.

A high energy drive allows new team members to keep up with the rest of the pack and work at whatever pace is set.

Finally, the team needs to be filled with people who are looking for ways to get things done, not reasons why they can't get done. Real team work means checking your ego at the door. It is not about the individual, it is about the team.

Perhaps your team needs other characteristics, but if you can fill these descriptions you will create a great group of workers to have on your side.

CAREER | WEDNESDAY

Don't expect others to defend you.
—*Anthony Parinello*

DONALD TRUMP'S SUCCESSFUL TELEVISION SERIES, *The Apprentice,* creates teams of individuals to work together. Generally, as the team takes shape, a clear leader emerges, along with legitimate team players, and at the bottom there's always a slacker, someone not interested in working with the team. If the team loses the challenge, the leader goes in front of "The Donald" and the board and explains what happened. Inevitably, the team leader blames the incompetence of the slacker. The slacker vehemently refuses to take the blame. The only way to get the truth is to listen to the story from the perspective of the other two team members. Yet, time after time, these two choose not to get involved. They don't come forward to defend either one of their teammates. They know staying neutral is their best strategy to look out for themselves.

Anthony Parinello learned that in business it's important to realize that, in the end, you have to rely on yourself. His book, *10 Secrets I Learned From the Apprentice,* examines how he realized there are plenty of times when you are left standing alone. Keep a paper trail of clear documentation about your actions so that you can defend yourself if necessary. If this happens, be ready to defend your actions, and not push the blame on someone else. Step up and take on the attack, and learn from your mistakes.

SALES | THURSDAY

> When you get to the end of your rope,
> tie a knot and hang on.
>
> —*Franklin Delano Roosevelt*

THE GREAT DEPRESSION CERTAINLY EXEMPLIFIED AN end–of-your rope situation. FDR surveyed his options and tied a brilliant knot, leading the country out of the Depression with the New Deal. He provided relief for the unemployed, helped the economy, and reformed the banking system. He helped the country recover from an economic disaster and adapt to the changing times.

Dark days in a sales career can feel like great depressions, but don't give up hope until you've examined what you still have to work with. Positive thinking, for example, is a tool you can use during these end-of-your-rope times. Positive thinking is grounded in optimism. Even if the facts say otherwise, and every sign you're getting may point to calamity down the road, think positively. Look around and see what your options are. For example, if you know that your sales technique is solid, look for alternative markets.

On the other hand: everyone can benefit from a little attitude adjustment. Examine your attitude toward each and every prospect. Is customer nonresponsiveness or resistance making you crazy? Back off and consider: have you offered everything you can to solve a problem? When you meet your customers halfway, you both win. You get the sale and the customer gets the benefits.

LEADERSHIP | FRIDAY

> Since love and fear can hardly exist together, if we must choose between them, it is far safer to be feared than loved. —*Niccolo Machiavelli*

MACHIAVELLI'S TAKE-NO-PRISONERS APPROACH TO governing, outlined in his famous book *The Prince,* is a provocative treatise, espousing the viewpoint that a ruler mustn't worry about unethical behavior if it is necessary to remain in power.

Misconstrued, Machiavelli's theories give people an excuse to behave badly. In Machiavelli's defense, during the Renaissance period, provincial governments were completely unstable and constantly being overthrown by warring factions. Rulers usually faced a certain degree of built-in hostility from their newly conquered subjects. While Machiavelli believed a leader must do whatever is necessary to retain power, he also maintained that one should at least try to cultivate positive relationships with those under his command. However, Machiavelli concluded that when push came to shove, the dictator with the strongest hand would survive the well-loved king.

A leader of a company must walk a fine line between being nice and being tough. Whether you are facing a union strike or a hostile takeover, if you can't maintain control over the situation you can't effectively run the company. Rather than being loved, Machiavelli would want you to show others why you are in charge.

ENTREPRENEUR | SATURDAY

> Brand loyalty and employee loyalty are
> both real assets, even if not reflected on
> balance sheets and income statements.
> —*Jeffrey Pfeffer*

THE DAYS OF LONG-TERM EMPLOYEES ARE RARELY NUR-
tured in contemporary business. Instead, young professionals jump from job to job seeking a promotion or a pay
raise if their company doesn't give them what they want in
the time frame they want. And the highest-paying jobs are
often the first cut when business shows a lengthy slowdown
and costs need to be trimmed.

Business, in general, would fare better going back to a
loyalty-based model. However, employee loyalty needs to be
two-way. Employees need to know that when the chips are
down, you won't forget who helped bring the company up
in the first place. You need to foster an environment where
loyal employees will be willing to make sacrifices to help a
loyal employer.

Brand loyalty needs to be bi-directional as well. If you
want customers to stick to your brand, you need to stick by
them. Learn what they like and don't like about your product
or service. The Coca-Cola Company found this out abruptly
when it tried introducing New Coke to the market in 1985.
Customers hated it and did not hesitate to let their feelings
be known. Coca-Cola dropped New Coke and brought back
the original recipe, to which their loyal customers flocked,
driving sales up higher than ever before.

MANAGING PEOPLE | SUNDAY

> Never tell people how to do things.
> Tell them what to do and they will
> surprise you with their ingenuity.
> —*Gen. George S. Patton*

M ANY MANAGERS MAKE THEIR JOBS INORDINATELY difficult by assuming too much responsibility. Worried that underlings don't know as much, aren't as talented, lack the same motivation, or simply don't share their passion, these managers refuse to delegate effectively. They take on eighty hours of work every week only to see their jobs, families, marriages, and happiness suffer. And when they do delegate, they often hover over their employees, explaining in tedious detail exactly how to perform in hopes of forestalling the errors that the managers assume will occur.

During World War II, General Patton liberated Morocco and Sicily and overran the German army. While many historians view the general as an insufferable and cruel megalomaniac, his knack for teaching and inspiring his troops was legendary. He was a master at identifying a goal and then drawing the best from his soldiers in the push to achieve it. Patton also wasn't averse to getting his hands dirty. He literally led his men into battle, getting shot along the way. But Patton didn't micromanage each gunshot. He didn't have time, and neither do the people in charge of today's companies.

To draw the best out of an employee, cede appropriate responsibility to him and then set him free to plan, revise, learn, thrive, and conquer.

MOTIVATION | MONDAY

The road to success is always
under construction. —*Anthony Robbins*

ONCE YOU'VE SET YOUR GOALS, DON'T MAKE THE mistake of assuming that the road to realizing your carefully crafted plan for success is going to be smoothly paved. Life doesn't work that way. Instead, you'll probably be faced with a street full of potholes. This is why you have to anticipate those potholes and construction signs. Learning from and adapting to change is part of the journey.

Tony Robbins, the powerful motivational speaker and bestselling author, knows full well about a journey that involves changing and adapting. First, his family name isn't even Robbins, it's Mahavorick. And he was not always the buff presence he is today—there was a time when he was overweight and depressed. But he got motivated (by another motivational speaker) and developed a unique neurolinguistic program that is the basis of his philosophy and teachings. His famous fire-walking seminars teach participants the strategies of control: mind over body and logic rules over pain.

His message is to always keep your wits about you. When unexpected obstacles block your path, use your head. Don't let a little thing like a hot coal burn your feet. Keep walking, with your goal of completing the path uppermost in your mind. Later, you can look back and say, "Ouch! Boy, that hurt . . . but it's over, and I won!"

TEAM-BUILDING | TUESDAY

> Most people's natural inclination is to judge themselves according to their best qualities while they measure others by their worst. —*John C. Maxwell*

HOW OFTEN HAVE YOU HEARD SOMEONE CRITICIZE another when you know that they have the same bad habits themselves? As a team leader, it's best to foster an atmosphere that isn't judgmental.

For example, just because someone is late all the time doesn't mean you have to talk about it endlessly when she isn't around, or even when she is. If a team member gets into a habit of being late for meetings, after the second or third time you should address it directly with that person. The team shouldn't waste time and build negative energy by grousing about it before the person gets there, or even later in a smaller group. Make it clear to the person when she finally does arrive that she is late and that being late is unacceptable. The offender should be put on notice that if the poor behavior continues there will be the consequences for being late.

Don't let meetings devolve into a place where people talk about others viciously. Unfortunately, it's a part of human nature to try to pump oneself up by bringing someone else down. But this personality trait isn't attractive at home or in the office. It's your job as a team leader to squash this behavior before it grows out of control.

CAREER | WEDNESDAY

> Debt brings on enough risk to offset any advantage that could be gained through leverage of debt. —*Dave Ramsey*

WOULD YOU GO TO WORK FOR A MAJOR PRESENTA-tion for the CEO half-dressed, starving, and unprepared? No, you wouldn't. You would plan ahead.

But how many people spend that same amount of time and effort preparing their financial future? The average American family has $11,000 in credit card debt, a car payment, a student loan, and a mortgage. And less than 1 percent are saving for a rainy day. These statistics show that many smart people don't have a clue about managing money. In *The Total Money Make-Over,* Dave Ramsey focuses on debt as a destructive financial position. He points out that the stress of having various interest payments has an adverse affect on your mental health, as well as your long-term financial goals.

Just as you have to organize your professional life, you need to apply the same discipline to your financial life. Stop running up your Visa tab, and focus on getting yourself and your family out of debt. See if you can forecast paying off your debts within a year. If you can't, get professional help to put you on a budget and teach you how to pay down your bills without accruing more debt.

SALES | THURSDAY

*Good luck is nothing but preparedness
and opportunity coming together.*
—*Deepak Chopra, M.D.*

I S IT LUCK WHEN YOU GET A NEW BUNCH OF CLIENTS through a referral or when you close a contract so complicated that you walk off with the Deal-of-the-Year Award? No, it's not luck. Rather, it's you doing your job like the professional you are, working hard, putting in quality time and providing top service. Thanks to your own networking and contacts, you're able to find new prospects and overcome countless obstacles and challenges to close a tough deal. When preparedness and opportunity come together, everyone can say you're lucky—but you know it wasn't luck that got you there.

Deepak Chopra's book, *The Seven Spiritual Laws of Success,* contains many pearls for the sales professional. Dr. Chopra has written extensively on spirituality, success, and mind-body medicine. His first spiritual law of success is the Law of Pure Potentiality. When you know who you really are, you are capable of infinite creativity, constantly aware of your desires and purpose in life. This is the preparedness you seek to carry with you in sales. So it follows that if you are not prepared for opportunities, good luck is not going to happen.

LEADERSHIP | FRIDAY

> Be civil to all; sociable to many;
> familiar with few; friend to one;
> enemy to none. —*Ben Franklin*

A S DAILY LIFE FLITS BY AT THE SPEED OF LIGHT, SOCIETY is being tested now more than ever. With the hallmarks of civility slowly dying, the boundaries that required us to use common courtesy and politeness have dissolved, giving rise to unbecoming behaviors that used to be held in check. Honestly, what would Ben Franklin make of all this!

If you think business relationships seem more fragile than ever, you're right. That's why you must set high moral standards for yourself. By keeping your boundaries clear, you can easily navigate through the different social scenes that are required of a modern professional.

For example, many people mistakenly believe that their co-workers are their friends, and expect their bosses to be their parents. Don't misconstrue the time you spend with co-workers as a substitute for building lasting and deep relationships elsewhere. These people didn't choose you as a friend; they have to talk to you everyday as part of their jobs. Don't confuse spilling your guts over last night's argument with your spouse for appropriate office conversation. Limit the number of people who know about your intimate life by keeping your personal life to yourself, especially when you're the one in charge.

ENTREPRENEUR | SATURDAY

> Any complex activity, if it is to be
> carried on with any degree of virtuosity,
> calls for appropriate gifts of intellect and
> temperament. If they are outstanding
> and reveal themselves in exceptional
> achievements, their possessor is called a
> genius. —*Carl von Clausewitz*

MOST ENTREPRENEURIAL ACTIVITIES ARE COMPLEX.
Even the smallest retail store requires thinking
through all sorts of details. For instance, you need to decide
on the best location and negotiate the best terms on a lease.

But, before deciding on a final location, you must analyze
the market and figure out how to reach that market.

The physical retail shop then needs everything from display units to throw rugs. And of course, the shop will have
to be filled with product. Decisions must be made about
which products are best for the store and how many and
what variety you need.

Next, you must make back-office decisions: professionals need to be hired to help with bookkeeping, taxes, and
legal concerns. You will also have to hire staff.

To get your store off the ground, you need to be a people-
person, a number-cruncher, and an opportunity-seeker all at
the same time. It's no wonder Clausewitz reminds us that
even smart and brave people need to keep a level head and
focus on the details.

MANAGING PEOPLE | SUNDAY

> In a hierarchy every employee tends
> to rise to his level of incompetence.
> —*Laurence J. Peter*

T HE PETER PRINCIPLE, DEFINED IN LAURENCE J. PETER'S seminal 1969 book, teaches that competent people get promoted into jobs they're not ready for, especially management jobs. Soon they appear to be incompetent—through no fault of their own—and the whole organization suffers.

The subtitle of Peter's book tells it all: *Why Things Always Go Wrong.* Today, highly effective companies have learned from this book and try to avoid the Peter Principle. Before promoting employees, it should now be common practice to train all employees to step up to the more difficult work that awaits them at the next level. Companies need to prepare their people for success.

Sometimes implementing this strategy means actually holding back ambitious workers until they're ready. Naturally, these workers may resent the delay. Competent managers address these concerns directly, explaining that their job is to help workers succeed and not fail. Competent managers also refuse to believe the Peter Principle is inevitable, despite how ingrained it has become. They don't promote unprepared people, because they realize their organization can't afford that kind of incompetence. If the Peter Principle seems inescapable in your company, do whatever you can to put a stop to it.

MOTIVATION | MONDAY

*One who sits between two chairs
may easily fall down.* —*Russian proverb*

WHETHER IT INVOLVES A MULTIMILLION-DOLLAR DEAL, an international merger, or something as mundane as choosing one stationery supplier over another, good opportunities can be lost by indecision. Business literature is full of great deals that have been lost by indecision. Usually, the problem was that one key player was unable to take a big risk.

While you can perform a balancing act, like straddling two chairs at once, the performance can't last for long. Soon you are going to hit a point when the crack between the chairs widens and it's too late—you're going to take a fall. Instead of trying to maintain the status quo, you need to create action. And if you react too slowly, you're going to lose ground.

Train yourself to act swiftly and confidently when faced with important decisions. Sure, you'll make mistakes, and your co-workers or your boss may even disagree with you. But if you are prepared to accept the consequences if it doesn't work out, you'll be able to relish the positive consequences of your actions.

As another (English) proverb says, "He who hesitates is lost." Take a stand. Action leads to success.

TEAM-BUILDING | TUESDAY

> I always tried to turn every disaster
> into an opportunity. —*John D. Rockefeller*

ONE WAY TO TURN DISASTER INTO OPPORTUNITY IS TO simply show clients or customers how well your company stands up for its product or service. It is amazing how many times a customer will come back to a company despite having received a bad shipment, a late delivery, or the wrong color order if the company goes the extra mile to fix the mistake.

The best-case scenario is that not only will you have a loyal customer, but you will also have a customer who relates her experience to someone else. What could be better than to earn great buzz about your company after you took care of someone when something went wrong?

Make customer service your number one priority. Often people just want to be heard or have something fixed. Remember: they wanted your product to begin with, and they still want it—they just want it a particular way.

Most successful businesses realize that every department that deals with the outside world is an offshoot of customer service. Sales, marketing, shipping, and even accounting need to put on their best business face with every interaction. This way, you can turn lots of disasters into opportunities.

CAREER | WEDNESDAY

Many people do not have a clear idea
about what is important to them.
—*Anthony Robbins*

I F YOU'VE EVER TAKEN A JOB OR COMMITTED TO AN OBLI-
gation that didn't seem right, but did it anyway, you're in
good company. It's not hard to make decisions for the wrong
reasons. Sometimes situations or people are not what they
appear to be, and, before you know it, you've been hood-
winked. Other times, circumstances change, affecting the
outcome. In *Unlimited Power,* Anthony Robbins writes that
one of the keys to successful decision making is to have clar-
ity of values: "Our beliefs about what we are and what we
can be precisely determine what we will be."

Amazingly, many of our beliefs simply aren't true.
Rather, they are modeled after influential people in our
lives, such as our parents. If you were told as a young child
that you were bad at math, you probably think that you
would stink as an accountant. The good news is, at any
given time you can change your beliefs and decide what is
most important to you. If you want to run your own company, it's as simple as believing that you can do it. Define
what your beliefs are. Write a list of those things that matter most to you and keep it close. This will remind you of
the hidden potential that resides in you, and make your next
career move that much better.

SALES | THURSDAY

> Content is a cause, an idea, trend, or skill—the unique subject matter on which you are an authority. —*Keith Ferrazzi*

YOU ALWAYS NEED TO BE AN EXPERT ON WHATEVER YOU sell. You're the ultimate authority on every aspect of your product/service, and your confidence in it enables you to sell it like nobody else. To get to this level of authority you have to believe in it—and believe in your product or service as strongly as you do any good cause. Content is, in effect, what fuels your passion about your product or service.

The combination of passion and content in any pitch is sales dynamite. Your passion and enthusiasm needs to be contagious in order to grow your business. Keith Ferrazzi, labeled as the "world's most connected individual," preaches that without content that you truly believe in, you can't share it effectively with the rest of the world. Indeed, content can become your gold mine and your calling card: the more you develop your communication skills to share what you know, the more contacts you'll make. Your own customers will even network your ideas for you.

Naturally, content will change over the course of a career. Your company will change its line or direction, or you'll change the company you choose to work for. But the skills you gain in presenting content can be taken from job to job and from one product or service to the next. Keeping content fresh and up-to-date ensures your marketability, no matter where you land.

LEADERSHIP | FRIDAY

> Resentment is like drinking poison and
> waiting for the other person to die.
> —*Carrie Fisher*

NEGATIVE OR DIFFICULT SITUATIONS OCCUR ALL THE time in business, and anger is a normal and even healthy reaction. However, letting anger run rampant throughout your day, and your workplace, just shows your colleagues that you aren't in control.

Actress Carrie Fisher is simply saying that if your anger metastasizes into resentment, it can destroy your sense of well-being. Cognitive therapy teaches how you can control your negative thoughts by redirecting them in an objective manner. When you start to feel anger or resentment toward others, try to clear your mind and force yourself to make an analytical assessment of the situation.

To avoid turning anger or frustration into resentment, acknowledge your feelings. Don't push them aside or punish yourself. Next, accept your feelings, but try to express them in a productive way. Expressing your anger at the appropriate person at the appropriate time is the most effective way to manage it. Speaking in terms of "I" instead of "you" keeps the focus on how you felt you were treated and shifts the conversation to a more productive conclusion. Lastly, forgiving and forgetting go a long way toward reestablishing a healthy equilibrium for yourself and your office.

ENTREPRENEUR | SATURDAY

> If general perception changes from
> seeing the glass as half full to seeing
> it as half empty, there are major
> innovative opportunities. —*Peter Drucker*

H OW MANY TIMES IN YOUR LIFE HAVE YOU BEEN chastised for taking the negative perspective? Peter Drucker believed that the entrepreneur must look at the half-empty glass and figure out what is missing that makes the glass half empty. Businesses have long been created by an entrepreneur sitting back and thinking about which need is currently not being met.

In the mid-nineties, grocery stores realized they were giving away business to the take-out food market. People were leaving work and stopping by the Chinese restaurant or the pizza shop on their way home to pick up dinner. Who had the time or energy to work all day, shop for groceries on the way home, cook a meal, and clean up after? Take-out typically meant a wholesome, hot meal, often with leftovers for tomorrow's lunch.

But the grocery business came to the conclusion that they could also satisfy the need for quality, ready-to-eat meals. Higher-end stores began installing pizza ovens and offering warm meals—and while you're at these stores, it's convenient to snag a carton of milk, eggs, cereal, or whatever else you might be out of at home.

The world never runs out of needs—imagined or real— to fill.

MANAGING PEOPLE | SUNDAY

Encourage your people to be committed
to a project rather than just be involved
in it. —*Richard Pratt*

THE WORD "COMMITMENT" HAS TURNED INTO BUSINESS jargon, a buzzword whose meaning has been lost through overuse and dilution. You want your people to be committed, to "buy in," so that their passion will drive up the energy level of the organization and produce stellar results. But employees are rarely committed to the degree you'd hope. It's not that they lack the requisite passion to feel committed (or that they aren't paid enough). Rather, Australian business mogul Richard Pratt believes that most of the time they simply don't understand the goal or strategy to which they should be committed. A staggering 95 percent of all employees are largely in the dark about strategy, according to research from Harvard Business School.

While encouraging employees to be committed is important, the encouragement will fail if it's simply rah-rah blather. Experienced employees see through this rhetoric in seconds. Instead, encouragement must also include a crystal-clear explanation of the company's adopted strategy, as well as answers to all employee questions. And this approach is even more important if the work on the table is a one-off project, the kind of job that is successfully done when the people involved are fully aware of the goals and how to achieve them. If you offer them substantive and valuable encouragement, commitment is sure to follow.

MOTIVATION | MONDAY

The average American millionaire realizes significantly less than 10 percent of his net worth in annual income.

—*Thomas J. Stanley, William D. Danko*

MOST PEOPLE THINK THAT ONCE YOU BECOME A MILlionaire all your worries will be over.

Stanley and Danko, authors of the bestselling business classic, *The Millionaire Next Door,* conducted a twenty-year study of how people become wealthy in America and found some surprising results. Annual income does not translate to net worth automatically. Smart entrepreneurs use their income to give their company the resources it needs to grow. The average millionaire then looks for ways to decrease income, pay lower taxes, and use what money is left over to increase net worth.

A story is related in their book about a Texan who had done so well in the business of rebuilding diesel engines that he was taking on British partners. The Brits flew to Texas to meet him and were rather taken aback by his ten-year-old car, his worn jeans, and his modest home in a lower-middle-class neighborhood. In fact, on meeting him, they thought he was one of the company's truck drivers. Then he showed them his spreadsheets, and they were blown away.

Besides hard work, accumulating wealth requires discipline and sacrifice, and that might mean living below your means. Keep your eye on the prize and don't be influenced by keeping up with the Joneses.

TEAM-BUILDING | TUESDAY

> Yesterday is history, tomorrow
> is a mystery, today is a gift.
> —*Eleanor Roosevelt*

I N THIS AUSPICIOUS QUOTE, ELEANOR ROOSEVELT ELO-
quently captures the Buddhist concept of living in the
moment. She knew you couldn't change history, and you
couldn't control tomorrow. We all know that in this day and
age, many feel uncertain that tomorrow will even come.
Eleanor Roosevelt knew how to live with both disappoint-
ment and triumph, and she will always be remembered for
her stoic attitude in the face of adversity.

Today is the gift you know about. Encourage your team to
use today and not to dwell on the past or plan too far into the
future. If the numbers were bad last month, think about what
you can do this minute to make the numbers better next time
around. Have them concentrate on the project at hand instead
of worrying if you will score another lucrative deal.

Instead, think about now. If the sale you hoped for
didn't go through, concentrate on the next sale you might
work. Don't regale your team with speeches about last
month's failures or next month's projections. Give your team
the gift of living in the moment. And let them go do it.

CAREER | WEDNESDAY

Your verbal IQ illustrates your business judgment. —*Roberta Roesch*

S ARCASM, INSIDE JOKES, AND SMIRKING ARE USUALLY shared in good fun, but in the work world these things may be considered highly inappropriate—just ask Don Imus. Professionals must have even better communication skills than they've needed in the past as the work force diversifies and cultures collide.

Roberta Roesch describes this phenomenon in terms of Verbal IQ. In her book, *Smart Talk,* she shows how successful business people grasp the importance of developing their Verbal IQ, which is measured by how well you use words to convey your thoughts and abilities. The goal is to project a positive self-image at all times. For example, verbally losing your cool when things go wrong in the office is an example of low Verbal IQ.

Roesch gives some handy tricks and tips to immediately increase your Verbal IQ. To soften any listener, your message should be preceded with words or phrases that show you are considerate of the listener. To soften the blow of criticism, start a sentence with "It is my understanding . . ." To deal with a conflict, you might say, "I know that we disagree, however . . ." And keep your offensive thoughts towards the opposite sex, other races, and religious affiliations to yourself.

SALES | THURSDAY

> A huge number of decision-makers
> use voice mail to screen virtually all
> their calls. —*Stephan Schiffman*

A LOT OF PEOPLE WHO DO COLD CALLING CONSIDER voice mail to be an obstacle. But cold-calling expert Stephan Schiffman's attitude is: Why let it stop you? Why hand over those customers to the competition because a machine answers? If you don't leave a message in voice mail, you may be damaging potential business.

However, it is not a good idea to leave ten messages on a new contact's voice mail. This can undermine a relationship before it begins. Instead of making multiple calls to the same voice mail, you should be cold-calling other prospects. Don't waste anyone's time with multiple messages.

The situation changes, however, once you've established contact with a human voice—you are now talking to a live prospect. From that point forward, it's entirely acceptable to leave follow-up messages on voice mail.

Lots of salespeople prefer leaving a compact, professional message on a decision maker's voice mail. Assuming you have perfected your pitch, your charm and professional skills must be at their best in that message. When the contact calls back, you can talk freely knowing you have her total attention because the return call is completely on her terms.

Another plus for cold calling to voice mail is that you can leave a message anytime, 24/7, which gives you a chance to work from home if you have some free time.

LEADERSHIP | FRIDAY

> As a top leader, you have the power the
> way nobody else does to create a positive
> leadership culture where potential leaders
> flourish. If you create that environment,
> then people with leadership potential will
> learn, gain experience and come into
> their own. —*John C. Maxwell*

GETTING YOUR DRIVER'S LICENSE IS A MILESTONE IN
everyone's life. It represents one more step toward
independence. However, before it can happen, white-knuck-
led parents devote their time to teaching their kids how to
drive. Even after their kids have been driving awhile, parents continue to coach them as they navigate the perils of
the road.

Developing the future leaders of a company is no different. Finding the next generation of talent often takes a
backseat to the everyday running of the show. While it's
currently in vogue for companies to say they value their people and offer token leadership programs, most never do any
real planning for the future. According to John C. Maxwell
in his book, *The 360 Leader,* leaders need to make long-term
commitments to outstanding employees and make sure that
they fully develop their potential. For example, Maxwell
writes that many bosses delegate tasks instead of facilitating
leadership opportunities to qualified managerial candidates.
Great leaders will seriously invest in the development of the
next generation.

ENTREPRENEUR | SATURDAY

> Subtlety and modesty are appropriate
> for nuns and therapists, but if you're
> in business, you'd better learn to speak
> up and announce your significant
> accomplishments to the world—nobody
> else will. —*Donald Trump*

D ONALD TRUMP'S ACCOMPLISHMENTS AS A SUCCESS-
ful real estate tycoon are far from fraudulent. He resurrected his career countless times from near disaster,
which is no small task for anyone. So, this quote is no surprise, as humility is not a quality readily associated with
Donald Trump.

He's not wrong, however. You do need to sing your own
praises, making sure both your customers and suppliers
know how good business is going. But you can learn to
announce your significant accomplishments to the world
while retaining a hint of humbleness and still get the
desired effect. One way is to use statistics—for example,
"Ninety-five percent of survey respondents said our widgets
outlasted any others that they had used." This statement is
more modest than saying, "My widgets are the greatest ever
produced, and anyone who doesn't think so is an idiot!"

Leave the sensational statements for the media, or better
yet, collect them from all your satisfied clients. When you
need a hit of hyperbole, talk to "The Donald." He'll be
happy to tell you all how fabulous he is whenever he gets
the chance.

MANAGING PEOPLE | SUNDAY

I handle gossip one way. I fire the person.
—*Dave Ramsey*

COMPANIES THAT TOLERATE GOSSIP ARE IN BIG TROUBLE. When employees entertain gossip, they aren't doing their job. There is usually one troublemaker in every department who volunteers to "officially" disseminate the "unofficial" news of the day.

The worst possible tactic is to ignore gossip, hoping that it will go away. Gossip can ruin company morale by spreading misinformation that can trickle out to the streets and damage the company's reputation. Today, as bogus law suits fill the courts, a disgruntled employee can turn around and sue the company if he feels his reputation was slandered at the office.

According to Dave Ramsey, whose books, speeches, and radio show preach self-discipline in personal finance, gossip happens when someone is frustrated with another person but feels that alerting management is futile. Sometimes this is because the boss doesn't adequately address problems, while other times the management just thrives on the controversy.

As a manager, you have to prove you are open and willing to listen to employee problems before they become "the word on the street." If you can address the problem, you can build an atmosphere of trust in your organization. If the problem directly relates to another person in the office, you need to be strong enough to address the issue with everyone involved.

MOTIVATION | MONDAY

It takes a long time to bring excellence to maturity. —*Publilius Syrus*

MANY OF US HAVE BOUGHT INTO THE FANTASY OF becoming an overnight success. We want it all to happen now.

Sometimes, your head is bursting with ideas, yet your career track isn't keeping pace with your perception of your talents. You may be past the initial entry-level post, yet you still have a supervisor or a manager above you whose job you covet because you know you can do it better.

Slow down. Give yourself time to learn everything you can in this period. Realize this is a golden opportunity to make money and learn your trade. For hundreds of years, apprenticeships have been a time-honored tradition. Indeed, Publilius Syrus, an Assyrian slave in Italy in the first century BC, served an apprenticeship of sorts with a master who educated him and became his mentor. Publilius's wit and talent were so remarkable that his master freed him. He became a writer of maxims like the one here.

Maybe you feel like a slave yourself on some days, groaning, "This career track is taking too long!" But when you start thinking like that, change your focus. Look at the larger picture and realize where you are now and what it's going to take to get where you want to be. You're not likely to become president of the company overnight.

If you want to be the best at your job, you need to mature in it. Excellence only comes with time.

TEAM-BUILDING | TUESDAY

Winning teams have players who make things happen. —*John C. Maxwell*

W E ALL CAN THINK OF TIMES WHEN WE APPRECIATED the one person on the team who just got the job done. When the company car broke down, he was the one who took control. When the projected numbers weren't making sense, the go-to guy picked up the phone and got clarification from the finance department.

Find these people and stack your team with them. Then when you ask them to go the extra mile you won't have to worry about task completion. Better still, you won't have to do it yourself because you know it will be taken care of.

When you are lucky enough to have these get-it-done people on your team, let them do what they do best. Don't request that they work on a report about how a certain widget is used, and then, before they finish, tell them what you found. People with a track record of making it happen despise doing double work. They want to find out the answers themselves.

Let these employees act as role models for other people who insist on jumping through hoops before they take on a task. Sooner or later, they'll learn: it's best just to dive right in.

CAREER | WEDNESDAY

> Ambition is a result of self-direction
> and self-direction is one of the six
> key principles necessary for building
> ambition. —*Jim Rohn*

MANY PEOPLE HAVE GREAT AMBITIONS, BUT LACK THE knowledge necessary to achieve them. How we choose to act, walk, talk, dress, and who we associate with—our self-expression—defines our true ambitions despite what we tell others. Motivational speaker Jim Rohn believes that finding the right direction or method to pursue your ambitions will dramatically affect your success rate.

Let's say your goal is to become the CFO of the company, but instead of taking the leadership class you need to get a supervisor position, you spend your nights playing in a band. No matter how much you practice or hang out in clubs, this is a not a direction that many successful CFOs have taken. Or, you might need to rethink the placement of your next tattoo, and be more realistic about how your choices are affecting your goals.

Choosing the right direction is paramount for realizing your ambition. By answering the question—"Is everything I'm doing now honestly helping me get where I need to go?"—you'll have a better picture of what needs to change, so that you can get back on the path to following your dreams.

SALES | THURSDAY

The smartest marketers profit from
protecting their customer's privacy,
not violating it. —*Evan I. Schwartz*

E VAN SCHWARTZ IS AN EXPERT ON THE INTERNET. IN
*Webonomics: Nine Essential Principles for Growing Your
Business on the World Wide Web,* he highlights informative
sales trends to profit any business.

Even if you don't actively sell over the Web, maintaining an Internet presence is virtually mandatory for most companies and/or their sales divisions. Keeping pace with the evolving technology of the Internet can make the difference between whether your marketing will succeed or fail online.

Security is the technology watchword today in Internet commerce strategies. With privacy issues and identity theft uppermost in users' minds, it's not only prudent but smart for a business to take its customers' concerns seriously.

Your Web site should highlight your ethical commitment to privacy. Spell it out clearly so that you won't violate anyone's privacy by sharing information with nonaffiliated third parties, and state that electronic safeguards are in place to protect the customer's security. A reticent prospect will be a lot more confident after receiving these assurances.

A breach in Web site security threatens not only your customer's personal identity; it will affect your company's bottom-line.

LEADERSHIP | FRIDAY

> You can't build a strong corporation
> with a lot of committees and a board
> that has to be consulted at every turn.
> You have to be able to make decisions
> on your own. —*Rupert Murdoch*

RUPERT MURDOCH HAS MADE A CAREER OUT OF HIGH-stakes business opportunities. No wonder people love to hate him. He believes that, even though collective decision making will always have its place in the business world, a leader needs to know when it's appropriate to consult others for advice and when to follow his own instincts.

A great team can accomplish great things. You should strive to assemble the best team possible for your organization, but this doesn't mean abdicating the responsibility for providing a vision. When controversial decisions need to be made, a leader needs a strong sense of self to push her ideas through and make them realities. When Murdoch was looking for business opportunities on the Internet, he picked a relatively unknown manager of a small Internet division of his company to spearhead the project. Ross Levinsohn was given carte blanche to do what he wanted and started the Fox Interactive division from the ground up. Before moving on from the company, Levinsohn increased its value by billions of dollars. Clearly, as Murdoch's track record proves, making decisions on your own and sticking to those decisions has merit.

ENTREPRENEUR | SATURDAY

> Nobody talks of entrepreneurship as
> survival, but that's exactly what it is
> and what nurtures creative thinking.
> —*Anita Roddick*

ANITA RODDICK WAS A BUSINESS SURVIVOR. SHE USED her fundamental instinct to be creative and become a pioneer in environmentally sound business practices long before such practices were in vogue. In fact, Roddick is partly responsible for the whole "going green" business movement. She opened her Body Shop stores in England to sell beauty products that were made of natural ingredients, sold in reusable containers, and labeled with handmade labels. The Body Shop soon became a symbol of environmentally friendly cosmetics. It grew into an incredibly successful franchise business, and Roddick's stores in Europe and the United States were hugely profitable for decades.

Roddick had a great ability to think creatively as she fought for her business to survive. She encouraged recycling of containers early on simply because the company did not have enough containers for the products. She also packaged her lotions and potions in several different sizes to give the appearance of having more products in her line than she did.

Although Dame Anita Roddick died in 2007 of a brain aneurysm, she leaves a legacy of forward-thinking entrepreneurship whose influence spans the globe.

MANAGING PEOPLE | SUNDAY

*Much of our language is nothing more
than wild generalization and assumption.*
—*Anthony Robbins*

TONY ROBBINS DOESN'T BELIEVE IN USING GENERALIZA-
tions, qualifiers, and universal phrases. They might
make you feel good, but the truth is they get in the way of
effective communication and decision making.

Let's say your goal is to unearth the roots of an office
conflict and then make sure it never happens again. One
deputy wants to spend a fortune on a marketing plan with
proof-positive results from the past, results so good they are
sure to pay for the plan three times over. Another deputy
wants to deemphasize the marketing plan so that deserving
lower-tier people can get bigger raises. Neither deputy can
see the other's point of view, leading to some nasty arguments. If you try refereeing with a statement such as "Maybe
we all want the same thing," you will never uncover the real
problem, which may be envy, disrespect, a slight from the
past, or something even more personal.

Instead, Robbins suggests you ask the deputies who,
what, where, when, and how questions—therefore giving
up any assumptions and generalizations in hopes of getting
to truth. Once the facts are on the table, apologies and
understanding will flow freely, not to mention compromise
and cooperation. Soon, the conflict will be solved and the
tools to root out future conflicts will be in place.

MOTIVATION | MONDAY

No matter where you are today, remind yourself daily, "Why limit myself? Why not open my life up to greater prosperity and abundance?"—*Ron Willingham*

OKAY, SUPPOSE YOU'VE MET THE GOAL OF YOUR LAST five-year plan and have been busy spending and enjoying the fruits of your labor. But then, when April 15 rolls around, you get gob-smacked with news from your accountant that you owe a lot more than you anticipated. You're not really moving ahead—you're basically treading water again, making ends meet.

You could go on like this indefinitely. But why should subsistence living be a life plan? You deserve much more.

Early in his career, Willingham realized that he was undervaluing his skills: he was charging too low a tuition for his sales training course. His ability to help other people succeed was not reflected in the money he was making. His fees were way too low compared to the wealth he was able to create for others.

Changing the way he perceived himself—realizing he was entitled to greater prosperity—was a turning point for Willingham. He convinced himself he was worth more. Which, of course, he was, as proven by the longevity and incredible success of the books he wrote, such as *The Inner Game of Selling,* and his subsequent development courses.

Believing in your abilities allows great things to happen. Repeat Willingham's mantra: "I deserve abundance."

TEAM-BUILDING | TUESDAY

An idealist is a person who helps other people to be prosperous. —Henry Ford

A S THE TEAM LEADER, YOU NEED TO BE THE ROLE model, not only in business practices, but in every aspect of personal interactions. By setting up "best practices," everyone will model your good behavior, and every aspect of the job will become easier.

At the same time, think about how the team should be constructed so that everyone can achieve individual as well as team goals. While the team goals need to be kept in the forefront, each team member will be more motivated to accomplish a team goal if she or he has a private goal to achieve as well.

Individual goals can be a monetary or competitive assessment. They can also allow team members to excel at a certain aspect of their job. Perhaps one person wants to become more proficient at business writing. Part of the team effort can include that individual spending time with the marketing department so that she can learn how to create next year's marketing brochure. When the team's goal is accomplished, that team member gets a nice addition to her resume, as well as the tools she needs to meet next year's challenges.

CAREER | WEDNESDAY

One of the symptoms of an approaching nervous breakdown is the belief that one's work is terribly important. —*Bertrand Russell*

BERTRAND RUSSELL'S CLASSIC TOME, *CONQUEST OF Happiness,* was written in 1930, but his advice holds true today. Russell, a melancholy youth who found solace pursuing the logical order of things, became one of the twentieth century's most gifted writers, mathematicians, and philosophers. He wrote *Conquest of Happiness* as a guide for those seeking to blame their unhappiness on others and the outside world.

Ironically, his views generated irrational hysteria and controversy. An uproar ensued when he was hired to teach math and logic at the City College of New York. In letters recorded in his autobiography, Bertrand Russell developed a sense of humor and a thick skin that protected him from criticism. To a student supporter at City College, he wrote, "I am afraid that if and when I take up my duties at the City College you will all be disappointed to find me a very mild and inoffensive person, totally destitute of horns and hoofs." Later, when Russell went on to lecture at Harvard, he mischievously added the line "judicially pronounced unworthy to be Professor of Philosophy at the College of the City of New York," to his listing of academic qualifications.

When you feel frustration because the work you are doing isn't garnering the kudos that you believe it deserves, remember not to take yourself too seriously.

SALES | THURSDAY

Much speech is one thing,
well-timed speech is another.
—*Sophocles*

AS THE PREEMINENT PLAYWRIGHT OF ANCIENT ATHENS, Sophocles honed speeches for a living. His idea to add a third actor to the standard two actors and Greek chorus shifted the attention to the actors' speeches, rather than the commentary by the chorus. He balanced the interplay of dialogue among the three actors according to the dialogue's importance, creating a revolutionary new structure in the art of playwriting.

Knowing what to say and how much time you have to say it is as important in sales as it is in playwriting. You only have a limited amount of time to structure your "dialogue" with a prospect, and developing your timing is a skill that demands craft and experience.

First, there's the right time to approach a prospect. You have to pack a lot of value into those introductory words, and at the same time you have to gauge if you're talking to the right person or the decision maker.

Then there's the well-timed speech that leads to closing a deal. Overemphasizing the closing in your sales process can undermine your efforts. You have to know when a probing question is appropriate and when going in for the close is your best option. Yes, speech is one thing, but timing is everything.

LEADERSHIP | FRIDAY

Education is what remains after one has forgotten everything one learned in school.
—*Thomas Edison*

T HOMAS EDISON HAD ONLY A FEW MONTHS OF FOR-mal education. After being told by his headmaster that he was unmanageable, his mother, a teacher, home-schooled him. Insatiably curious, Edison sought answers for why things happened. He tried hatching eggs by sitting on them. He accidentally burned down his father's barn attempting an experiment, and he gave a friend some gas-producing potion to drink to see if the gas would make him fly. He drove adults crazy with his constant questions of why, how, and if. His bedroom was a minefield that no person would dare enter without fear of harm. In truth, his headmaster was right: Edison was unmanageable. But he was also brilliant.

Edison viewed the world as a place full of strange and wonderful things, and he wanted to know about everything. He became the most prolific inventor of our time by pushing his questions into discovery.

We need to be reminded that so much to be learned in life isn't learned at school. Each day presents a chance to figure out a new way to view your life. Look for the opportunity to learn new things about yourself and your business that no graduate school course could possibly teach.

ENTREPRENEUR | SATURDAY

*There are many gaps and voids, many
unmet needs in our complex world.*
—*Martha Stewart*

I T MAY APPEAR THERE IS NOTHING IN THE WORLD LEFT TO invent, no new business to start, or no product not already on the market. Yet savvy entrepreneurs look to fill the gaps and voids often created by new businesses themselves.

Take the iPod, for example. Apple created this piece of equipment and its fundamental operation. But anyone who has an iPod knows that the accessories available to enhance your iPod experience almost rival those available for the best-dressed Barbie doll. Ipod enhancements include docking stations to use your iPod like a stereo and knitted socks designed to protect an iPod in a backpack, briefcase, or purse.

If you are looking for a business, look around this complex world for the gap you can fill. What is the next iPod sock? And why can't you be its creator? Read business magazines and find out what new products will soon land in the marketplace that might create voids that you can fill. Keep a notepad nearby as you go through your day and jot down the possibilities. Then take the next steps. Brainstorm with others. Have prototypes made. Invent something. The world is waiting.

MANAGING PEOPLE | SUNDAY

> Our perspective is so skewed toward
> weakness and illness that we know
> precious little about strength and health.
> —*Marcus Buckingham and Donald Clifton*

P ERFORMANCE REVIEWS, RAISES, BENCHMARKS, QUOTAS— the list measuring a worker's value is endless. But, according to Buckingham and Clifton, who turned the life-coaching field on its head with their book, *Now, Discover Your Strengths,* most of these assessments actually devalue and demoralize employees.

It's counterintuitive but true. When hiring someone, the usual tack is to find out what a person is good at. Obviously, there needs to be a level of competency to land the job. Yet, just because someone is good at something doesn't mean that it is what they are best at. An excellent personal assistant that wants to be on the sales force might succeed at her current position, but will not get personal satisfaction and growth from staying a personal assistant. Good employees who are unwittingly encouraged to keep the status quo eventually quit.

If you want to retain good people, it's up to you to look at their potential success, rather than current success. If you can allow someone to pursue work that really gives him a sense of purpose, he will be that much more productive. It's a win-win for everyone.

MOTIVATION | MONDAY

I always cheer up immensely if an attack is particularly wounding because I think, well, if they attack one personally, it means they have not a single political argument left. —*Margaret Thatcher*

NEGOTIATING THE MINEFIELD OF OFFICE POLITICS IS A part of your job—and your survival depends on it. Disagreements and rivalries are going to happen. Besides understanding the intricacies of the office hierarchy, you also have to learn how to gain the upper hand when friction occurs. The "art of war" between you and your colleagues can become brutal.

Don't resort to personal abuse when office politics suddenly invade your office space. When co-workers resort to insulting you in an argument it only means one thing: they've got nothing on you and feel threatened. Don't overreact and become offended; understand you hold the advantage. You may have already won the battle if you play it right. If someone resorts to personal barbs, it spells desperation. Restate your argument from your position on the high ground you've just gained.

The flinty Margaret Thatcher took delight in her nickname, "Iron Lady"—a tribute to her steadfast character in the face of opposition. She did not flinch when attacked. She remained rock-steady and cannily played it to her advantage. Take a tip from her and stand true to your beliefs, even in the face of mudslinging.

TEAM-BUILDING | TUESDAY

Trust lies at the heart of a functioning, cohesive team. —*Patrick Lencioni*

I F A TRUE FRIEND ASKS YOU FOR A FAVOR, YOU PROBABLY don't first say, "That depends on what it is." You simply say, "Sure"—not because you'd do anything for your friend, no matter how crazy the request, but because you can trust a true friend not to ask you to do something you wouldn't want to do.

Develop this same trust within your team. Without trust the team can't effectively communicate, and they certainly can't work together. Nothing much will get accomplished if team members are always looking over their shoulders worrying that one person will steal another's ideas.

Trust within the workplace can mean many things. It can refer to trusting the team not to divulge what is discussed in meetings with other departments or those outside the company. It might mean trusting your team members to do what they say they will do. Or, it may mean each team member will be honest in dealing with the team—saying what is really meant. Each type of trust is critical to the creation of an effective team. Without trust, you're only a bunch of people operating alone.

CAREER | WEDNESDAY

Financially independent people seem
to be better able to visualize the
future benefits of defining their goals.
—*Thomas J. Stanley and William D. Danko*

ACCORDING TO THOMAS J. STANLEY AND WILLIAM D. Danko in *The Millionaire Next Door,* your average millionaire tends to be a small-business owner in his or her fifties who lives a frugal lifestyle and values saving instead of spending. The authors discovered that people who successfully became millionaires methodically planned to achieve this goal. They all inherently understood accruing wealth wouldn't happen overnight: keeping the goal in mind and following their plan is what made them millionaires. All of these efforts, the frugal shopping and saving for retirement, when combined together, produced long-term gains created from a plan that was set in motion when they were very young adults. With singular focus and discipline, they bypassed the consumer-driven social circle that many people get trapped in.

Becoming a millionaire requires you to think about the future and about how you want your life to unfold. Having a plan is half the battle, but having the discipline to execute the plan is the real challenge. Don't be afraid to map out your financial success. After all, it might be your first step to becoming a millionaire.

SALES | THURSDAY

When you are making a difficult decision, decide what you absolutely must get out of the transaction and what you are prepared to do to get it. —Abraham Lincoln

ABRAHAM LINCOLN IS NOT THE FIRST PERSON WHO comes to mind when thinking about modern sales techniques. But, sales and politics have a lot in common. Lincoln handled the warring factions of his own Republican Party by bringing key members into his cabinet and forcing them to cooperate. He gave up on placing his own allies in his cabinet because he knew he couldn't reach his higher goals—ending slavery and winning the Civil War—without the help of the diverse leaders he chose.

Closing a deal doesn't necessarily mean you have to conquer the enemy. It means getting what you want out of the sales transaction and meeting your key objectives. Sometimes you will need to analyze what you are willing to give up. Examine the obstacles to closing the sale and think of some possible solutions. Knowing your customer is vital in this situation. You must know how customers will react in most situations; armed with such valuable data, you have a good chance of knowing how much they'll give before you have to give up anything. Sound like game theory? Yes—it's played in politics, and it's played in sales.

LEADERSHIP | FRIDAY

You keep moving and the enemy cannot hit you. When you dig a foxhole, you dig your grave. —Gen. George S. Patton

WHEN THE DUST SETTLED AFTER WORLD WAR II, nobody could believe the performance record of General Patton's troops. The Third Army fought more German troops and advanced faster than any division during the war. Patton had his reasons to keep moving. During World War I, the U.S. army suffered tremendous losses engaging in trench warfare against the Weimar Republic, resulting in a stalemate. Life in the trenches bred disease, and thousands of soldiers who were never shot died nevertheless. Knowing this, Patton kept his troops aggressively moving forward during WWII. "Never let the enemy rest," he told his men, "once you have them on the run, keep them on the run."

A business is strikingly similar to an army. Complacency can strike at any time. Although the results aren't literally bloody, the fallout of a failed business hits many levels of society—employees lose their jobs, or perhaps a great product or service disappears.

Remember there is no safety in staying the course. Innovation must win over complacency. By being flexible and finding new ways to do business or new products to sell, you can keep your business humming along. Stand still and you become a marked target for the competition. All business leaders should have a plan to keep their companies moving forward and avoid the foxholes.

ENTREPRENEUR | SATURDAY

> Do not fear to be eccentric in opinion,
> for every opinion now accepted was
> once eccentric. —*Bertrand Russell*

TECHNOLOGY IS JUST ONE AREA WHERE REALITY OUT-
paces popular opinion. Steve Jobs and Bill Gates
thought personal computers would become the new chicken
in every pot. But the two men had no idea that families
would need more than one laptop, or that corporations
would upgrade their systems every five years. When they
started out to create the PC, computers were considered the
playgrounds of geeks. Yet, in twenty short years, personal
computers, the Internet, and e-mail have become an almost
indispensable part of everyday life.

The telephone is another prime example. Even Alexander
Graham Bell surely didn't think that his telephone would
be in every home, let alone in every pocket in the developed
world. He could never have imagined the popularity of
cordless phones, or certainly could not have foreseen the day
when the number of cell phones would exceed the number
of home phones.

Your opinion is yours. Don't let anyone talk you out of
it just because it is eccentric. Eccentric only means deviating from an established or usual pattern or style. It doesn't
mean that an eccentric opinion can't be accepted. You
formed your opinion for good reasons. Don't give up on your
dream easily—and especially not just because someone says
it's eccentric.

MANAGING PEOPLE | SUNDAY

> Nothing others do is because of you. What others say and do is a projection of their own reality, their own dream. When you are immune to the opinions of others, you won't be the victim of needless suffering.
>
> —*Don Miguel Ruiz*

WHETHER A CO-WORKER IS COMPLAINING ABOUT pointless meetings, an office manager is moaning about vacation days, or the CEO is having a conniption about cost cutting, someone is always on stage, and there is always some kind of drama. That's why Don Miguel Ruiz's wisdom—from the 1997 masterpiece *The Four Agreements*—should serve as a guidebook for any manager.

The actual name of the agreement that incorporates his wisdom is, *Don't take anything personally.* It's liberating advice. Employees who direct their anger at managers may have legitimate grumbles, but chances are they'll embellish their complaints with all kinds of personal attacks. A manager who takes these complaints to heart will suffer from needless emotional turmoil and soon make unproductive decisions like making excuses for a poor performer or even punishing a complainer too harshly. Nothing good will come of those decisions. In fact, they are in direct conflict with another of Ruiz's agreements: Always do your best. Managers who avoid playing key roles in the dramas of colleagues create the space to star in their own command performances.

MOTIVATION | MONDAY

If winning isn't everything,
why do they keep score?
—*Vince Lombardi*

VINCE LOMBARDI STARTED PLAYING COLLEGE FOOTBALL at Fordham University in the Bronx, New York. He was a lowly guard, a mere slip of a guy at only five feet eight inches and 185 pounds. His small stature says great things about the man who went on to create the mold for a great coach. A master motivator, he inspired his players with his own values of hard work and deep faith.

Winning was the central concept of Lombardi's philosophy. He found a million different ways to say it and urge his players on. His words were blessedly simple but packed with wisdom that is just as appropriate on or off the football field.

Business is a neat parallel to sports. That's why so much sports lingo has entered the boardroom. And why not? You're on a playing field, usually with a team, and your ultimate goal is to win.

So, who's keeping score? Look around—the only one in your game who can keep score on you is you. You know that winning is everything, so keep the score high. Train everyday and work hard to hone your skills to win the big game. Don't kid yourself—the score counts.

TEAM-BUILDING | TUESDAY

Achieving a balance of power between the board and CEO requires trust, the free flow of ideas, and a board that is comfortable challenging even the most powerful CEO.

—*Bill George*

BEYOND BILL GEORGE WRITING TWO BESTSELLING books, *True North: Discovering Your Authentic Leadership* and *Authentic Leadership: Rediscovering the Secrets to Creating Lasting Value,* he also knows something about boards of directors. This Harvard professor of management practice and former CEO of Medtronic sits on the boards of ExxonMobil, Goldman Sachs, Novartis, and the Carnegie Endowment for International Peace.

A board of directors is a unique team. Although they are not employees of the company, all members are crucially involved with the company's mission.

Communication is key to ensuring the board is in line with the company mission. The company needs to provide each new board member with a thorough orientation. Board members need to be familiar with the company's product or service. They need background information that enables them to put all the pieces together and go out into the world and talk about the company with confidence.

If you are building a board of directors, choose people who have interests in your industry, or knowledge of your specific products or services. Use them as a sounding board, and get them to contribute to the big-picture goals of the company.

CAREER | WEDNESDAY

Keep you friends close, but your enemies closer. —*Michael Corleone,* The Godfather *(1972)*

DON'T THINK EVERYONE IS SINGING YOUR PRAISES even if you are smart, hardworking, and motivated. After all, smart people routinely show up dumb people. Hard workers make it impossible for the lazy folks to skate by. Motivated people make the status quo extremely cranky. So before you start waxing on about how great your career is going, take a long hard look and see what your enemies are up to. Don't pretend you don't have any. You are probably the number one target on many a co-worker's list. The higher you move up the corporate ladder, the worse it gets.

To figure out whom your enemies are you must be skeptical of any and all efforts made by others to get close to you. As the movie *The Godfather* taught us, it is usually someone in your inner circle who is your nemesis. Once you determine who your rival is, proceed with caution and protect your own interests.

Marginalizing your enemies is the next step. Pay attention to their body language and pick up nuanced messages in their speech to give you some insight into their motivations. If you've met your match, worst case scenario, offer a truce—it doesn't have to be them or you. You can work it out so the both of you can get ahead. But stay alert, and be careful who you trust.

SALES | THURSDAY

> The more you chase money, the
> harder it is to catch it. —*Mike Tatum*

M IKE TATUM, VICE PRESIDENT OF STRATEGY AND
development for the online CNET Network, evalu-
ates new Web markets and products for possible acquisition.
He's in a good position to comment on patterns emerging
in the new Web economy because he gets e-mails and calls
all the time from people wanting to sell their Web sites.

Starting an online enterprise with the hope of turning it
over to make a fast buck is not the way to do Web business.
People frequently contact him claiming, "Things are moving quickly on our end," and pressuring him to make a deal.
Tatum is all for Web entrepreneurs selling because they want
to grow their business; but from his point of view, using a
hot pickup line effectively destroys the deal or decreases the
value of what you're selling.

The reason? The seller is chasing the cash instead of having a real passion for the product or service. Tatum is interested in products or services that can combine with one of
CNET's own existing businesses and can increase profits for
both parties. He also wants a product with tremendous
growth potential that can benefit from the resources CNET
can provide.

A useful nugget of Web wisdom comes from the Web
technologist Niall Kennedy: Building to flip is building to
flop. So go slowly, keep your enthusiasm for your product,
and you'll know the right time to sell.

LEADERSHIP | FRIDAY

*What you cannot enforce,
do not command.* —*Sophocles*

EVERY SIX YEARS, EAGER NEW SENATORS DESCEND ON the Washington, D.C., political scene determined to make their mark in government. A flurry of government policy making commences after the swearing-in ceremonies. Bills that are highly touted but are never actually read become federal laws that are overly complex, impossible to decipher, and completely unenforceable. When people must hire a lawyer just to decode the language of the law they are accused of breaking, you know something has gone too far.

The same can be said for many company policies, especially those created from multilayered acquisitions and mergers. Contradictory policies kill office morale, eat up valuable work hours, and irk your employees. Leadership must keep the company's corporate vision in line by streamlining corporate policies. Revisit the rules of the workplace often and make sure that these policies reflect the reality of the work environment.

Another mistake that companies make is using e-mail to inform employees of major changes. It's not the right medium to disseminate important information.

Streamline your corporate policies, base them on sound principles and not current fads, and make them easy to follow. You'll have a better chance of employees actually following these policies by doing so.

ENTREPRENEUR | SATURDAY

A goal without a plan is just a wish.
—*Antoine de Saint-Exupéry*

P ILOT ANTOINE DE SAINT-EXUPÉRY LIVED JUST FORTY-
four years (1900–1944) but became a legend due to a
short book he wrote called *The Little Prince.* This literary
classic tells the story of an aviator who has crashed in the
desert. There he encounters a small, young man, a prince
from another planet, and profoundly experiences the meaning of life.

Saint-Exupéry lived a life of adventure and turmoil, and
he liked it that way. He was severely injured in several plane
crashes, but none stopped him from wanting to fly again.
His words are intriguing: he may never have had a specific
goal beyond flying airplanes right until the end of his life.
Saint-Exupéry died in a plane crash, the cause of which has
never been certain—either his plane was shot down, the
crash was an accident, or his death was a suicide.

In his lifetime, Saint-Exupéry conveyed the importance
of passion. He was a firm believer that you need to be passionate about something in life, and that passion can itself
become a goal for which one needs a plan to accomplish.

MANAGING PEOPLE | SUNDAY

> I consider my ability to arouse enthusiasm
> among men the greatest asset I possess.
> The way to develop the best that is in a
> man is by appreciation and encouragement.
> —*Charles R. Schwab*

DURING GRADE SCHOOL CHARLES SCHWAB SEEMED destined for a life of mediocrity. Labeled a slow learner by the nuns at his Catholic school, he frequently scored poorly in English and reading.

Charles didn't let his poor grades get him down. Instead, he found academic success at math and science. After failing English and French at Stanford University, nobody believed he'd graduate, but he did. He said his upbeat personality and winning demeanor got him through some difficult classes at school, allowing him to concentrate on science, math, and entrepreneurial activities.

It's no surprise that Schwab believes in using encouragement and appreciation to motivate people. When an employee is having a difficult time completing her assignments or following through on a big project, a good manager will explore the reasons instead of automatically giving her negative feedback.

Managers often forget that employees are individuals with completely separate lives outside of work that are full of both negative and positive influences. Every employee dreams of having a boss who believes in him or her, so its up to you to encourage all of them to do their best.

MOTIVATION | MONDAY

*If we can stop excusing ourselves,
we can get better at almost anything.*
—*Marshall Goldsmith*

T HE SUBTITLE OF MARSHALL GOLDSMITH'S BOOK,
What Got You Here Won't Get You There, is *How Successful
People Become Even More Successful.* In his role as a highly
sought-after executive coach, Goldsmith zeros in on the
details of what it takes to bring you to the top of the ladder.
One area that can make the difference is recognizing trans-
actional flaws. These are mistakes in everyday transactions
which, unbeknown to you, might be holding you back.

One of these flaws is making excuses for yourself. When
you continually give excuses for plans that don't work, or
lose your temper if things don't go your way, you're promoting a perception about yourself that you're not really
responsible for your actions.

Using the phrase, "I'm sorry, but . . . " too often is not
good, either. Steer clear of the word "but." (This is a major
Goldsmith rule—other words to avoid are "no" and "however.") And drop the rest of the excuse. Instead, don't say
anything unless it's constructive. Accept responsibility for
your part in what went wrong.

Taking responsibility for how you act will make you better at almost everything you do. Correcting the small flaw
of making excuses—polite as they may seem—may be all
that is standing between you and where you want to be.

TEAM-BUILDING | TUESDAY

> Without beliefs or the ability to tap into them, people can be totally disempowered. They're like a motorboat without a motor or a rudder. —*Anthony Robbins*

WHEN STEPHEN COVEY'S BOOK *THE SEVEN HABITS of Highly Effective People* first was published in 1989, the concept of a mission statement was completely novel. But soon companies around the country started creating their own mission statements. Mission statements are the core beliefs of a company. Motivational speaker Tony Robbins suggests that living by your mission statement creates the integrity that clients are looking for.

Internally, company-wide mission statements are important tools because employees need to know what is expected of them—just as they need to know how the company perceives itself. For example, customer service reps can't call their manager every time a customer calls with a little gripe. They need to understand the corporate philosophy and apply it to a customer's concerns. Sales people also need to be able to make deals and offer contracts that are consistent with the mission statement.

Empower your people with solid information on your goals and expectations. Then give them the ability to make decisions based on your philosophy, and then be able to broadcast your ideas to the rest of the world.

CAREER | WEDNESDAY

The cure for boredom is curiosity.
There is no cure for curiosity.
—*Dorothy Parker*

EVERYONE GETS BORED WITH THEIR JOB AT SOME POINT. Boredom is often what pushes people to leave behind a well-paying job for a new and exciting endeavor. But where does that lead you—especially if you aren't quite sure which job is going to excite you? Before you hand in your notice, look around and take stock of whether you should give your company one more try.

Take witty writer Dorothy Parker's words of wisdom to heart. Inspire yourself through curiosity. Make sure you know your job—and your industry—inside and out. Perhaps there is another department within your company that better meets your interests. Are you better suited for marketing than crunching numbers? Would you prefer to be on the road in a sales position rather than strapped behind a desk? Or do you feel like moving from the corporate side to the client side of the business?

Reinventing yourself to become a more fulfilled person is fine. But, before you go through all the work of finding a new career path, make sure you examine the situation fully and clearly. You might be in the right industry but just trapped in the wrong job—and all you need is fresh start.

SALES | THURSDAY

> A sale is made on every call you make.
> Either you sell the client some stock or he
> sells you a reason he can't. Either way a
> sale is made, the only question is who is
> gonna close?—*Jim Young,* Boiler Room *(2000)*

B EN AFFLECK, PLAYING JIM YOUNG IN THE FILM *BOILER Room,* delivers a pep talk to the new recruits in this movie about a group of stockbrokers working out of a strip mall "boiler room" in Long Island. He's fiery and passionate, and Seth Davis (played by Giovanni Ribisi) is hooked. He doesn't know yet that the firm, JT Marlin, is a "pump and dump" operation. All he knows is that he might become a millionaire overnight.

Young's inspirational message offers a lot of truth. When you're cold calling, someone is always going to close the deal. Make sure that person is you, and not the prospect on the other end of the line. You must be relentless to avoid being on the receiving end of a "thanks, but no thanks" sign off.

Of course, this is where we part company from the high-pressure, fast-talking sales techniques on display in his boiler room. For one thing, not many sales close on the first approach. The first chat is your opportunity to tip the balance, with you in control making the right points and asking the right questions. You begin to build a rapport with the prospect as you explain how the solution you're offering is the best one for his situation. And you hope that future meetings will build on that rapport and turn into trust.

LEADERSHIP | FRIDAY

> Bureaucracy defends the status quo
> long past the time when the quo has
> lost its status. —*Laurence J. Peter*

THE INTERNAL STRUCTURE OF A STAGNANT COMPANY rarely reflects a healthy corporate system. Outdated and outmoded bureaucracies perpetuate the status quo. That leaves management supporting a system that may no longer be relevant to the current business climate.

Unfortunately, bureaucracy is virtually impossible to eradicate. Bureaucracy is even more lethal when combined with Laurence J. Peter's other famous proclamation, the Peter Principle, that states that everyone rises to their own level of mediocrity. At some point, those in a leadership role need to take the necessary steps to correct this corporate malaise.

Finding a new direction for the company is the first step. Concentrate on making basic processes better and continue to make company-wide innovations. Change will keep the status quo from choking the life out of the company. Even though rules are important, you must resist the temptation to overregulate. Employees work better when they are allowed to keep their individuality. While you're at it, throw out meaningless policies and have the discipline not to replace them.

ENTREPRENEUR | SATURDAY

> If a foreign country can supply us with a commodity cheaper than we ourselves can make it, better to buy it of them with some part of the product of our own industry, employed in a way in which we have some advantage.
>
> —*Adam Smith*

F AMED ECONOMIST ADAM SMITH'S QUOTE IS A TWIST ON the old proverb: don't put all your eggs in one basket. If you set up your business to rely on one supplier, the consequence of any changes occurring with that supplier could be drastic. Worse yet, if that manufacturer also supplies every component of your product, you can't go elsewhere for manufacturing.

Think back to the pet food recall in spring 2007. Wheat gluten imported from China was found to be tainted with a product used in making plastic. The United States didn't run out of pet food when all that food was removed from the market. Many pet food manufacturers either didn't use wheat gluten or got it from another source. Also, most manufacturers produce several different products, so they still had others on the shelves.

If your product becomes hugely popular, spread out your suppliers so you can also spread the wealth. The Harry Potter franchise was a great example where many facets of the entertainment industry shared in this enormously successful product.

MANAGING PEOPLE | SUNDAY

Life is too complicated not to be orderly.
—*Martha Stewart*

MARTHA STEWART CLEARLY SEES THE VALUE OF ORGAN-
ization. Her business empire routinely offers tons of
clever solutions that can be applied to any overworked person. Creating a to do list, dealing with paper work, using an
organizer, and maintaining a clean e-mail inbox should be
top priority for every employee.

Make sure you start each day at the office on the right
organizational foot. First, make a to do list. At the end of
the day, carry over things that didn't get done to the top of
the next day's list. Each morning take a few moments to sort
through your loose papers. Don't touch a paper and then say,
"I'll get to it later." That's inefficient. If you are done with
something, toss it, file it, or forward it to the appropriate
person. Third, use the calendar function of your e-mail program or cell phone to remind you of important appointments—or use both devices as many of these functions can
communicate with each other. Nothing is worse than running into a potential client and not being able to nail down
a time to meet her in the future because you don't have your
calendar up to date—or even with you. Lastly, stay on top of
your e-mail in-box, sorting, saving, and deleting as you read
them. Create folders on your desk top for easy access to
important information.

Now go clean off your desk, so you can concentrate on
more important things—like being successful.

MOTIVATION | MONDAY

Be determined to handle any challenge in
a way that will make you grow.
—*Konrad Adenauer*

K ONRAD ADENAUER BRAVELY MET MANY CHALLENGES
before and after he became the first chancellor of
West Germany in 1949. His life during World War II
consisted of alternately hiding from the Nazis and being
imprisoned by them. He was famously implicated in the
assassination attempt on Hitler, then imprisoned before
being released later.

After the war, the Americans appointed Adenauer mayor
of Cologne, and in 1949 he became chancellor of the new
republic of West Germany. He served until 1963, when at
eighty-seven-years-old he was the oldest chancellor ever to
serve Germany. He then served as chairman of the Christian
Democratic Union until 1966 before dying in 1967.

Adenauer's long life and career is a monument to determination. The challenges he faced were extraordinary, yet he
greeted each obstacle as a way to build character. No matter
how difficult the challenge, he made it work for him instead
of letting it hold him back. It was not just about basic survival for Adenauer; it was about proving himself and becoming a stronger person.

Often you don't know your potential until you're challenged to prove it. If you set your mind to excel, you may
surprise yourself. Look at each new challenge in your business career as a way to grow as a person.

TEAM-BUILDING | TUESDAY

I don't believe in team motivation. I believe
in getting a team prepared so it knows it
will have the necessary confidence when
it steps on a field to play a good game.

—*Tom Landry*

HOW DOES SOMEONE LIKE FORMER DALLAS COWBOYS coach Tom Landry not believe in team motivation? First, lots of motivational-speak comes across as insincere. People know insincerity when they hear it, and motivational pep talks can often backfire.

Landry believes that by preparing a team with knowledge and resources, the team can become self-motivating. The team will have confidence and know they can be successful. What more motivation would a team need?

But this preparation needs to be thorough. For a football team, that means practicing key moves needed to complete a play and having an updated play book that puts the right plays at the team's disposal. Players need to be in shape and well-rested. The team needs to consist of the right combination of players, and the administrative staff needs to know their roles as well. Ownership needs to be willing to pay out a large sum of money to capture key players to fill out the roster.

Give your team what they need to win. Whether it is technological resources, additional team members, or seminars to build skill levels, your team must feel like they are prepared to win. If you don't know what they need—ask. And when they tell you—listen.

CAREER | WEDNESDAY

Be who you are and say what you feel
because those who mind don't matter
and those who matter don't mind.

—*Dr. Seuss*

A S MUCH AS WE'D LIKE TO CHANGE FOR THE BETTER, there is logic and sanity in accepting who we are right now. Theodor Geisel, aka Dr. Seuss, was the beloved author of children's books and wrote frequently about individuals whose characters needed attitude adjustments. He also realized that we are all a bit different, and those differences should be celebrated. One of Dr. Seuss's most famous characters, Horton, in the book *Horton Hears a Who,* is an enormous elephant who finds himself caring for a variety of characters quite unlike himself. He realizes that, "A person's a person, no matter how small," and protests against the indifferent and unjust treatment of those that are not like him.

You may not be so lucky to have a Horton on your side in the business world. There will always be people in business who will not appreciate your work, or who simply don't like you. Stay grounded and continue to be yourself when you find yourself in this situation. Changing your opinions to make other people happy is a recipe for disaster.

There will be many critics, but hopefully just as many cheerleaders, over the course of your career. Finding your true calling and a path to happiness is complicated enough. Be true to yourself, and others will accept you.

SALES | THURSDAY

*Success usually comes to those who
are too busy to be looking for it.*
—*Henry David Thoreau*

A LOT OF TIME AND EFFORT IS INVOLVED IN FINDING innovative ways to improve sales. Keeping up with technology is a challenge, requiring frequent upgrades to both electronic equipment and your skill set. The modern sales process mandates that you be in constant communication with your customers by e-mail, voice mail, cell phone, and/or Blackberry.

You must also be comfortable multitasking. You have to be able to manage your contacts and locate information for them fast, whether you're ensconced in your home office, at the corporate desk, or waiting in the Dayton airport for a storm in Chicago to pass so your flight can leave. Your customers count on you so your system of communication, no matter where your location, has to be reliable.

You need to always be nurturing your customer base, solving individual problems, and exceeding your customers' expectations. Building such reliable relationships takes hard work and polished people skills.

But suddenly one day you'll turn around and notice something: you're a success! You were just too busy to realize it before now.

LEADERSHIP | FRIDAY

> The number one managerial productivity
> problem in America is, quite simply,
> managers who are out of touch with
> their people and out of touch with their
> customers. —*Tom Peters*

TOM PETERS WRITES IN *A PASSION FOR EXCELLENCE,* "Customers love being appreciated and hate supervisors or managers who pull a disappearing act." Who doesn't, for that matter? Peters says, "Bad leaders are invisible, while good leaders employ MBWA," an acronym he coined that stands for "managing by walking around."

If you want to be informed about your company and provide useful direction to employees and managers, you need to get out of your office and change your focus from analyzing yesterday's trends to witnessing the daily operation of your company. By asking questions in person, you will get answers to problems you didn't even know existed. By listening to employees, you can give real input into the processes of your company. By talking to customers, you'll know if the business is hitting its target or just missing. Talking to a customer is much more valuable than looking at the results of marketing surveys.

So, the next time you want information, take a walk. Good things are sure to happen.

ENTREPRENEUR | SATURDAY

*You always pass failure
on the way to success.*
—*Mickey Rooney*

S UCCESS RARELY COMES WITHOUT A VISIT FROM FAILURE.
Look at legendary actor Mickey Rooney. He was already
a successful child star when he moved to Hollywood to
audition for the original cast of *The Little Rascals.* He didn't
make the cut, but that didn't stop him from pursuing his
dream. In fact, he went on to star in more than three hundred films spanning from 1926 to as recent as 2008.

Like Rooney, most business people don't think that "failure" is a negative experience. A failure is a great opportunity
to learn what not to do. Even if you don't move forward with
your rejected idea or product, you can take the knowledge you
gained from the so-called failed business, tweak it a little, and
use it to create a new business opportunity.

The key word in Rooney's quote is "pass." Don't get
hung up lingering over a failure—that is a waste of your
valuable time. If you get far enough along in something to
actually fail, you can surely get that far again and succeed!

MANAGING PEOPLE | SUNDAY

A vintner making a fine wine chooses his grapes from a number of varieties.

—*Roger Fisher*

VARIETY IS THE SPICE OF LIFE, OR SO THE SAYING GOES. Why not consider this when hiring your staff? With the amount of diversified skills required to make any organization run smoothly, you need to blend the right mix of personalities. If you have too many type-A personalities, you'll be mediating egos all day. On the other hand, if you hire a host of big dreamers who have lots of great ideas, nobody will notice when the office supplies are gone.

Part of managing is figuring out who gets along with whom or who can handle certain tasks better than others. Similar to creating a fine wine, a certain balance will achieve great results. Getting the right mix takes time, effort, and experimentation. Since the manager's responsibility is to craft a team that thrives in a productive working environment, you must be fairly flexible in your personal management style to effectively manage different types of people. Barking orders to an insecure employee isn't going to bring out the best in him. Instead, you might place that employee with a nurturing personality to help mentor him in the company.

Constructing a fine team is a great way to add your mark to the company. Your goal should be to craft a group that has camaraderie and is cooperative and productive. It will not only make your job easier, but will get you noticed by the boss upstairs.

MOTIVATION | MONDAY

In life and business, there are two cardinal sins. The first is to act precipitously without thought and the second is to not act at all.
—*Carl Icahn*

BILLIONAIRE CARL ICAHN BUILT HIS FORTUNE ON investing in other people's undervalued companies. His first investment involved the Tappan Company. As a major shareholder, he wanted changes made in the way the company was run. The corporate executives resisted, but it was clear to them that Icahn, who was set on acquiring a controlling interest, would try to take over the company if they didn't strike a deal with him. They offered him a $10 million profit if he'd just go away. The offer was a surprise to Icahn, but he accepted it on the spot, and thus began his stupendous career as a corporate raider.

Icahn was not acting precipitously with Tappan; he had a well-thought-out plan. Yet, it didn't turn out the way he expected. But look what happened—he profited anyway. If he hadn't acted, he wouldn't have made $10 million.

Not everything in business is going to work out according to your grand plan. Road bumps are part of life. It is important to have a grand plan and keep your eye on your goal. Know full well what you want to achieve, so that you act when the opportunity presents itself.

Remember the tale of Carl Icahn: he thought he was going to take over the company but instead began a whole new career.

TEAM-BUILDING | TUESDAY

I've always found the speed of the boss is the speed of the team. —Lee Iacocca

I F LEE IACOCCA IS SETTING THE PACE, YOU'D BETTER HAVE your running shoes on! This is the same executive who saved Chrysler Corporation in the 1980s by creating the minivan and bringing back the American convertible. Prior to that, he also worked at Ford Motor Company where he helped design the now-legendary Ford Mustang. Although he has certainly reached retirement age (he was born in 1924), Lee Iacocca continues to be an active business executive. When his wife died of complications from diabetes in 1983, he established a foundation for research to find a cure for diabetes, a cause with which he is still associated.

Iacocca is a great business leader because he knows his products. Everything he got involved with took off because he was 100 percent committed. Iacocca knew the speed at which the automobile industry moved, and he expected the teams he built to keep up. If Iacocca was slow and deliberate, families might still be trying to pack themselves into sedans.

It was often difficult for Iacocca's co-workers to keep up with his pace, but when they did, they were rewarded with success. As a team leader, you need to set an appropriate pace for your team—and you need to keep that pace and lead by example. If the person at the helm is in no hurry, the team will not be in a hurry. And then you'll be sure to watch innovation pass right on by.

CAREER | WEDNESDAY

A good reputation is more valuable than money. —*Publilius Syrus*

PUBLILIUS SYRUS CERTAINLY KNEW THE RELATIVE VALUE of money and reputation. Brought to Italy as a slave, he started with neither. Nevertheless, his talent for inventing witty maxims and performing mimes bought his freedom and his education. The reputation he built performing in the provinces eventually reached Rome, then Caesar. The emperor wanted to see if Syrus's reputation was valid and ordered a contest between Syrus and Decimus Laberius, one of the most celebrated performers of the time. After a performance from Syrus that equaled his outsized reputation, Caesar named him the victor.

A good reputation ensures that your customers and clients will help grow your business through their word-of-mouth advertising, leaving you to concentrate on maintaining and improving the quality of the products or services you provide. Successful companies are built through repeat business—building a customer base that is loyal and will come back again and again. The stronger your reputation, the more likely these customers will pass along your name to their friends. Take care of your reputation by servicing your customers to the best of your abilities, and, in turn, their praise will take care of you.

SALES | THURSDAY

> The terrible thing about pride in the business development process (and relationships in general) is that it squelches what could have been.
>
> —*John L. Evans*

USING A KNOWLEDGEABLE AND CONFIDENT APPROACH with a prospective customer is paramount to closing the deal. But there's a fine line between conveying solid information about your product and boasting about it. Pride is, after all, one of the seven deadly sins. In business, pride can kill a deal in the cradle.

With a successful career in medical sales and real estate behind him, John L. Evans parlayed his business experience into a unique system to train "persuasion executives"— salesmen—to grow their business. Evans places a high value on giving advice in the art of persuasion. By advising a prospect rather than telling him—or worse still, lecturing him about the product or service—the customer will feel like the two of you are in partnership. The grateful customer will in turn generate more business for you by bringing in others to share what they've learned from you and take advantage of your product.

Arrogance or hard-sell boasting to new prospects can squelch the possibility of establishing an enduring partnership. To develop a winning and lasting business relationship, sincere interest in wanting to help your customer is sales gold.

LEADERSHIP | FRIDAY

Good leadership consists in showing average people how to do the work of superior people. —*John D. Rockefeller*

WE ALL ADMIRE THOSE INDIVIDUALS WHO HAVE A high IQ. But how important is it to hire highly intelligent people, and is having them around directly proportional to the success of a company? As any boss knows, smart people learn faster, making training them easier. But it's impossible to fill every job with a genius.

John D. Rockefeller, the first American billionaire, funded many colleges and universities. He knew that educational opportunities could make a difference to the average person in achieving success. His General Education Board, founded in 1902, eventually funded many colleges throughout the country, including the Ivy League as well as many small black colleges.

A good leader needs to know how to motivate people to see beyond their abilities. New training and job-swapping programs that expand duties and opportunities offer your employees a direct challenge. Even if an employee isn't highly motivated, you can structure her job so what she is asked to accomplish is more than what she is presently doing. Once your employees see learning as a tool for earning, they'll jump at the chance to participate in these programs.

ENTREPRENEUR | SATURDAY

> Your largest wealth-building asset is your income. When you tie up your income, you lose. —*Dave Ramsey*

INCOME REPRESENTS MONEY YOU CAN INVEST TO MAKE more money. If you tie up all your future income, you will always be living in the past. As Dave Ramsey tells his listeners every week, you can't jump at an opportunity without the necessary cash on hand.

Entrepreneurs need to plan ahead for business expenses—and planning ahead includes collecting the funds you need to start your business. Some people do this with credit cards, which are useful if you keep your debt to a manageable level. Risks arise as you go overboard buying things you don't need.

Your business plan can help you keep track of the financing amount you need and provide you with a blueprint for the necessary purchases you need to make before opening your doors. If you are starting a business that requires an inventory, your start-up capital needs will be greater than if you are starting a service business where you will make money from your labor.

Successful entrepreneurs also know the value of keeping cash at hand to take advantage of unexpected opportunities. And they know the importance of saving for the future, by not paying for the past.

MANAGING PEOPLE | SUNDAY

*There is nothing to compare with family
if they happen to be competent, because
you can trust family in a way you can
never trust anyone else. —Donald Trump*

T HE FAMILY DYNAMIC CAN PROVE TO BE A POWERFUL
tool in successfully running your company. As Trump
tells us in *Trump: The Art Of The Deal,* he'll take a smart,
hardworking member of his family over just about anyone
else because he feels he can trust them more.

Family-owned businesses have a unique advantage over
corporate entities because the relationships within a family
are usually firmly prescribed. What's more, any problem
the business encounters will become a family problem.
That means everyone has a stake in how things turn out.

Trust can't be based on bloodline alone, though. A family member should really prove his or her competence before
reaping the benefits of a high-profile position in the company. After all, the company's reputation is at stake. Too
often, the favored son or daughter doesn't have what it takes
to move the company into the future, but it's discovered too
late. Trust between family members can also facilitate better
deal making. After all, sharing your thoughts with someone else who has the same motivation to succeed greatly
enhances your chance for success. On the other hand, you
can't hire incompetent family members and hope they work
out. They should prove themselves first. But once they do,
you can count them in.

MOTIVATION | MONDAY

Adversity can strengthen you if you
have the will to grind it out. —*Ray Kroc*

WHEN A FRANCHISEE'S INEPTITUDE RESULTED IN THE
possibility of a detrimental lawsuit against the fast-
food giant McDonald's, founder Ray Kroc quickly hatched
a plan to buy back the problematic properties, using loans
from his suppliers. After the crisis passed, the corporation
went on to grow progressively bigger. It doesn't claim,
"Billions served" for nothing!

Adversity never stopped Ray Kroc—he thrived on it.
Kroc was a door-to-door salesman for seventeen years before
he founded McDonald's. Kroc's tremendous resolve to hang
in there even when sales were down allowed him to view
adverse situations as mere potholes on the road to success.
He was able to stay focused on winning because he knew
that, somehow, every pothole could be filled.

Setbacks happen in every business. Possessing the tenac-
ity "to grind it out," to see problems through, and to overcome obstacles requires enormous strength of will. That
will is powered by perseverance.

If you persevere, troubles can always be resolved, and
your will to succeed will strengthen you and your business.
Even if your business never grows to reach the levels of
worldwide domination such as McDonald's, you're chances
of success are far greater than if you throw in the towel.

TEAM-BUILDING | TUESDAY

> You cannot generate heartfelt debate
> unless the participants believe that the
> outcome is not predetermined.
> —*Rudolph Giuliani*

W HO IN A COMPANY WOULD CONSIDER IT WORTH-while to share his or her views or speak up at a meeting knowing that their opinion didn't matter? How many times have you not bothered to express your views on a subject simply because you thought that no matter what you said, the outcome had already been decided?

In such cases, when you think the outcome is predetermined—or at least perceive it to be predetermined—you still can make a difference. You need to go into the debate or discussion fully prepared and motivated to show that someone might want to think twice about the decision at hand. If you surprise everyone with your mastery of the topic, then you (or your idea) will become a serious contender. Perhaps you can turn the whole corporate atmosphere around, so that the next time a debate is on the horizon, the outcome is not predetermined.

CAREER | WEDNESDAY

> You may have to fight a battle more than once to win it. —*Margaret Thatcher*

T HE 1970s LABOUR PARTY STRUGGLES IN GREAT Britain presented Margaret Thatcher with an opportunity to make history. She rode the wave of public disapproval into the office of prime minister in 1979. Long a staunch conservative, she was a firm believer in individual freedom over state interference. She sought the demise of the Soviet Union because the release of the Eastern European countries from the Communist hold would dilute German and French power and give England a change to regain prominence on the European economic and political stage.

Margaret Thatcher had to reestablish Britain's reputation both politically and economically because of Britain's isolated geographic position. She accomplished a great deal by keeping the bigger picture in mind, all the while accomplishing smaller goals. Still, her innovative thinking toward reinventing Britain was routinely criticized. Her many speeches, expounding the same concepts over and over in the Parliament, secured the support she needed to make the changes she wanted.

Persistence pays off whatever your business or career goals are. Sticking with your convictions, even when they are unpopular, will be rewarded as long as you've done your research and know that your decisions are correct. Make sure you do your homework before sharing your big-picture ideas with others, especially if they are earth-shattering ideas.

SALES | THURSDAY

Plans are only good intentions unless they immediately degenerate into hard work. —Peter Drucker

PETER DRUCKER, "THE FATHER OF MODERN MANAGEment," combined plainspoken common sense and genuine concern for the employee and the consumer in his myriad business philosophy books. He believed that management's mandate was to free people to perform at the top of their capacity. Being free to perform, however, requires planning as well as the responsibility for being accountable for your actions.

Your primary plan should be to create—and keep—your customers. As Drucker said, "The customer is the business." In this way, every part of your company is tied to sales.

You can absorb this concept, but unless you move out of the planning stage your strategy is one of inaction—procrastinating, which never gets anyone anywhere. Move past the planning phase and leap into implementing your plans and fine-tuning your strategy. Creating intimacy with the customer, establishing trust, negotiating with integrity— along with everything you do in the sales process—have to be part of your strategy. Any plan is going to stay in the "good intentions" stage unless you convert it into sweat-and-tears hard work.

LEADERSHIP | FRIDAY

They are the lions. I am the roar.
—*Winston Churchill*

M ANY PEOPLE CREDIT WINSTON CHURCHILL'S WEEKLY
fireside chats as the single most influential reason
that Germany and its allies were defeated. A great orator,
Winston Churchill understood that he needed to communicate hope and determination to keep the British people
motivated and supportive of the war.

Anyone interested in being an effective leader can
employ some of Churchill's techniques. First, he provided a
vision. He spoke about the big picture and outlined the goal
of the war: a world free from dictatorship. Second, he motivated people by generating enthusiasm and personalizing
the message individually. When people can see personal
gain, they are more committed to the outcome. Third, he
demonstrated determination. By staying in London and not
running away from the bombing, he showed resilience and
discipline during England's darkest hours.

Leadership is about providing individuals what they
can't provide for themselves. But, just as important, the
leader must share some of the credit with his followers.
Churchill often said that it was the combined efforts between
the people of England and his cheerleading that really won
the war. A big part of leadership is giving credit where credit
is due.

ENTREPRENEUR | SATURDAY

I'm convinced that about half of what separates the successful entrepreneurs from the non-successful ones is pure perseverance. —Steve Jobs

SOME PEOPLE ARE EASILY DISCOURAGED. IT OFTEN doesn't take outright failure for them to give up their pursuit; they can be stalled just as easily from a relatively minor drawback. They are ready to call it quits after one order gone wrong, a bad financial month, or a sale that didn't quite close.

As Steve Jobs says, perseverance means hanging in there time after time, not letting any one single event get you down. If you get close to a big sale that doesn't materialize, at least you know it is possible—and you can work on lining up a similar sale again. A bad financial month can be turned around by a subsequent good one—but not if you close up shop. If an order gets botched, find out what went wrong, and make sure it doesn't happen again.

A true entrepreneur enjoys the journey as much as the destination. Hang in there and learn to appreciate the process. The setbacks will become the war stories you will tell years later when you answer those questions about how you got your successful business off the ground.

MANAGING PEOPLE | SUNDAY

> Managers who are blind to the changes
> in this new cohort of free agents are
> operating like dangerous, deluded
> executive bigots. —*Marshall Goldsmith*

P EOPLE HAVE MORE CHOICES ABOUT THEIR PERSONAL AND professional lives than ever. With this in mind, managers shouldn't make any assumptions about employees staying on the job one second longer than they have to. Marshall Goldsmith reminds us that employees no longer have the same loyalty to the company. Most people look to the company and see how much it can do for them, and then they move on. Assuming the employee needs the company more than the company needs the employee won't get your company or department where you need to go.

Instead, management has to make a concerted effort to retain the best and the brightest. People want to spend their time where they can make a difference. Rewarding employees with money, additional responsibilities, and freedom to make decisions can pump up job satisfaction. Younger workers often want frequent slaps on the back and monetary incentives, while older workers may covet flexible scheduling and job-sharing. Work-life balance incentives also make employees think twice about jumping ship.

Get to know your employees, and find out what incentives will make them happier in their jobs. If you want to create loyal employees, you need to offer them something they can't easily get anywhere else.

MOTIVATION | MONDAY

Unless a man undertakes more than he possibly can do, he will never do all that he can. —*Henry Drummond*

NINETEENTH-CENTURY SCOTSMAN HENRY DRUMMOND gained early renown as an evangelist and a natural scientist. Not settling for either career track, the energetic Drummond combined his scientific and theological training to become an inspirational writer. His books sold millions and his quotations about how people can achieve their goals are still widely read.

Drummond's life was devoted to undertaking challenges. As a result, he achieved fame and notoriety as a writer that he had never imagined.

These days, doing more means packing your day planner or Blackberry with more meetings and appointments than it seems you can handle. That's just a start. When you have a full schedule, you're forced to be efficient. You learn to prioritize tasks and appointments, and you learn to do things faster. In the process of becoming more efficient, you open unrealized potential.

Never underestimate your capacity to do more. Continuous effort to succeed and undertake new challenges on a consistent basis is bound to unlock doors to new opportunities and business success. You will never know all you can do unless you experience as much as you can.

TEAM-BUILDING | TUESDAY

> Obstacles are what you see when you
> take your eyes off the goal. —*Vince Lombardi*

EVERY SPORTS TEAM IS JUDGED BY ITS CHARACTER. EVEN when a team is losing by a score they cannot overcome and defeat is certain, a respectable team will still play its heart out until the final whistle. Often, when the going gets tough, the true heart of a team will shine through. Each player helps his teammates stay focused, and sometimes they'll overcome the odds and pull off a miraculous come-from-behind victory.

In a traditional SWOT analysis, you set out to conquer a task—such as opening a new business—by reviewing the four basic parameters that will determine success or failure. In this analysis, you outline your plan's Strengths, Weaknesses, Opportunities, and Threats. Obstacles or threats are the things you can immediately identify that will stand in your way of success. In the case of a new business, a threat or obstacle could be a well-financed competitor or a downturn in the economy. If you have some idea in advance how you might handle these threats/obstacles, you won't have to waste time floundering when they appear—you can keep your field of vision looking to the future and at the goal ahead.

One way to successfully deal with threats or obstacles is to plan for them. Talk through your strategy ahead of time. At the risk of being accused of focusing on the negative, anticipating obstacles can then jump-start your readiness to overcome them if they arise.

CAREER | WEDNESDAY

If I only had a little humility, I'd be perfect.
—Ted Turner

IN 1980, TED TURNER HAD A VISION TO CHANGE TELEvision news programming forever by introducing the first twenty-four-hour live news broadcast channel, Cable News Network (CNN). Going head to head against the entrenched broadcast news giants took guts. Many people called him a crackpot. But, Turner took no heed of his critics; rather, he seized the opportunity and moved forward. The result? He built a media empire. CNN has become the channel to watch during any crisis, from covering the space shuttle *Challenger* disaster in 1986 and the first Gulf War in 1991, to today's headlines.

Unfortunately, Turner's strong sense of ego was only matched by his inability to resist insulting people. Ultimately, his abrasive personality affected his business relationships. Always quick with a comment, Turner earned the nickname, "The mouth of the South." Throughout his professional career he managed to insult many ethnic groups, as well as potential business partners. Forced out of his own company, he was eventually turned into a figurehead with little power.

If you have big dreams, and the skill set to do it, you can accomplish great things. But it's important to remember that we aren't always the best judge of our own actions. A little humility goes a long way.

SALES | THURSDAY

> The challenge in every conversation
> is to try to transcend the trivialities of
> polite chitchat. —*Keith Ferrazzi*

TODAY YOU HAVE TO WORK A LOT HARDER AT DEVELOP-ing deep and lasting relationships with your customers.

Doing your homework before you go out prospecting is invaluable. People are flattered when you know something about them. Keith Ferrazzi, CEO of FerrazziGreenlight, a marketing and sales consulting firm, practices what he calls "the deep bump"—a fast and meaningful personal comment that creates an intimacy, an emotional bond with the prospect.

For some salespeople a deep bump is instinctive—establishing intimacy with someone else comes easily. If you don't have this facility naturally, it's a challenge to develop it, though not a monumental one. You can start by reading a lot—not just business books, but all books—to help you become a better conversationalist. If you know your potential customer likes fly-fishing, you don't have to learn how to tie trout lures or study up on classic bamboo fishing rods. You can read a good novel about fishing, like Ernest Hemingway's *The Old Man and the Sea,* or ask him about the movie A *River Runs Through It* and how that compares to his experiences. He'll be glad to fill you in on everything you ever wanted to know and more. Find common ground, and your potential customer will respond to it.

LEADERSHIP | FRIDAY

> Good tactics can save even the worst strategy. Bad tactics will destroy even the best strategy. —*Gen. George S. Patton*

A S COMMANDER OF THE THIRD ARMY, GENERAL Patton was known for getting the job done. Patton succeeded because he was a realist. He always took into account the overall plan and analyzed what needed to get done—and then did it without any delay or excuses. More than anything, he hated orders that didn't make sense or put his men in harm's way. If the orders were outrageous, he modified them so that his troops could still achieve success.

Patton wanted no part of bad strategy. When he was told to stand by and not advance, he sharpened his troops by sending out small fighting units to keep the enemy guessing.

When it comes down to being successful in business, a leader should make sure her "troops" have what they need to execute the grand plan, or that plan can quickly become a nightmare. Whether you are selling shoes to customers in a retail setting or delivering parts to an oil rig in the middle of the Gulf of Mexico, how well you perform the task will indicate your level of success. On the flip side, great plans are ruined when the execution suffers. Bottom line—grandiose strategy plans won't sell more shoes, but solid customer service will.

ENTREPRENEUR | SATURDAY

*Don't be afraid to give up the good
to go for the great. —John D. Rockefeller*

THE ROCKEFELLER NAME IS SYNONYMOUS WITH GREAT-
ness. Even in his youth, John D. Rockefeller saw
greater options than those prescribed by society, as evi-
denced by his leaving high school to go to business school
instead. His greatness was quickly recognized in industry.
He founded Standard Oil and became wealthy. Rockefeller
did everything within his power, some of it controversial,
to make sure that Standard Oil was the greatest oil company
in the country. He knew the value of putting profits back
into the business and was rewarded with a highly efficient
and successful company.

Rockefeller went on to become the first billionaire in the
United States. He made a conscious decision early in his
career not to be just good in business, but to do what great
people do and give generously to charity. Philanthropy is
where he perhaps shone the brightest. He spent the last
forty years of his life (he lived to age ninety-seven) in retirement, giving him plenty of time to devote to his charitable
practices.

MANAGING PEOPLE | SUNDAY

It's only when the tide goes out that you discover who's been swimming naked.
—*Warren Buffett*

AT EVERY COMPANY THERE'S SOMEONE WHO'S MADE IT to the top with the consensus that she doesn't deserve to be there. Either she got the job from an uncle who went to kindergarten with the CEO, or she said all the right things at all the right cocktail parties. That's all fine when profits are pouring in and the coffers are overflowing. But when profits threaten to head south, and they eventually do for every company, if you can't handle the position you are in, you might be seeing yourself to the door.

Proving your worth when times are tough is what will set you apart from your nepotistic counterparts. When a company has a downturn, it often must reinvent itself. Be prepared to offer evidence as to why it should keep you. When it sheds underperforming divisions, and that usually includes those in the ranks who have been difficult to deal with, you won't be the one with a pink slip if you have solid evidence to prove your worth. It's more important to have thought of ways to diversify or solve some problems that will lead the company where it needs to go before profits take a nosedive. Make sure leadership knows they need to take you with them.

MOTIVATION | MONDAY

> Nothing of great value in this life comes easily. The things of highest value sometimes come hard. The gold that has the greatest value lies deepest in the earth, as do the diamonds. —*Norman Vincent Peale*

NORMAN VINCENT PEALE, THE CHAMPION OF POSITIVE thinking, built an industry on his powerful philosophy, including dozens of books, thousands of lectures, fifty-four years of radio programs, and the widely read magazine, *Guideposts.* But positive thinking alone did not make him such a success—underlying all was hard work.

Peale's hard work involved mining deep into believing in yourself in order to attain your dreams. Like miners who dig deep for gold, you also have to dig deep to find your own gold and diamonds—the priceless personal values that make you who you are.

Hard work to attain business goals requires a lot of effort that few will ever notice. It often involves confronting your fears. For example, it's hard work to remain positive when presenting a new business idea if it generates nothing more than an initial lukewarm response. Taking action and not giving up produces solutions.

Mine your inner values of perseverance and dedication to achieve your goals. If you think you can do it, you will do it. It may often be rough-going at times, but no one ever said success comes easy.

TEAM-BUILDING | TUESDAY

> Groups of three, four, or five perform better on complex problem solving than the best of an equivalent number of individuals. —*Paul Laughlin, Ph.D.*

THE OLD SAYING GOES, "TOO MANY COOKS SPOIL THE broth." But for problems more complex than cooking broth, the saying that would be more useful is, "two heads are better than one."

In a 2006 psychological study performed at the University of Illinois Urbana-Champaign, Dr. Paul Laughlin found working in small groups brings out creative ideas and thought processes that no one individual will have on his or her own. However, even the best teams often need to be coached in how to solve a complex problem. One good way to get the creative juices flowing is by letting everyone contribute their ideas on how to proceed. None of these first ideas are likely to be the right one, but part of this messy process may include a single word, phrase, or concept that triggers someone else's thinking.

Keep everyone focused and keep these brainstorming sessions contained. Reel in tangential conversations or wandering to an unrelated topic. But don't shut down tangents altogether—they can provide useful springboards to get to the right answer.

CAREER | WEDNESDAY

Let the other guy go first.
—*Mark H. McCormack*

WHEN IT COMES TO NEGOTIATING A PAY RAISE, OR even working out a deal with a new client, follow the lead of the current crop of television's police dramas. While you can't threaten your customers with a sentence of "fifteen-to-life" if they don't acquiesce to your demands, you can learn a lot watching how TV detectives question their suspects. One thing they never do is talk first. Instead, they always encourage the suspected perpetrator to tell all, finding out what the suspect knows before divulging their position on the case. By doing so, they gain, or retain, a stronger position if they need to bargain with the criminal.

Negotiating is similar in business. Keep the conversation short and sweet. Use your adversary as a source of information, and let him do all the talking first. Listen to his proposition, and ask questions to clarify what you've heard. Active listening shows the other party that you understand their position. It also builds trust. Then, wait at least thirty seconds, silently, while you think through your response. You'll only have one chance to counteroffer and keep your position high. Take in all the information you've received and make your best response. Most likely, you'll be able to get what you want.

SALES | THURSDAY

High profiles fit businessmen
like a cheap suit. —*Harvey Mackay*

W HEN YOU'RE IN A CAREER AS PUBLIC AS SALES, IT'S important to always make a good impression. But that doesn't mean you have to mortgage the house just to look sharp. Sales isn't about the clothing label or the gold Rolex; it's about your relationship with your customer. Your customer should regard you as a trusted and indispensable adviser, not a wardrobe consultant.

Legendary salesman Harvey Mackay knows that success at sales isn't about being a high-flying personality or controversial figure either. Ultimately, all that glitter and flash get in the way of the customer's ability to see who you are and what you're offering. Even more important, it gets in the way of communicating with your customer.

Communication is how you build an enduring sales relationship. You need to remember that when you are speaking or writing, you are communicating to your customer as her trusted business adviser—and recognizing who she is as a person. This means knowing all you can about your prospect or customer. Collect information about her interests inside and outside business and be eager to talk about them.

Selling isn't about you or your showmanship. It's about your customer and making him or her want your product. Keep it real.

LEADERSHIP | FRIDAY

> Keep your fears to yourself, but share your
> courage with others. —*Robert Louis Stevenson*

ACCORDING TO THE WRITER JACK LONDON, STEVENSON'S approach to writing was to "put all yourself into your work until your work becomes you, but nowhere let yourself be apparent." London's observations were accurate. Stevenson, like the many adventurous characters that fill his novels, traveled with willful abandonment, seeking refuge from the cold winters of his native Scotland because of his sickly constitution. Ignoring pleas of caution, he lived wildly, smoking daily cigars and traveling in sordid conditions, while minimizing the gravity of his condition.

To write *Across the Plains,* Stevenson crossed the Atlantic in steerage class to experience the dismal surroundings. He recounts, "I had a fixed sense of calamity and to judge by the conduct, the same persuasion was common to all of us." Obviously, Stevenson felt apprehensive after he committed to the long journey. But, he wrote, when you are in a situation that you can't escape, the worst thing to show is fear. Fear overwhelms the natural instincts of survival and can make a bad situation even worse.

In business, fear can paralyze even the keenest leader. Too much fear causes a drop in emotional stability, which leads to bad decision making. Whether you are fending off corporate lawsuits or facing jeering union workers, contain your fear and limit your stress response. A true leader hides his fear and shows courage, confidence, and perseverance instead.

ENTREPRENEUR | SATURDAY

> In a crowded marketplace, fitting in
> is failing. In a busy marketplace,
> not standing out is the same as being
> invisible. —*Seth Godin*

THERE ARE MANY WAYS TO STAND OUT IN A CROWDED field. In some industries, it can be as simple as giving topnotch customer service, or maybe offering an additional value that no one else provides. Standing out can be as easy as making use of color—both FedEx and UPS prove that a color can distinguish your business, whether the color scheme is bright or dull. Or you could blast your message across every conceivable advertising resource: TV, radio, print, and the Web. Perhaps your product stands out by being the only CD wrapper that's easy to open.

What are the ways your company can stand out in its own crowded marketplace? The current interest in going "green" is ripe for finding ways your company can contribute to protecting the environment. And don't forget the importance of attracting the best employees your industry has to offer—this is always a surefire way to stand out.

MANAGING PEOPLE | SUNDAY

*Why is it drug addicts and computer
aficionados are both called users?*
—*Clifford Stoll*

CLIFFORD STOLL, AUTHOR OF *SILICON SNAKE OIL*,
makes an astute point when he says we all hide behind
our computers. We spend too much time surfing the Web
at work, researching just one more way to get the answer we
are looking for. Or, we spend so much time perfecting the
way a letter or business document looks, changing fonts,
moving margins, and aligning boxes, that we don't have the
time left to work on the content.

True, this book would be nothing without a computer.
But computers are taking over the office in unforeseen and
unintended ways. Take e-mail, for example. If you have a
problem with a co-worker or employee, it's become much
easier to e-mail him your complaint instead of actually confronting him face to face. But that's a potentially dangerous
habit. First, you come across as unapproachable, which is a
trait that no manager wants. Second, your message may not
come across on the screen in the same way you intended.

Kick the computer habit whenever possible. Talk to
people face to face, instead of hiding in your office. A handwritten note wouldn't hurt, either. And while you're at it,
erase your computer games from the hard-drive: how many
hands of solitaire do you really have time for?

MOTIVATION | MONDAY

Every cloud has its silver lining, but it is sometimes a little difficult to get it to the mint. —Don Marquis

MAYBE YOU THINK YOUR LATEST PROJECT IS GOING SO well that you've already put in a bid on that new Porsche you've had your eye on. Or you've made a deposit on the safari vacation in Tanzania, or that dream week in Anguilla.

Slow down. Stick to reading the glossy car magazines and watching the Discovery Channel until you know it's a done deal and the commission or the bonus check is not just "in the mail," but in your bank account.

It's wonderful to be an optimist. In business, it is a blessed gift, especially if it's genuine. A lot of people do an excellent job of faking optimism, so who's to say if genuine enthusiasm breeds greater success than false hope? Pessimism has no place in business, though you might reveal a little of it to your spouse or your best friends outside the office when times are particularly rough.

But optimism can get out of hand. Some exuberant types can't be held down—they build their castles in the sky at the slightest glimmer of silver. They've got the money all spent even before there's any ink on the paper to dry.

Learn from famed nineteenth-century humorist Don Marquis when he advises you to monitor yourself. Stay optimistic, but don't spend the precious ore until you've taken it to the mint.

TEAM-BUILDING | TUESDAY

The nice thing about teamwork is that
you always have others on your side.

—Margaret Carty

WORKING AS A TEAM CAN BE DEMANDING. A TEAM is composed of many different personalities that each person on the team has to learn to work with. There are often issues to deal with, like someone not doing his or her share of the work, or someone doing the work that was assigned to another. Even the most intimate team of all— the family unit—has its share of ups and downs.

But, being part of a team can be a rewarding experience as well. Sharing makes successes more joyous and failures easier to take. If a team works well together, there is nothing better. And the best way for a team to work well together is for the team to have a team leader who understands group dynamics.

True team members stick together under pressure. When a deadline is looming, you don't work overtime at the office alone; rather, the rest of your team will be there with you. If something doesn't go quite right, the whole team shoulders the burden and knows that every team member has a role whether the outcome is good or bad.

Don't avoid teamwork just because it can be hard. Learning to be a good team member and a good team leader can open doors to future work opportunities.

CAREER | WEDNESDAY

Given a choice beyond love and physical
attractiveness, I prefer to marry a woman
who can manage a business.

—*Thomas J. Stanley*

S UCCESSFUL PROFESSIONALS KNOW THAT HAVING A
supportive spouse is a huge asset. According to Thomas
J. Stanley in *The Millionaire Mind*, your spouse will also influence how well you do in business. Stanley's research reveals
that most millionaires consider their spouse one of the main
reasons they were able to achieve their financial goals. From
being a support team when you decide to change careers, to
cutting coupons when you lose your job, or being a cheerleader when you close a great deal, your spouse's actions affect
your ability to do your job well. And while a good partner is
integral to the profitability of any company, a supportive
spouse who understands your business is just as critical to
your personal success.

Just like a business, running a household requires keeping
a balance sheet. Compulsive spending, wasteful purchases,
and lack of saving all add up to the number one reason people get divorced: irreconcilable differences over money. Planning a life with someone often does not include discussions
about financial habits, but it should. If you already have differences in spending habits and you need to make changes, do
so by setting a good example. Whatever you do, don't ignore
it. Angry, bitter, broke, and alone is not the way to retire.

SALES | THURSDAY

*A mediocre idea that generates
enthusiasm will go further than a
great idea that inspires no one.*
—*Mary Kay Ash*

F ROM A STOREFRONT IN DALLAS AND BACKED BY A
$5,000 investment, Mary Kay Ash founded a cosmetics
empire with the goal of giving other women an equal chance
to succeed in business. Her famous pink Cadillac incentive
awards were emblematic of her unconventional approach to
selling with a feminine touch.

Mary Kay trained her sales force—now over one million
strong and spread throughout thirty countries—with techniques she learned from previous employers. She made a list
of the positive and negative things she'd observed in sales
and invented her winning formula. Indeed, her book, *Mary
Kay on People Management,* is now taught in business courses
at Harvard.

Mary Kay chose the Golden Rule as her credo: "Do unto
others as you would have them do unto you." Accordingly,
she trained her saleswomen to not be too forceful and to deal
with customers on an equal basis.

It's a wise doctrine. When you're in the negotiation phase
of the sales process, strive for a deal that allows both sides to
walk away happy. Don't oversell your product. The terms
should be fair and satisfactory, and no one should feel com-
promised. When both sides are negotiating with skill and
integrity, you'll both get a feeling of accomplishment.

LEADERSHIP | FRIDAY

Successful people become great leaders when they learn to shift the focus from themselves to others. —*Marshall Goldsmith*

C LAWING YOUR WAY TO THE TOP REQUIRES A DEGREE of self-centeredness. Unless you're the CEO's son or daughter, in order to get promoted you've probably demonstrated determination and focus, maintained high work standards, and achieved or exceeded your company's expectations. These are characteristics that people need to get to the top.

However, once you are at the top, it's not these traits that will keep you there. In his book, *What Got You Here Won't Keep You There,* Goldsmith writes that people routinely assume that certain traits they've relied on to become successful are the same traits that they can rely on to be effective leaders. They couldn't be more wrong. A highly competitive person will soon realize that one upping your subordinates is a surefire way to create a disgruntled staff. Taking all the credit is another one of Goldsmith's pet peeves. Once you are at the top, your focus needs to shift from reveling in your own success to facilitating your employees' success. By highlighting staff contributions, sharing credit, and giving everyone else a pat on the back, you'll create a team that will keep you on top.

For a leader, success boils down to parking your ego and getting your employees fired up. That won't happen if you act like you already know everything.

ENTREPRENEUR | SATURDAY

*What's possible won't happen just
because it's possible.* —*Al and Laura Ries*

IN ORDER TO MAKE THE POSSIBLE HAPPEN, IT TAKES
someone with foresight, imagination, and drive to see it
through. But, how many business ideas or inventions never
get off the ground? So-called idea people can sit around and
think up ideas all day long, but ask them to implement an
idea and see it through to fruition and their brains seem to
freeze.

Statistics prove that a great percentage of patents pending
are never fully realized and brought to market. To accomplish this last important stage takes dedication to your idea
and a penchant for details, says the father-daughter marketing team of Al and Laura Ries. You have to find the right
people to make a prototype, research the market, figure out
what kind of advertising you should do, and then determine
how to get your product to the market in the form of sales
and distribution.

Creative types often don't believe they have the ability
to be practical and work through the mundane details it
takes to pull off an idea. But they probably do have those
skills; they've just always assumed they couldn't take the
next step.

If you have a great idea, but you don't have the confidence to pull it off, you may need to bring others on board.
Pull your team around you, and you can be an idea person
who still makes things happen.

MANAGING PEOPLE | SUNDAY

*We can draw lessons from the past,
but we cannot live in it. —Lyndon B. Johnson*

EMPLOYEES CAN BE AGGRAVATING. THEY WILL NOT listen to you. They will make mistakes constantly. And they will never be as good as you were when you had their job.

It's time for a reality check if this is your attitude toward those that work for you. It doesn't matter if these statements may be true. It doesn't matter how well you did your job back when you had their job. What matters now is getting everyone to perform at levels that are productive, profitable, and acceptable.

The same holds true for employee mistakes. Don't hold past errors against anyone when you are analyzing present performance. It's quite possible that even the hugest error was simply an accident. It doesn't mean that they will screw up the Excel file every time they use it or mess up every sales presentation. What's done is done—so as Lyndon B. Johnson stated, learn to let go and move on.

MOTIVATION | MONDAY

In the depth of winter, I finally learned that within me there lay an invincible summer.

—*Albert Camus*

F RENCH NOBEL PRIZE-WINNER ALBERT CAMUS HAD A philosophy of life which, while influenced by John Paul Sartre's existentialism, was uniquely his own. He believed that the world and human beings are essentially absurd, but at the same time he thought it possible to find meaning in life by concentrating on your own existence. Living your life to the maximum, savoring being alive, is the point of our time on earth.

Everyone reaches a point where events seem to conspire to bring you down. During the winter of your discontent, you wonder if you will ever get past this point. Finding a ray of sunlight during the worst times is sometimes impossible to imagine, but it's not impossible to achieve.

Working toward a solution on your darkest business days requires skills, all of which you can learn from years of experience. But to use those skills effectively, as a member of a team or as the team leader, requires a strong foundation of trust and belief in yourself. Knowing how to draw on that strength is how you will ultimately triumph over the bad times.

Finding that "invincible summer" within you will make you invincible as well. When everything looks dark and bleak, draw on that summer within to bring light to the situation.

TEAM-BUILDING | TUESDAY

> My responsibility is to get my 25 guys
> playing for the name on the front of their
> uniform and not the one on the back.
> —*Tommy Lasorda*

T HE *HARVARD BUSINESS ESSENTIALS: MANAGER'S Toolkit* lists the following six characteristics of an effective team:

- Competence
- A clear and compelling goal
- Commitment to a common goal
- Every member contributes; every member benefits
- Supportive environment
- Alignment

Tommy Lasorda's words of wisdom certainly support these characteristics. After fifty years in major league baseball, Lasorda knows the challenges of team building.

Team members who are only concerned with themselves do not show commitment to the common goal. Sometimes that common goal is an individual team member—everyone devoted to getting the football to the running back or, all members of the Discovery Channel Tour de France cycling team geared toward getting Lance Armstrong to the winner's podium. But these micro-goals culminate in the common goal of an overall team win. When every member contributes toward that common goal each member benefits by being on the winning team because of how it will enhance their personal resumes.

CAREER | WEDNESDAY

When you substitute "thank you" for "I'm sorry," the results will lead you closer to the truth. —Jeffrey Gitomer

I T'S HARD TO BELIEVE THAT THE WORDS "I'M SORRY" CAN ever be the wrong thing to say. But in business, that is often the case. Most people don't say "I'm sorry" enough. But, for someone who fears criticism or worries what others might think of him, he might use the words as a way to get out of being reprimanded. From a psychological perspective, "I'm sorry" can have a negative effect on one's self image. When you say the words, "I'm sorry" all the time, you can internalize it to mean that you are a sorry person.

Jeffrey Gitomer, the king of positive thinking, states in his book *The Little Gold Book of Yes!* that if you substitute "thank you" or "I understand" for "I'm sorry," you change the content of the conversation from one of subservience to self-empowerment. By saying, "Thank you for bringing this problem to my attention" instead of apologizing for the problem, you are showing that you welcome criticism and want to move forward in a positive direction. Accepting criticism without apologizing also keeps your attitude upbeat because you aren't concentrating on what you didn't do right and then wallowing in self pity.

This is not to say that you should never say, "I'm sorry." There are clear instances when "I'm sorry" is absolutely the only thing you should say—but such times might be less common than you imagine.

SALES | THURSDAY

Learn to count the no answers.

—Stephan Schiffman

I T'S A HARD FACT OF THE SALES LIFE THAT YOU'LL HAVE to master the simple yet effective sales technique of the cold call. In his book, *Cold Calling Techniques (That Really Work!)*, Stephan Schiffman posits that cold calling is the most economical way to find prospects on an ongoing basis, and that its dynamic cumulative effect is foolproof.

Based on his own research and sales experience, Schiffman maintains that out of all the cold calls you make, one-third of them are going to net you a sale—no matter what. The second third is sales you'll never get, and the last third is up for grabs. That last third is the most important. This is your target market—these prospects that you stand a chance of getting to a negotiation phase—potential customers that make cold calling worth your while.

Your number one competitor is status quo when you talk to potential customers in this crucial third. That means, in Schiffman's terms, what people are doing right now. In other words, most people are happy with what they've got—it is your job to convince them otherwise.

The more people you reach with cold calling, of course, the more likely you'll eventually make more sales. But it's equally important to take advantage of having the prospect—a live human voice and not an answering machine—on the phone, and that you make the most of the opportunity.

LEADERSHIP | FRIDAY

Leadership is often about providing
options when there are none.

—*Alan Axelrod*

IN THE 1920S, BUSINESSES STARTED A WIDESPREAD
practice of using credit for acquiring and growing their
companies. Banks eagerly complied, and consumers got on
the bandwagon by taking out personal loans and mortgages.
Eventually the economy slowed and demand for products
plummeted, resulting in debt-ridden businesses becoming
vulnerable. By the time the stock market crashed in 1929,
the confidence in the U.S. economy was at an all-time low.
President Franklin D. Roosevelt, who was inaugurated in
1933, proposed a radical restructuring of the economy, which
is still controversially discussed in economic circles today.

Whether or not you fall on the left or right of the equation, Alan Axelrod, author of *Nothing to Fear: Lessons in Leadership from FDR,* offers some keen insight into FDR's
leadership abilities. To lead the country during several profound crises, FDR believed he had to reinvent the government's role in the economy. The New Deal was his legacy, a
huge bureaucratic intervention that allowed the United
States to build up confidence and move forward.

In business, whether it is bankruptcy, a hostile takeover, or a defective product nightmare, when the outcome
looks bleak, all eyes will be on the leader. Finding a progressive solution is what true leadership is about.

ENTREPRENEUR | SATURDAY

> Success is a lousy teacher.
> It seduces smart people into
> thinking they can't lose.
> —*Bill Gates*

WHILE SUCCESS IS WITHIN YOUR REACH, DON'T GET duped into thinking you have the proverbial Midas touch. Not everything you create will turn to gold. Every success you have is the result of thorough research and hard work. Effort needs to be continuously put into everything you attempt to do. Even Bill Gates, who is phenomenally successful, doesn't assume that everything Microsoft creates will overpower the market, or that a strong global economy will always be in place.

Getting complacent, skipping a step or two, or thinking you've been so successful you simply can wing-it, is a sure way to almost guarantee future failure. Yes, success does breed success but there will always be variables that are out of your control, affecting your chances of succeeding again.

That's not to say you shouldn't enjoy your successes. You certainly should. But luck, timing, and a good business sense are all necessary for every venture to get off the ground. You need a bit of each, every time you go to market with your next big thing.

MANAGING PEOPLE | SUNDAY

Life is a long lesson in humility.
—*James M. Barrie*

J AMES BARRIE, THE CREATOR OF *PETER PAN*, IS IN GOOD company with Elton John, sharing the sentiments of "(Sorry) seems to be the hardest word." While Elton John was swooning about love gone wrong, the same message applies to the drama at your office.

Your employees will make mistakes, and it's quite possible that you will make mistakes as well. Just as you expect others to 'fess up, they also are waiting for you. So, if you reprimanded another too sharply, and then it turns out you were wrong, apologize. If you laid blame where it wasn't due, apologize. And if you learn that you embarrassed an employee for whatever reason, apologize.

It's difficult to admit error, but once you do, you will realize that it is truly liberating. Apologizing for something goes a long way toward mending broken relationships and getting your staff back on a productive track. Making a mistake and moving on makes good business. And in those rare times when others are expecting an apology, yet you know you were right, do it anyway.

INDEX